DATE DUE

AG 14 '92	OC 23 '03		
NO 20 '92	JE 9 '04		
AP 9 '93	OC 14 '04		
DE 10 '93	NO 29 '04		
JA 28 '94			
AP 18 '94			
MY 13 '94			
JE 10 '94			
FE 17 '95			
FE 24 '95			
MR 31 '95			
FE 23 '96			
OC 3 '02			
NO 22 '02			
NO 17 '03			

DEMCO 38-296

THE BLACK FAMILY

A Ministry Resources Library book

THE BLACK FAMILY

Past, Present, & Future

Perspectives of
Sixteen Black Christian Leaders

EDITED BY LEE N. JUNE

PREFACE AND SPECIAL ASSISTANCE BY
MATTHEW PARKER

ZondervanPublishingHouse

Academic and Professional Books

Grand Rapids, Michigan

A Division of HarperCollinsPublishers

The Black Family: Past, Present, and Future
Copyright © 1991 by Institute for Black Family Development

Requests for information should be addressed to:
Zondervan Publishing House
Academic and Professional Books
1415 Lake Drive, S.E.
Grand Rapids, Michigan 49506

Library of Congress Cataloging-in-Publication Data

The Black family : past, present, and future / edited by Lee N. June.
     p.   cm.
   ISBN 0-310-45591-X
    1. Afro-Americans–Families.   I. June, Lee N.
  E185.86.B52554   1991
  306.85′08996073–dc20   90-19567
                                          CIP

Edited by Susan Lutz
Designed by Nancy J. Wilson

Printed in the United States of America

91 92 93 94 95 96 / AK / 10 9 8 7 6 5 4 3

CONTENTS

PREFACE

Black (African-American) families are most often portrayed as being in crisis. Problems of teen pregnancy, crime, substance abuse, family dissolution, and unemployment are extremely severe.

One challenge that Black America faces is similar to that experienced by the twelve tribes of Israel, who wandered for forty years because they lost the faith. When they had sent out scouts to the Promised Land, all but two returned fearful of what they believed existed; they saw large fruit and assumed that the land was occupied by giants. They discouraged the people from continuing. Only two of the scouts saw the promise that the land held and saw it as God's fulfillment of his covenant with Israel. Their views were unpopular with the people. However, they were the only two adults of their generation who entered the Promised Land with the children of the others. The rest of their generation perished.

There are at least two lessons that we can draw from this. The Black community is similarly lost because it no longer sees the vision of what is possible. We only see the failures. This is reinforced by society's tendency to focus on failures and obstacles to understand success. But the only thing one can learn from a focus on failures and obstacles is how to create more failures and obstacles.

If one wants to be successful, one must learn from those who have achieved it. For example, if one wants to learn how to play the piano, one wouldn't go to ten people who failed and ask, "May I study your failures, so I can learn to be successful?" One would go to those who have mastered the instrument, seeking to learn their techniques.

We at the Institute for Black Family Development believe that some of the solutions to the crisis of the Black family are being generated by the Black community itself. To that end we have identified individuals and Christian organizations nationwide who are dealing with the problems of the Black family in imaginative and innovative ways. These successful self-help activities and models are rooted in the premise that solutions can be found by capitalizing on the strengths and successes of the Black community.

This book, one of several projects initiated by the Institute for Black

Family Development, serves as an example of how Christians from the African-American community can work together to provide knowledge, wisdom, and how-tos on biblical family life.

Dr. Lee June, as the book's General Editor, has invited grass roots people to give grass-roots solutions to several grass-roots problems facing the African-American community. This approach has yielded a book that will reinforce scriptural values while promoting an agenda that will assist Black families, Black churches, Black communities, and those working with these institutions to thrive in the years ahead.

Matthew Parker, President
The Institute for Black Family Development
16776 Southfield Road
Detroit, Michigan 48235

INTRODUCTION

This book presents the perspectives of sixteen writers on fifteen issues of vital importance to the African-American (Black) community. Each writer was deliberately chosen for his or her expertise (educational and/or experiential) in a particular area.

Although there have been several excellent books written on the Black family (some of which are referenced in this volume), this book is unique in the following ways:

1. It is comprehensive in scope, covering several topics of crucial importance to Black families and churches in a single volume.
2. Its authors are persons who write from an experiential and/or scholarly perspective *and* who make deliberate efforts to integrate a Christian perspective in their treatment of their subjects.
3. It is written with both a lay and professional readership in mind.
4. It analyzes a topic and also suggests practical solutions.
5. It makes use of writers from a range of backgrounds and disciplines.

The book begins with an examination of the unique heritage of the African-American family. Hank Allen, a sociologist and educator, describes the legacy of the Black family, outlines current issues, and suggests future challenges.

Darlene Hannah, a psychologist and educator, outlines the history and current status of the extended family in chapter 2. She sees several contemporary challenges to the extended family and points out ways the extended family can continue to be viable in future generations.

Chapter 3 is written by a counselor experienced in working with single mothers. Sheila Staley brings a practical and Bible-centered approach to a topic of growing concern within African-American communities. The suggestions she offers can aid pastors, other church leaders, and professionals, as well as persons who are themselves single parents.

Carolyn Thompson-Wallace, in chapter 4, shares her wealth of experience in working with inner-city teenagers. In this chapter, one can get the "feel" of her deep commitment to, and knowledge of, a group of persons that too many have abandoned. She shares the elements of a successful program and cries out to the church and broader society to get more involved in "saving" this segment of the population.

Chapter 5 addresses a topic that has gained increased attention over the last two decades—Black male/female relationships. This will remain an extremely critical area into the twenty-first century, given the devastating plight of Black males. In this chapter, Sherrill Burwell cogently analyzes the nature of the problems between the sexes and offers solutions. She appropriately refers to "improving" and "strengthening" in the title, which is the major focus of the chapter.

Chapters 6 and 7 look at two institutions—the church and the home—and analyze the role of each in the development of society's most valuable resource—our children. Shirley June, a homemaker for the last thirteen years, makes a strong biblical case for the deliberate and systematic use of the home in the spiritual development of the child. She challenges parents to use the time that they have with their children to carry out the biblical mandate for training. She offers concrete suggestions and resources to aid in the completion of this formidable but rewarding task.

Bonita Pope Curry, a psychologist and associate professor, evaluates the role of the church in the educational development of children. She suggests ways in which the church, like the home, can be more systematic and deliberate in the educational process. Several national, educational, church-related programs are presented.

Chapter 8 covers a topic that is too often neglected in contemporary society, even in our churches—values. Fred Lofton, a pastor, makes a compelling case for the family to focus more intentionally on values formation and transmission. Ways are suggested for doing this.

Lloyd Blue, pastor and nationally known evangelist, covers in chapter 9 an area that will need increased attention in the century ahead—pastoral counseling. This chapter argues that pastoral counseling is biblical and needed. The specific issues in establishing a pastoral counseling program are outlined.

In chapter 10, family therapist Derek McNeil takes the reader on a journey through the marriage counseling process. Couples experiencing difficulties, persons working with couples, and those learning how to work with Black couples all will profit from this analysis of the marital counseling process. He also offers methods for improving relationships.

Joan Ganns, a child and family therapist, thoroughly examines sexual abuse in chapter 11. She makes a strong case that sexual abuse is an issue requiring the intervention of both the church and the Black community. After describing the signs of possible sexual abuse and at-risk situations, she offers numerous suggestions for the church and broader community as they make an effort to prevent this most serious violation.

Lee June, a psychologist and professor, covers an area that is often neglected in the Black and broader church community. He outlines the biblical viewpoint on sex and sexuality, discusses why sex and sexuality issues tend to be problematic for many in the church community, lists resources available on the topic, and offers several suggestions for improving the sex education of Christians.

Michael Lyles, a psychiatrist, makes a compelling argument for the church to be more involved in the area of drug abuse prevention. He points out in chapter 13 that this area definitely affects the church membership. After reviewing the types of drugs and their impact on the user's body and family, he discusses treatment issues and concludes with several realistic approaches that churches can use to combat this epidemic.

Black male participation in churches lags far behind Black female participation. Black males who are involved in church are only a small percentage of the total Black male population. Willie Richardson, a pastor and national seminar leader on issues regarding the Black family, offers concrete ways to reverse this phenomenon in chapter 14. He provides a model for reaching and discipling Black males. His suggestions reflect his knowledge of the resources available in the field as well as his experiences as pastor of a church with a systematic and effective program in evangelizing Black males.

The final chapter, chapter 15, covers an area that haunts the entire world of money management. Marvin Lynch, a personnel administrator and financial management consultant, and Jackie Lynch, a financial aid counselor and a financial management consultant, share the biblical viewpoint on finances, present principles of money management, and suggest how proper financial management will promote a more hassle-free and biblically centered life.

The reader will note some variations in writing styles and formats across chapters. This is typically a feature of an edited work and often adds to its richness. Each contributor has had the freedom (within certain guidelines established by the editor) to treat the topics according to one's unique perspectives. As such, the views expressed in the chapters do not necessarily reflect those of the editor or the Institute for Black Family Development

Three comments need to be made regarding terminology. First, while the book was being assembled, the use of the term "African-American" became more prevalent. It was considered whether or not to use African-American rather than "Black" in the title of the book and chapters, while maintaining terminology that was being used by the various contributors within the chapters (thus one will find the use of both "Black" and "African-American" within some chapters).

Second, there was the question of the use of the terms "Black family/families," "Black child/children," "Black community/communities," and "Black church/churches." McAdoo (1988) discussed this issue in the preface to her book and pointed out the potential dangers of using these terms in their singular forms. However, contributors were allowed to handle this in their own manner and, at various points, used both the singular and plural forms. When this was done, the intent was not to suggest that the Black family and the Black child, etc., are monolithic entities. We recognize, as do McAdoo (1988) and Billingsley (1988), that there is diversity within the Black community. In the end we decided to use the word "family" in the overall title while recognizing the diversity within the African-American community.

Third, with regard to the issue of Black church/churches, it is common within Black communities to refer to Black churches as "the Black church." C. Eric Lincoln (1974), among many others, has described what is connoted by the term "Black church." Again, diversity is recognized in such a characterization, and the contributors were given the freedom to use the term of their choice.

My deepest appreciation goes to each contributor. A special thanks is extended to Matthew Parker, President of the Institute for Black Family Development, for his assistance in selecting writers. Likewise, a special thanks to the entire Board of Directors of the Institute for Black Family Development for their foresight in launching this project and their persistence in seeing it to completion.

As editor, it was a rewarding experience to assemble the topics and writers. It is my hope that this book will be of great value to the entire community, and particularly those who are interested in being effective with the Black (African-American) population.

Lee N. June, Editor
Lansing, Michigan
March 1990

References

Billingsley, A. (1988). *Black Families in White America*. New York: Simon & Schuster.

Lincoln, C. E. (1974). *The Black Church Since Frazier*. New York: Schocken.

McAdoo, H. (1988). *Black Families* (2d ed.). Newbury Park, Calif.: Sage.

1

The Black Family:
Its Unique Legacy, Current Challenges, and Future Prospects

Hank Allen

HANK ALLEN is Associate Professor of Sociology at Calvin College, Grand Rapids, Michigan. He has a Biblical Studies degree from Wheaton College and a Doctor of Philosophy degree from the University of Chicago. Born in Joiner, Arkansas, and raised in Phoenix, Illinois, he is married to Juliet Cooper Allen. They have six children: Jonathan, Jessica, Janice, Justin, Julia, and Janel. Hank is actively involved at Community Bible Baptist Church in Grand Rapids.

1

The Black Family: Its Unique Legacy, Current Challenges, and Future Prospects

In March 1986, Bill Moyers—then a CBS television correspondent—hosted a controversial documentary on the Black family. Moyers interviewed a sampling of teenaged mothers, as well as jobless males who had fathered multiple children. Although the documentary closed by soliciting the comments and prescriptions of Black experts, the overall impression many viewers received was that the urban Black family was in a pathological crisis. In the years since that program, journalists, educators, religious leaders, opinion-makers, and public officials have focused increasingly on problems of the Black family.

The predictable political polemics have likewise erupted, stirring further public debate. Treating Moyers' somewhat limited case studies as irrefutable empirical evidence, many politically conservative leaders have used them as an argument against government welfare programs for poor Blacks, maintaining that the economic disadvantages these Blacks experienced were merely a function of their family dissolution. Those opposed to Moyers' presentation have assailed it as an unrepresentative caricature. Because politicians influence the lives of millions for good or ill, these kinds of debates on the Black family will have serious repercussions for the future of all Blacks.

How might a Christian perspective assist in understanding the current status of the Black family? Can Christian faith enhance our understanding of the social science data and the political polemics that surround the debate over the Black family's survival? As a Christian and a sociologist, I believe that a more transcendent appraisal of the

17

strengths and weaknesses of Black family patterns is desperately needed before further progress can be made. Thus, this chapter will provide a commentary on the Black family, stressing its unique heritage, present challenges, and future possibilities.

THE BLACK FAMILY'S LEGACY

Casual observers often assume that Blacks have had social experiences that closely resemble those of their own ethnic group. To illustrate, other ethnic and racial groups will often say that their ancestors overcame prejudice, discrimination, poverty, and oppression—so why cannot Blacks do the same? This type of thinking ignores pertinent sociological evidence (Feagin, 1984). The sociological experiences of Black Americans are not comparable to those of any other ethnic group in the United States, despite social science prognostications to the contrary (Lieberson, 1980).

Blacks alone have experienced the irreparable complications of attempted genetic genocide, of being uprooted from their ancestral families and simultaneously deprived of names, culture, legacy, inheritance, and sponsorship from the old country. Blacks alone have survived the vicious dehumanization of slavery across generations, only to find themselves ushered into segregation and economic dependency by a society unwilling to make appropriate restitution for its atrocities against them. Blacks alone have watched as their labor, creativity, and productivity have been exploited from generation to generation. No other ethnic group has come close to this pariah status (Omi and Winant, 1986).

Thus, from the very beginning, Black families in the United States have faced complications that have persistently threatened their survival (Grier and Cobbs, 1968; Bennett, 1969; Franklin, 1980; and White, 1984). Blacks, most of whom were from pastoral societies in western Africa or along its continental coastlands, fell into the common predicament of slavery from several distinct tribal backgrounds (Goode, 1976). They came into slavery with varying languages, cultural traditions, rituals, and kinship networks. This, along with an unfamiliarity of American geography, effectively prevented slaves from developing the kind of complex social organization, technology, and mobilization that would be necessary to alleviate their plight (Franklin 1980). Moreover, to reinforce their brutal social and psychological control, slaveholders often eliminated any bonds of kinship or culture by dividing captured Africans into groups of mixed tribal origins before selling them to plantation owners.

These and other intergenerational social pressures associated with slavery weakened many of the original cultural and network barriers among slaves. However, the resulting ethnicity among Blacks has always been somewhat artificially induced, because of the impossibility of reconstructing indigenous tribal cultures, symbols, and lineages. To fill the social void, therefore, other status distinctions emerged from the slavery context to replace tribal affinities, as typified by the well-known status distinction Blacks still make between "field-niggers" and "house-niggers." The former group experienced greater social separation from European cultural and social influences, while the latter encountered much less social isolation, having been more fully assimilated into the dominant culture by virtue of their accessibility to and interaction with slave masters and their kin.

The reason for citing this distinction is to demonstrate that from the very beginning, Black families have been divided by superficial criteria of class, culture, and kinship foreign to them. Thus, the recent "race versus class" debate is merely the latest chapter in the continuous saga that began when Blacks were brought to this nation. Black ethnicity, being ideologically imposed on atomized family units, has always had a superficiality to it that has stymied efforts to promote unity.

Progressively across generations, ancient tribal differences among captured Africans were replaced by the more artificial cultural traditions and kinship ties adopted en masse by slaves during their captivity. Added to this complexity, which emanated from the division of labor within the plantation economy, were further regional and other subcultural distinctions between slaves. Finally, the genealogies of numerous Black families were fragmented even further by miscegenation, violence, and slave transfer. No other ethnic group has had to experience such an onslaught of sociological complexity while being denied the basic resources of humanity by their oppressors. Black families have had to create or recreate the norms, roles, culture, institutions, and ethnic ties other groups take for granted.

The point is that the failure to recognize the inherent limitations of such an artificial or aggregated ethnic experience contributes to our bewilderment over the lack of Black unity. This does not mean that specific groups of Blacks have not been able over the generations to establish powerful social networks and/or communities, nor does this suggest that ethnic unity is not an admirable or feasible goal. What it does imply, however, is that we need to visualize the Black community as a collectivity composed of individuals variously located in diversified, and sometimes extremely complicated, social networks which, like the larger White society, are competing within and among

19

themselves for power, prestige, wealth, and more recently, opportunity. These networks portend different lifestyles and standards of living for the people or families included within them. Black sociologists like E. Franklin Frazier, in *Black Bourgeoisie* (1962), and William Julius Wilson, in *The Declining Significance of Race* (1978) and *The Truly Disadvantaged* (1987), have both recognized and demonstrated the reality of social stratification in Black communities. In short, neither the Black community nor the families that have comprised it have ever been monolithic.

Thus, Blacks cannot be defined by a single, simplistic stereotype in the formulation of public policy. Prescriptions that do not recognize the complexities of Black families are destined to fail miserably. An exclusive preoccupation with the group's phenotype (skin color) obscures the historically distinct cultural parameters, institutional features, network liaisons, and universal human dimensions that describe real personal experiences within families. Just as Jews vary significantly *within* their ethnic group (a fact of ethnic life shared by European descendants such as the Germans, Scandinavians, Italians, and Irish), so diversity characterizes African-Americans. Because relevant inter-tribal comparisons are not obtainable for African-Americans due to slavery's impact, interethnic comparisons of Blacks with Jews, Poles, West Indians, and Vietnamese are also quite dubious, leading logically to an ecological fallacy of momentous proportions.

All of this reveals the complicated legacy inherited by Black families today, a heritage made more complex by our failure to acknowledge that many Blacks do not always view those Black Americans outside their families or social networks as genetic kin falling under the moral purview of their corporate responsibilities. To that extent, Black ethnicity is more atomized than that of other ethnic groups who have voluntarily entered this nation with their cultural, institutional, and network structures intact, and have not faced the multidimensional, repeated onslaught of ethnocentrism, racism, prejudice, discrimination, poverty, and segregation to the same degree.

Can Black families who desire a common ethnicity find solace in the heritage of their ancestors? As a parent coping with my own place in the saga of African-Americans, I think that there is much in our roots to embrace and salvage for future generations. However, in my experience, I have observed that many Blacks of all generations make a fatal mistake whenever they reflect on the heritage of the Black family. That is, there is a tendency to focus disproportionately or exclusively on the tragic era of slavery. This tendency is a direct consequence of being raised in a society that presents Black history and culture primarily from the viewpoint of White Americans. Indeed, one of the greatest difficulties that Black families have faced in America is to determine who we are as a people in a land in which we have been culturally, historically, and geographically exiled.

Many of us do not know much about the heritage of the Black family prior to slavery, during slavery, and subsequent to slavery. We have failed to organize evening or weekend schools devoted to the task of transmitting the history of our people. Therefore, one of the most important things we can do is to teach ourselves and our children the truth about our history as a people. We and our children need to know that Black people once had one of the most advanced civilizations on earth in ancient Egypt and Ethiopia (Snowden, 1970, 1983). Blacks have been leading intellectuals, businesspersons, engineers, lawyers, politicians, and religious officials. Moreover, in West Africa (Ghana, Mali, and Songhay), where many of our African ancestors were kidnapped, there were great kings and great civilizations. (Franklin, 1980).

Why is it important for Black families to recognize and preserve their heritage? The heritage of any ethnic group serves as the basis for its identity, social organization, productivity, planning, and responsibilities. Thus, recognizing the strengths and weaknesses of prior Black civilizations encourages a healthy self-concept. Consequently, no Black person can ever excuse himself or herself from being the most productive human being possible.

One article suggests that general feelings of inferiority may be disposing Black students to accept mediocrity in intellectual competition with others (Howard and Hammond, 1985). However, a broader view of our heritage rescues us from the paralysis of mediocrity. It is helpful to understand how societies have declined and what factors contribute to such declines (Lenski, 1970; Roberts and Brintnall, 1983; Williams, 1976).

A second reason why the Black family must recognize and preserve its heritage is to gain a global perspective on the responsibilities and needs of Black people. The reason that all family members must strive to do the best, according to God-given talents and capabilities, is because, as Jesse Jackson says so poignantly, "No one can do for us or save us but us." Blacks must assume leadership and responsibility for the problems of Black people and others, not only in words but in deeds. There is a tremendous need for Black professionals to use their resources, talents, expertise, contacts, and influence to serve Blacks in their American communities and abroad. This communal ethic must be taught and exemplified by the Black family.

A third reason for recognizing and preserving the heritage of the

21

Black family is to anticipate and rejoice continually in God's goodness. Black people can rejoice that we have endured the most degrading onslaughts of human evil and yet, through God's grace and blessing, we have more than survived as a unique people. Given the obstacles we have had to overcome, we are truly an amazing people. Despite many devastating handicaps imposed on us, we have achieved excellence in many fields of human endeavor. We have our great humanitarians, our great athletes, our great entertainers, our great professionals, and our great religious leaders.

When I remember the heritage of the Black family, I visualize millions of fathers and mothers sacrificing themselves to promote a better future for their children. We are the beneficiaries of a heritage that can in turn be made better or worse by our contributions in each successive generation. We need to remind ourselves and our children of the blood, the sweat, and the tears of our forefathers and foremothers, who eagerly embraced the moral instructions God gave to the nation of Israel in the Bible. Understanding our heritage helps us remember the ways God has blessed and disciplined our families. Family members should never forget that their lives and freedoms were purchased by human and divine sacrifice. We will curse ourselves and our descendants if we neglect the lessons of our unique heritage.

THE CURRENT STATUS OF THE BLACK FAMILY

Black families en masse must actively seek to preserve, critique, and enhance our heritage. We must not depend on the media and others to inform us about our own strengths and weaknesses. We are, can, and should be the writers and experts on the current status of our families.

The statistics and research unfortunately indicate that many types of Black families are experiencing the pressures of internal fragmentation and external social forces (Pickney, 1984; Staples, 1986; Wilson, 1987). There are multiple reasons for this, but I shall highlight a few of the neglected ones. The ones that have received more attention include the exodus of business from urban areas, a changing occupational structure, imbalanced sex ratios, the reconcentration of poverty, and racial discrimination.

An additional threat to Black civilization in cities across the nation is moral (Loury, 1985). As Christians, we must recognize that many Black families are in danger of breaking apart because Black men and women are disregarding biblical standards for sexual relations and other behaviors. Without a genuine sense of who we are before God

22

and others, we will not visualize or relate to each other as sacred human beings. Furthermore, when we violate moral principles, we are bequeathing to our descendants a burdensome legacy that they must overcome in addition to the other pressures they face as members of a captive people. The Bible offers a number of consequences associated with immorality (Job 31:1–12; Prov. 5:4–10; 29:3; 1 Thess. 4:1–8).

Black men and Black women must examine their view of sexuality and masculinity. Black women must not allow themselves to be victimized by males who would steal their purity for selfish gratification. Black women and men who ignore biblical standards for marital and family relations will suffer the consequences that result from perverting God's sacred order for all human beings (Prov. 14:34; Gal. 6:7–8).

Among the things that Black men and women must do to build better relationships is to stop listening to exploitative music and imitating media characters who promote distorted notions of romance and fidelity that ignore our accountability to God and responsibility to each other. We need to provide models of Black male and female relationships that exemplify integrity, sacrifice, lifelong commitment, and loyalty. Our communities have always been blessed with men and women who raised families in an environment of genuine love, despite the hardships of slavery, segregation, and poverty. Positive, wholesome masculine and feminine identities must refute and replace the caricatures (created for cheap profit) that pervade the entertainment industry. None of these changes can occur without churches and leaders whose priorities are to seek to restore essential moral foundations.

What is the situation for single families? One has to grieve over men or women who have willingly abandoned spouses and families, thereby inflicting harmful spiritual, psychological, sociological, and economic consequences on future generations of Black people. No amount of material comfort can replace the loss of a loving relationship. We need to recover an "extended family" or "tribal" ethic that stigmatizes those who abandon family responsibilities for personal pleasure. Obviously, we have single parent families because of divorce, marital discord, male unemployment, and teenage pregnancy, as well as from the death of a spouse. With the exception of the death of a spouse, the problems of single parent families (though complicated) could be reduced significantly by teaching and modeling corrected notions of sexuality, valuing marital relations and responsibility, and applying community norms that negatively sanction all forms of sexual promiscuity. The Black church must play a critical role in this regard.

Redefining our ethnicity and reconstructing an ethic of sexual fidelity in themselves will not provide the complete solution to the problems of the Black family. We must also focus on the external social forces that affect the Black family. One major force is economic. Whether middle class or underclass, Black families are affected by the struggle for survival. Dual parent and single parent families must concern themselves with acquiring the material resources necessary to preserve life. To achieve this, we must seek to have jobs available to all who are desirous of work.

✱ We acknowledge that Black families participate in an economy that has stolen the labor of our ancestors for generations. At the same time, it has penalized each generation for lacking the financial, cultural, and physical capital to compete on equal terms with White America. Yet we cannot wallow in self pity or paranoia. Black families must teach spouses and children to be creative, productive, diligent, and resourceful. We have both biblical and historical examples of people who have overcome obstacles and prospered.✱

Despite racism, discrimination, and poverty, Black families, rich and poor, must network within and outside the church to sponsor each other in investments, education, and business. In other words, we must strive to be at the cutting edge of all fields of work or professional endeavor, viewing our work as a sacred trust from God. Black parents, whatever their occupation or social background, must socialize their children to have positive self-concepts, to be willing to take risks and fail in order to achieve, to tackle tough jobs that require rigorous training and competition, and to organize with other Blacks to build the cultural, material, and technological resources of our communities. Teaching a correct view of our history and our successes, as noted earlier, will assist in achieving this.

We must not limit the financial, intellectual, and spiritual horizons of any generation. As parents, we must continually invest in our own spiritual, intellectual, and physical development even as we encourage our offspring to tackle science, mathematics, medicine, physics, and other areas of work. Our renowned excellence in sports, music, and entertainment must be duplicated in these other endeavors. Productivity liberates (Prov. 12:24; 22:29; Col. 3:17, 23). To meet the economic challenges, Black families must become much more productive, network more effectively, invest our material and financial resources wisely in our own enterprises as much as is feasible, and seek to creatively achieve in all types of work. As industries and jobs leave our communities, rather than panic, we must productively organize our families, schools, churches, elected officials, and businesses to create or attract new ventures.

The Black family must also combat sinister political forces. The current Black liberal versus conservative public policy debate has profound ramifications for Black families. We must inform, sponsor, and endorse candidates who have the wisdom to recognize that an uncritical adoption of either ideological position would be detrimental to the future of Black Americans and to the nation as a whole. I say this because neither the moralistic strategies of self-reliance promulgated by Black conservatives nor a messianic confidence in legislation designed to bring White America to repentance (and favored by Black liberals) are sufficient policy positions in and of themselves to address the multidimensional needs of Black families in the 1990s and beyond. Both alternatives identify crucial issues, but neither alone nor in combination can miraculously deliver Black families to the Promised Land.

To positively impact Black families, we need to understand and shape political agendas formally (through the system) and informally (by influencing coalitions within White America). We must control or contribute resources or expertise that are highly valued by the dominant society to increase our political influence. We must prepare our members to assume political office. Our political status will be enhanced to the degree that we develop and improve our creative talents in strategic areas of service and productivity (such as solar technology, business, and research). When in office, the goal of our political leaders must be to help organize the personnel, institutions, and resources of our communities in a way that enhances families.

Perhaps the most difficult obstacle Black families face is not moral, economic, political, or organizational, but psychological-cultural. Jesse Jackson aptly termed this "the grasshopper complex" during a sermon based on Numbers 14. We often have an inflated sense of White America's unity and capabilities, and conversely, a deflated sense of our own God-given resources. In essence, we devalue God's creative genius in our history and abilities.

Black families must consciously work to correct our distorted self-concepts by spearheading or controlling the educational experiences of our children. As much as is possible, we should expose them to quality, excellence, rigor, and discipline in a variety of spiritual, cultural, intellectual, and social endeavors. We must inoculate them against an excessive paranoia about racism even while we immunize them from racial schizophrenia. In short, we must (and do) significantly influence the way our family members view themselves.

To enhance our self-concepts, therefore, we must shun hurtful,

25

put-down humor along with sarcastic innuendos about the inability of Blacks to achieve or to work together. Black families must teach respect for each other and all humans. We must teach responsibility, wisdom, integrity, and cooperation with our own people. As members of the Black church, we have a unique opportunity to do this.

However, Black families must also attack notions of Black inferiority, whether these are found in the ivory towers of the academy or the cultural ghettos (Taylor, 1980). Blacks are not intellectually, culturally, nor spiritually inferior to Whites, and we should not compete or act as if this is so! But neither are we innately superior to Whites. Because God has blessed all people with talents and capabilities, Black families must avoid any sense of racial superiority or ethnocentrism. We have no right to obscure God's glory by taking exclusively selfish pride in the talents and abilities he has given us through his sovereign will.

Black families must also aggressively attack the waste and destructiveness typified by Black-on-Black crime in all its forms, from murder to violence to drug addiction. One way to do this is to become leaders or experts in the professions of law enforcement, criminal justice, and jurisprudence, as well as psychology, social work, education, and sociology.

Not only must we oppose evil behaviors when we are their objects or victims, we must aggressively seek to deliver our brothers and sisters from these self-destructive habits through evangelism, discipleship, and direct yet proactive social involvement. Indeed, one of the reasons why the Muslims have been so successful among street people and criminals is because they inform the street people about their Black heritage and give them a sense of spiritual destiny. Every Black criminal, pimp, prostitute, and drug dealer was born and raised in some relation to a Black family. One wonders how many lives might be changed if Black families would begin a massive offensive with a goal to network and socialize their members into their heritage without any thought of casualties or retreat.

THE FUTURE OF THE BLACK FAMILY

What can be done for Black families as we approach the twenty-first century? First, on the individual level, I recommend that every Black man and woman research their racial heritage, develop a biblically based self-concept, and commit themselves in their sexuality, identity, and relationships to God and his standards for morality, integrity, and excellence. This recommendation presupposes that all are committed to a biblical working knowledge of God's truth. Because the fear of the

Lord is the beginning of wisdom and knowledge (Prov. 1:7), we must individually recognize that our personal success depends on how we practice or experience God's truth in our own lives. There is no excuse for this generation of Black Americans to ignore the God who delivered us from the bondage of slavery, segregation, oppression, poverty, and ignorance. We must realize that we are accountable to God for our gifts, talents, opportunities, attitudes, actions, and motives in life.

Second, Black men and women who possess the qualities outlined above must enhance their dating and marital standards, refusing to surrender their purity or legacy for a moment of sexual pleasure, thereby modeling biblical femininity and masculinity for the next century. Ephemeral romance must be abandoned; achievements in character, education, career, and finances must take priority. All temptations to illicit sex must be resisted. Black parents must rediscover the African tribal tradition of making marriage a corporate affair, involving two families whose destinies become intertwined by the union of man and wife. Moreover, our families should create norms that reinforce family responsibility even as we give needed support to single parent families. Black families should also be responsible for channeling the talents of their members into economically productive activities and occupations, as well as exposing members to excellence in all human endeavors.

Because the family is the fundamental social institution that holds the key to the future status of the Black church and community, families must be formed with an evidence and pledge of faith and character. True love between a mature man and woman recognizes a responsibility to bequeath a healthy and productive legacy to their children.

Third, the task of the Black church is—like that of Ezra and Nehemiah in the Old Testament—to promote spiritual, ethnic, and psychological rejuvenation among a people recovering from captivity; to model and proclaim God's truth to Black men, women, and children through evangelism and discipleship so that Christ's sovereign rule will be acknowledged in the family. Weak families suggest weak churches and vice versa! Satan thrives where spiritual authority is weak (Mark 3:27). Could the destruction rampant in certain communities reflect a vacuum of true spiritual leadership? Are many of our churches neglecting their biblical responsibility?

God, our Creator, controls and distributes the creativity, talents, resources, and opportunities we need to bless the lives of our families and others (Prov. 2:5–11; James 1:5). By giving our lives and resources first to him, submitting to his Word, and obeying our true spiritual leaders, we can expect God to meet our families' needs through our own creativity and productivity or through the resources of others. The church cannot fail at its task without also damaging the potential of Black families and, ultimately, the Black community. This is not to say that the church must endorse the theological fallacy of separating spiritual concerns from material concerns. Indeed, the church must be the means through which Black families unite to invest their time and resources to accomplish essential economic, social, and political objectives for the Black community.

Because churches are still the central, most indigenous social institution in most communities, they might network to sponsor periodic workshops on child-rearing, on writing religious literature for all ages, on business development, career planning, and investments. They could also organize political or educational forums, as well as sponsor recreational activities. However, the church leadership must not abandon their primary spiritual mission. Laity must execute these supplemental activities (but not at the expense of family nurture). In short, the church must be the resource center for enhancing the Black family and reconstructing the foundations of our communities.

Finally, each urban area with a large population of Black families could incorporate a philanthropic foundation that would research changes in the Black family. Funds could be combined to provide the investment capital required to establish this key entity. Over a decade, millions of dollars might be easily secured to sponsor all kinds of ventures that would enhance the quality of life for Black families. Private schools and corporations, for example, might be started with such funding.

CONCLUSION

This chapter has explored issues in the heritage, current status, and future prospects of the Black family. Seeking a balanced viewpoint, the chapter has promulgated a respect for the past as well as the encouragement to meet the challenges of the present and future. The problems of ethnicity, morality, organization, internal fragmentation, and external pressures, and their impact on various Black families have been examined.

God desires to have a cadre of Black men and women whose ambition is to serve our community and not neglect it for the temporal luxuries of our adversaries. We need Black women and men with the character and courage of the biblical Esther to do whatever is righteous to preserve our families before God! We need people who have the faith to raise godly and productive families! My hope is that everyone will decide to be that kind of person, by understanding the positive aspects of our heritage while preparing oneself spiritually, academically, and in every relevant way to liberate other Blacks from the internal chains of sinful oppression, as well as from racism within society.

References

Bennett, L. (1969). *Before the Mayflower* (4th ed.) Chicago: Johnson Publishing.

Feagin, J. R. (1984). *Racial and Ethnic Relations* (2d ed.). Englewood Cliffs, N.J.: Prentice-Hall.

Franklin, J. H. (1980). *From Slavery to Freedom* (5th ed.). New York: Knopf.

Frazier, E. F. (1962). *Black Bourgeoisie*. London: Collier Books.

Goode, K. (1976). *From Africa to the United States and Then*. Glenview, Ill.: Scott, Foresman and Company.

Grier, W. H., and Cobbs, P. M. (1968). *Black Rage*. New York: Bantam Books.

Howard, J., and Hammond, R. (1985). Rumors of Inferiority. *The New Republic* (September): *193*, 17–21.

Lenski, G. (1970). *Human Societies*. New York: McGraw-Hill.

Lieberson, S. (1980). *A Piece of the Pie*. Berkeley: University of California Press.

Loury, G. C. (1985). The Moral Quandary of the Black Community. *Public Interest* (Spring): *79*, 9–22.

Omi, M., and Winant, H. (1986). *Racial Formation in the United States*. New York and London: Routledge and Keegan Paul.

Pinkney, A. (1984). *The Myth of Black Progress*. Cambridge: Cambridge University Press.

Roberts, R. E., and Brintnall, D. E. (1983). *Reinventing Inequality*. Cambridge, Mass.: Schenkman Publishing.

Snowden, F. M., Jr. (1970). *Blacks in Antiquity*. Cambridge, Mass.: Belknap Press.

————. (1983). *Before Color Prejudice: The Ancient View of Blacks*. Cambridge: Harvard University Press.

Staples, R., ed. (1986). *The Black Family: Essays and Studies*. Belmont, Calif.: Wadsworth Publishing.

Taylor, H. F. (1980). *The IQ Game*. New Brunswick: Rutgers University Press.

The Holy Bible: New International Version (1978). Grand Rapids: Zondervan.

White, J. L. (1984). *The Psychology of Blacks*. Englewood Cliffs, N.J.: Prentice-Hall.

Williams, C. (1976). *The Destruction of Black Civilization*. Chicago: Third World Press.

Wilson, W. J. (1978). *The Declining Significance of Race*. Chicago: University of Chicago Press.

————. (1987). *The Truly Disadvantaged*. Chicago: University of Chicago Press.

2

The Black Extended Family:
An Appraisal of Its Past, Present, and
Future Statuses

Darlene B. Hannah

DARLENE HANNAH is Assistant Professor of Psychology at Wheaton College, Wheaton, Illinois, and a member of the Philadelphia Church in Chicago. She received her Bachelor of Arts degree in psychology from the University of Virginia and her Master of Science and Doctor of Philosophy degrees in social psychology from Northwestern University, Evanston, Illinois. Born in Newport News, Virginia, and raised in Hampton, Virginia, Darlene is married to Blair Hannah and mother of one daughter, Danica.

2

The Black Extended Family:
An Appraisal of Its Past, Present, and
Future Statuses

Next to the myth of the domineering Black matriarchy, the structure of the extended family is perhaps the most misconstrued aspect of the Black family lifestyle. Those overestimating its frequency fail to realize that the extended family structure is but one of a variety of kinship forms found among Blacks. Others lauding its strengths have often simultaneously ignored weaknesses found in many of these families. Still others predicting the ultimate demise of the extended family as a viable relational unit for Blacks have neglected its resilient nature. Taken in sum, the views pertaining to the Black extended family need to be carefully scrutinized in order to obtain an accurate appraisal of its present state. The goal of this chapter is to develop a working definition and description of the Black extended family network and to examine how historical forces have shaped its current status. Strengths and weaknesses that contribute to this unique relational unit will also be discussed, along with an analysis of projected trends that will impact the future of the extended family.

TYPOLOGIES OF FAMILY STRUCTURE

A proper examination of the extended family begins with a brief exposition of the classification of family structures. In general, social scientists have identified three basic structural categories: the nuclear family, the polygamous family, and the extended family (Reiss, 1976).[1] Nuclear families, the nominal structure in American society, consist of one husband and wife and their offspring. Historical research suggests that Black families had been primarily nuclear for many decades (Hall and King, 1982; Krech, 1982). Polygamous families include extra husbands and/or wives and their children. Legal restrictions, for the most part, prohibit the official recognition of such families in the United States. Consequently, the polygamous family will not be considered as a viable Afro-American family grouping.

In contrast to the relatively simplistic definition of the nuclear family, the extended family unit has been classified in a variety of ways, depending on whether one's definition of a family is a residential group or a kinship group. The former construct identifies all individuals living in the same household as a family unit, while the latter restricts family membership to related individuals. Krech (1982) notes that census data tends to obscure this distinction by describing households (residential groups) only, ignoring the vast array of relationships between persons residing in a household setting. But the extended family household can include non-kin residential groupings as well as nuclear kin residential clusters. Taking these variations into account, the extended family unit has been defined by researchers in the following manner:

> A household including any relatives other than spouse or children of head of the household . . . does not require three generations. (Anderson and Allen, 1984, p. 149)

> Any living arrangement that includes family members other than the respondent's spouse and children. (Beck and Beck, 1984, p. 283)

> Other relatives or in-laws of the family head sharing the same household with nuclear family members. (Billingsley, 1988, p. 16)

> Primary family units that take in (a) two or more related persons (i.e., subfamilies), (b) one related person (i.e., secondary members), and (c) non-relatives. (Hill, 1977, p. 36)

Section (c) of the last definition listed is actually a variation of the extended family structure that some researchers define as a fourth distinct entity, the augmented family (Billingsley, 1988). Augmented families consist of a nuclear family plus members in the household not

---

[1]An obvious omission in the family structure category listing is the single-parent family unit. Admittedly, this is a category that is increasing in quantity and warrants attention. However, a significant number of single parent family households (in contrast to nuclear family households) are a part of extended family units. Thus, I have decided not to address them separately

related to the nuclear family members. If we include augmented families in our operational definition of an extended household, the percentage of Black extended families in the United States increases from 25 percent to 33 percent. The special relationship between the augmented and extended structures will be discussed further in another section of this chapter.

All of the definitions listed above limit family members to a single household. While the focus on a common residence is the prevailing norm for studies of the extended family using census data, the extended family is not necessarily restricted to a single residence. Multihousehold extended families dispersed across geographical regions are found extensively in the anthropological/case studies of Black extended families (e.g., Aschenbrenner, 1975; Martin and Martin, 1978; Shimkin, Louie, and Frate, 1978). Hence, for the purposes of this chapter, the extended family can be described as an interactive and mutually supportive unit consisting of multigenerational kin and non-kin members, living in the same household or in connected households dispersed geographically.

HISTORICAL PERSPECTIVE OF THE BLACK
EXTENDED FAMILY

To comprehend the unique nature of the Black extended family, as well as the value-laden views developed by many White Americans toward this system, it is necessary to juxtapose the African-American variant of this kinship form to its Anglo counterpart. The extended family network was never a dominant family form for the Anglo-American populace. Skolnick (1986) comments that the "Era of the Extended Family" in American society was, to a great extent, nonexistent. Contrary to popular belief, America was never a nation dominated by extended family households. Whenever a significant number of American families were found to contain non-nuclear persons in the home, these individuals were usually strangers boarding in the household instead of relatives or close associates (Skolnick, 1986). The rationale for the development of an extended family household unit was primarily economic in nature, as opposed to any "traditional desire to maintain generational ties" (Reiss, 1976). Thus, the idea of the multigenerational household was more fantasy-oriented than reality-based.

Crucial to this fantasy was the implicit assumption that the Anglo multigenerational household should be financially solvent, not a unit based on mutual need or reciprocal aid. This romanticized view of the extended family system was reminiscent of the few wealthy family lines established during the pre-Revolutionary war era. Numerically, however, America reflected the trend of most industrial societies in its movement toward nuclear families as the norm (Popenoe, 1987), and the extended family structure as the exception to the rule.

How does the genesis of the Black extended family compare to the Anglicized version? First, it is imperative to note that in contrast to Western culture, the extended family is the prevailing mode of family organization throughout Africa and other Third World settings (Al Faruqi 1978; Obikeze, 1987). It is primarily African culture, as opposed to a European framework, that is believed to be the foundation of the Black American extended family network. Some African-American scholars assert that the Black extended family can only be comprehended as a derivative of the African family system that was altered by its transition into American society (e.g. Nobles, 1974). The entry of the African family unit into American society reflected the impact of slavery, yet the unit still retained a strong African influence (Sudarkasa, 1981).

The institution of slavery attempted to destroy the solidarity of the African extended networks, which were based on consanguinous (i.e., bloodline) ties, and that were predominantly polygamous in structure. This was systematically accomplished by eliminating polygamous family units and by providing a quasi-monagamous ideal for slaves to emulate (Du Bois, 1908). The new foundation provided by slavemasters was "quasi" in the sense that slave marriages and families were not legally acknowledged, nor were the offspring of slave unions under the authoritative control of the parents.

Nevertheless, the disruption of formalized family units only served to encourage obligations between whatever blood kin could be identified. Often it was the case that slave relatives struggled to save money in order to purchase each others' freedom (Gutman, 1976). If acquiring freedom for family members was an impossible goal to accomplish, more drastic measures were taken to maintain bonds between relatives. History is replete with accounts of runaway slaves risking their lives to be reunited with family members about to be sold or sent away. Although African-American slave families may not have been initially recognized by the government, the perception of family and the subsequent obligations entailed were salient realities in the eyes of the slaves.

Thus, the transmission of African culture onto American soil produced a variant of American and African family styles that combined elements of both societies. The resulting product structurally resembles its American counterpart in that it was monogamous, conjugal, and had a bilateral emphasis (Aschenbrenner, 1974). The values inherent in the Black extended family, however, reflect much more of a consanguinous focus, like its African counterpart. Nobles' (1974) characterization of the present Black extended family household as being "African in nature, American in nature," aptly depicts the contributions of these two cultures in the formation of this distinct family structure.

PERCEPTIONS OF THE BLACK EXTENDED FAMILY BY ANGLO-AMERICAN RESEARCHERS

Because the Black extended family stands in stark contrast to the White middle class nuclear family, it is often perceived as a deviation of this prevailing American familial lifestyle. Comparisons are made with the assumption that the two units (White nuclear and Black extended) are culturally equivalent (Dodson, 1981; Myers, 1982), when, in fact, the Black extended family functions more as a cultural variant. The comparisons usually generate a depiction of the Black family structure as abnormal, pathological, and undesirable (Heiss, 1975).

To illustrate this point, consider the case of the sub-extended family. These are family members not residing in the primary household, yet depending on the extended family for financial and emotional support. Martin and Martin (1978) observe that "taking a sub-extended family for a nuclear family can easily distort the perception of Black family life. A sub-extended family household with the father absent appears to be a broken home, but it may really be a vital part of a strong and flexible extended family" (p. 9). Hence, comparisons are often value-laden and misleading, with White middle class cultural norms being used as the standard for judgment. A more profitable approach to studying the extended family is to examine the function it serves for African-Americans. By identifying the characteristics of the Black extended family and the values embraced by this kinship system, a clearer picture of its role in African-American society should emerge.

CHARACTERISTICS OF BLACK EXTENDED FAMILIES

What are some of the attributes affiliated with extendedness in Black families? One distinctive is its multigenerational composition. Although many Black extended networks are comprised of a family taking in additional adult siblings or a household absorbing extra nieces or nephews, a significant number of extended families are three-generational households. Beck and Beck (1984) report that over a ten year period (1966–1976), approximately 25 percent to 33 percent of their Black survey sample lived in households composed of aged parent/grandparent(s), adult children, and grandchildren. The formation of these multigenerational units is often prompted by a temporary need for an older parent to house an unmarried child and his or her children, or by economic hardships experienced by elderly parents.

The head of the extended household is usually forty-five years old or older (Anderson and Allen, 1984). Many of these heads of households are the eldest in the family and are female, although Martin and Martin (1978) hasten to contend that the latter is due to the fact that female spouses live longer than their husbands. They corroborate this point by noting that in their case study examining thirty Black extended families, many of the households originally began with a husband/wife dual headship structure. This finding corresponds with other observations that the Black extended family is a bilateral unit, albeit one with a matrilineal focus (Aschenbrenner, 1975, 1978).

A very interesting trend in Black nuclear family networks is the way many of these households evolve into a variant of the extended structure, the augmented family unit. As identified earlier in this chapter, an augmented family includes non-relatives living in the residential unit. These individuals, mostly children, are informally adopted by the household. They can include foster children as well as adult family friends and neighbors (Wolf, 1983). Statistics suggest that 8 percent of the children living in nuclear homes are not related to the family members, in essence, belonging to an augmented structure (Hill and Shackelford, 1986). That this percentage may indicate a growing trend is reflected in the increasing number of children absorbed by augmented families (National Urban League, 1981). With respect to how these individuals are treated, there is no data to suggest that members of augmented households treat kin and informally adopted non-kin residents differently. Indeed, we may even go so far as to assign the role of "para-kin" to these non-related household members. The augmented variation of the extended family structure depicts a very special quality of the Black extended family. The taking in of non-related individuals reflects the elasticity of these households, for informal adoptions of this nature often begin as temporary arrangements and end up becoming permanent (Hall and King, 1982; Hill and Shackelford, 1986).

38

Geographic Locale

African-American extended families are found primarily in the southern region of the United States, specifically in rural areas (Anderson and Allen, 1984; Shimkin et al., 1978). The South functions as home base for many sub-extended families that migrated to the northern regions of the United States. Interestingly, extended kin networks do not fare as well in the western states. Shimkin and his colleagues (1978) attribute this finding to the relatively young age of the Black population that migrated to the West. An elderly, mature head of household was less likely to be found among these families. Thus, the age status that is such an integral component of the Black extended family was missing in the western region of the country, resulting in its relative lack of extended networks.

Socioeconomic Status

Perhaps the most controversial demographic characteristic of the Black extended family is its socioeconomic standing (SES). Whereas Heiss (1975) argues that the relationship between lower class standing and the extended family structure for Blacks is illusory, other data (e.g., Anderson and Allen 1984; Martin and Martin, 1978; Stack, 1974) suggest that extendedness is strongly associated with lower SES levels. In the Martins' (1978) population sample, high incidences of unemployment existed and despite maximum effort, the families were barely subsisting. Anderson and Allen (1984) note that Blacks living in extended family residences tend to form the network as an adaptive response to their low economic condition. On the other hand, extensive research by Harriet McAdoo (1981) suggests that upward mobility in many Black families is a result of support from the extended family network. McAdoo asserts that extended family bonds transcend economic status and will be found at middle as well as lower-class levels.

How do we resolve the conflicting findings? An important factor to consider is the definition of the extended family that is used. Anderson and Allen (1984) note that "when definitions of extended family structure based on interaction and exchange are used, results seem to be mixed. However, when a residential definition of extended structure is used, it has consistently been found that socioeconomic status is inversely related to the probability of extendedness." (p. 144). Not only must we examine the definition of extendedness, it is also necessary to scrutinize the distinction between "lower" and "middle" class standing. It has been suggested that current social class indicators have been structured using a White population base system that overestimates the number of lower-class Blacks (Dodson, 1981). Thus, if we adjust for this bias, we will find Black middle-class families embracing an extended network. Nevertheless, even in Black middle class families, the rationale for embodying extendedness can often be related to financial struggles (Tatum, 1987).

Functions of the Extended Family

Paramount in the existence of the extended family unit is its function as a mutual-support system for all family members. The form of support is predominantly economic sustenance, but to assume that the function of the network is limited to this one crucial element is an error. The extended family also provides emotional stability for its members (Martin and Martin, 1978) and serves to encourage social support and emotional obligation (Shimkin et al., 1978; Taylor, 1986). The role of a social support system is an extremely important function of the extended family. In many Black communities, needy people turn to their extended family, not to the government institutions that were established as public service organizations but are not viewed as very supportive of minorities (Hays and Mindel, 1973). The police force, for example, may not always provide the protection needed against gang intimidation, violence against family members, and damage to personal property. It may be deemed more practical to depend on a relative known by the perpetrators to intervene for the family's safety. Thus, without this ongoing exchange of goods and services within the extended network, many of the family members would not be able to survive (Stack, 1974).

The Extended-Family Value System

Whereas the functions of the extended family correspond to needs exacerbated by the structure of American society, the value system embraced by the extended family reflects its African heritage. Rokeach (1968) has collected data that shows significant differences in the relative rankings of values held by Black and White Americans. One of the primary differences existing is an African-American emphasis on obedience. With regard to the extended family, this value is reflected both in its adherence to strict discipline and in its overwhelming respect for parental authority (Martin and Martin, 1978). A respect for elders is a crucial component of the Black child's socialization process in the extended network system. In an extended family, the responsibility for child rearing is shared by many adult members. It is important for the maintenance of order that the child learns to heed not only his/her parents or just the household head, but also any other older relative who may be tending to the child for a set period of time. Children learn rapidly that any and all of the caretakers in the family possess the right to administer discipline.

A heightened respect for elders is also one of the reasons why multigenerational extended families exist in African-American society in the first place. Black families are reluctant to place their incapacitated elderly members into nursing homes. Such placements are perceived as tantamount to abandonment, and are viewed as a poor means of reciprocating the years of care provided by parents and grandparents. Thus, although great expense may be incurred, taking in the elderly member is considered to be a much better alternative than the impersonal assistance provided by a nursing home facility. Only when we acknowledge this respect for the elderly held by the extended network can we begin to understand why a struggling household will choose to risk further financial strain by absorbing elderly members.

Another value embraced by the Black extended family is a high priority placed on motherhood and children. Anti-abortion attitudes are more prevalent among Blacks (Hall and Ferree, 1986), and reflect, in part, a greater acceptance of unwed motherhood. While being pregnant and single is not considered a desirable situation, Black unwed mothers are nevertheless encouraged to have their children. "Motherhood is nothing to be ashamed of," is the stance adopted by the Black community. The support system established by the extended family attempts to secure the welfare of these children born out of wedlock. As noted earlier, responsibility for child rearing is diffused, and whatever household (in sub-extended networks) can best support the child in question is the household that child will live in. There are even circumstances in which children are shared with other relatives who may desire to be parents but are childless. The common denominator linking both of the above cases is a generalized positive regard for children.

A final value embraced by the extended network is the perceived importance of religious belief (Martin and Martin 1978; Shimkin et al. 1978; Tatum 1987). This particular value is stressed more by the elder members of the family, who may often feel that younger family members do not depend on or believe in God as they ought. The elderly members are the transmitters of religious instruction; they are the ones most concerned about exposing the children to religious training. A respect for their position in the family serves to facilitate the transmission of religious belief to other family members.

STRENGTHS AND WEAKNESSES
OF THE EXTENDED FAMILY

Besides the aforementioned value system embraced by the extended unit, there are a number of strengths reflected in this particular family structure that merit attention. Elasticity is one of these attributes. The Black extended family, by necessity, must be able to expand in order to accommodate additional members. The encouragement of informal adoptions by the extended family certainly demonstrates an important aspect of flexibility (Hall and King, 1982; Hill, 1977). In like fashion, however, the extended unit also needs to be resilient enough to function when the household size is reduced. The ability of the family to cope with a diminishing household depends, in part, on the nature of the support withdrawn by the departing family member. If the individual in question played a crucial role in generating emotional or financial support, his or her absence will produce a significant void. Of course, this problem is not unique to the extended family structure. But because a strong mutual support system is essential to the very existence of extendedness, the loss of supportive members may exact an even greater toll on the extended family's welfare than would be the case for the nuclear family. We may conclude then, that a strength of the extended unit is its ability to expand when necessary, but that this flexibility is not as obvious when the family starts to get smaller.

Interconnectedness, a sense of oneness with family members, is regarded as another prominent strength of the Black extended family. In an extended structure, the family provides a sense of belonging to each member, so that one's personal identity becomes defined and shaped by the household. The "I" is often enveloped by the "we"; what is "mine" or "yours" becomes "ours." Nowhere is this concept so explicitly revealed as in the familial sharing of material possessions and achievements (Martin and Martin, 1978). "Cousin Barbara's" new car becomes communal property; in a tightly knit extended network, supportive kin take advantage of the availability of her vehicle. Likewise, the pride evoked by a brother's athletic or academic accomplishments is shared by relatives, who may boast as if the achievements were actually their own. Both of the previous examples illustrate how acquired possessions and accomplishments of individuals in the network gain family ownership. The resulting status-heightening is shared by the unit as a whole.

The cohesion exemplified by the extended family's interconnectedness is yet another reflection of its grounding in African heritage. In African society, emphases are placed on tribe members' horizontal relationships with relatives currently living, and vertical relationships connecting ancestors and those family members yet to be born (Nobles, 1974). A similar process occurs in African-American culture via the extended family structures. The interdependence displayed by the extended family network acts as a springboard for the unity displayed by the Black community at large. In both cultures, the Black individual finds him- or herself integrally related to other Blacks. There is an unspoken sense of obligation and shared destiny, resulting in what *Ebony* publisher John H. Johnson (1986) describes in its ideal state as a "love for each other whether we're related or not." Such a philosophy easily translates into the practice of establishing fictive (non-related) kin ties and encouraging foster support in the extended network (Wolf, 1983).

The egalitarian view of sex roles held by the extended family is one that promotes the functioning of the unit and thus also serves as a strength of the network. Predating the feminist and men's liberation movements, the perspective of the Black family in general was—and still is—to acknowledge the complementary and interchangeable roles of the sexes and to reject rigid sex role dictates. Both males and females are expected to perform a variety of household tasks, with an emphasis placed on a job being completed as opposed to focusing on sex distinctives that may be associated with the task in question (Chimezie, 1984; Peters and Massey, 1983). Consequently, sex-stereotyped traits such as nurturance and assertiveness are deemed desirable for all family members to possess. This seems to be particularly the case for the eldest child (male or female) who often finds him- or herself in the role of sibling caretaker (Peters, 1988). Furthermore, that these behaviors are acquired via a social learning process is reflected partly in the positive correlation existing between maternal employment and children's egalitarian sex role identity in Black families (Brookins, 1985). Children living in extended structures are accustomed to their mothers working outside of the home, and to having male relatives frequently serve as caretakers. Experiencing assertive female and nurturant male role models in their home setting promotes the modeling of egalitarian behaviors by youngsters in extended families.

Elasticity, interconnectedness, and egalitarian sex role views are just a subset of the strengths found in the extended family. Other positive attributes mentioned in the literature on Black families as a whole also apply to the specific case of the Black extended network (e.g., see Hill, 1977).

Like any other social structure, the extended network is not without its liabilities. Some of the criticisms leveled against it, however, are subject to reproof. Consider, for example, the concern raised by Baughman (1971) with regard to the instability of the extended family. He maintains that the composition of the family is subject to such fluctuations that the younger dependents are uncertain as to who will be present from day to day. Case studies (e.g., Martin and Martin, 1978; Zollar, 1985) clearly refute this charge of residential flux and suggest, to the contrary, that the extended family network provides a sense of stability for its members (Peters and Massey, 1983).

While the charge of instability is unsubstantiated, a valid criticism of the extended family structure involves its overemphasis on consanguine loyalties. In a sense, this weakness can be perceived as a strength of the extended network—the interconnectedness of kin—gone awry. The high rate of divorce and separation plaguing Black marriages may partly stem from an undermining of conjugal ties when conflicts with blood kin occur (Skimkin et al., 1978). In her examination of the support system of the extended network, Aschenbrenner (1978) found that the solidarity of family frequently worked to the detriment of the spouse linked by marriage to the extended family.[2] Often, family members are expected to place the needs of relatives before the needs of a husband or wife. The consequence of such a decision is a strain on marital relations, especially when a spouse's siding with blood kin is unquestioned and recurrent. The preservation of Black marriages will depend, to a certain extent, on an increased effort by extended networks to perceive the special needs of the nuclear families within them.

A related weakness of many extended families is an unqualified acceptance of the human frailties of members within the network (Shimkin et al., 1978). Adult family members who violate norms of reciprocity, expecting support from the family while concurrently providing few, if any, benefits for the family, are often not just tolerated, but are actively supported by the network. While negative reciprocity is not deemed desirable by the network, the family still manages to encourage such selfishness by its ongoing aid to the

[2]Even though spouses are part of the extended structure, in many cases they still have not been afforded "kin" status. Contrast this position to the one held by "informally adopted" non-relatives (fictive kin). The former become part of the family by legal sanction, the latter by family consensus.

offending member. Zollar (1985) provides a prototypical example of this problem in one of her case studies:

> Once again, Brenda is the only member of this family who is dependent on welfare payments. Her mother and sisters are at the point of saying, "We give up on that girl. We just give up." They explain their willingness to give up on Brenda in a number of ways. First, she has had a second child (by a different man than her first child!). Second, she refuses her family's offers to pay for schooling, and turned down an offer to work for her sister Louise. Finally, she seems content with her situation. Even with this aid, they continue to make sure that she has her rent paid, some food to eat, and clothes for herself and her two children to wear. (p. 43)

In the case of this particular family, Brenda (the youngest sister) has placed the family in a constant state of crisis. They must subsidize her minimal welfare payments and have grown accustomed to receiving little help from her in return. In essence, she has placed the family's economic position in a precarious pattern. Worse yet, Brenda seems to have no intentions of changing her behavior. Note that the weakness in this practice lies not in the network's unconditional support of kin. Rather, the problem is grounded in the family's unconditional support of a parasitic relative to the detriment of the network as a whole. An important element in this weakness, as well, is the family's submission to violations of their code of moral conduct without rigorously demanding and effecting change in the wayward adult members. Whereas children are administered swift discipline to correct unacceptable behavior, the transgressions of many teenage and adult members often go unchecked.

Despite the serious consequences resulting from the weaknesses of the extended family, none of the problems identified are immutable. It is important, however, to recognize these faults as true shortcomings and neither justify them nor dismiss them as "cultural variants" that are part and parcel of Black family lifestyle. To do so, suggests sociologist Walter Allen, is to accept the false premise that "any aspect of Black life which exists, no matter how perverse or harmful, must serve a useful function" (Allen, 1978, p. 126). Accurately assessing these frailties as faults is the first step to eradicating the weaknesses found in the extended network.

ISSUES IMPACTING THE FUTURE OF THE BLACK EXTENDED FAMILY

If we anticipate the survival of the extended family network into the twenty-first century, it is imperative not only to identify assets and deficits within the structure, but also to examine external factors that impinge on its functioning. The next section of this chapter addresses sociological trends that will have a definite impact on the future of the Black extended family.

Urbanization and Remigration

In their broad research on extended families, Elmer and Joanne Martin (1978) discovered that a majority of their interviewees believed urban life to be detrimental to the existence of the family network. The availability of adequate housing was foremost among urban problems; extended families in large cities are faced with either living in cramped quarters or trying to find a slightly larger residence that would most likely be prohibitively expensive. Even if the family could find an affordable, sizable apartment, rental policies may limit the number of residents allowed to dwell in the premises or place restrictions on which persons (e.g., relatives, non-related adults) may subsequently come to reside there. Availability of rentals in urban areas has also been impacted by the widespread conversion of moderately priced apartments into expensive condominiums (Ploski and Williams, 1983), further reducing the number of affordable residences. Clearly, extended family bases that relocate in an urban setting are faced with a housing crisis that discourages long-term residency. Consequently, a number of Blacks previously living in the northern and western regions of the United States have been, since the late 1970s, remigrating back to the South (Farley and Allen, 1987). Whether remigration is attributed to the high unemployment rates, abundant crime, or lack of adequate housing plaguing urban environments, this trend ultimately favors the strengthening of the extended networks. With a number of Black families returning to the South, the geographic dispersions of sub-extended families will be over shorter distances, enabling more interaction between family members residing outside of the home base.

Changes in Value System

A negative consequence associated with urbanization is a drift away from many of the traditional values embraced by the rural-based extended network. Replacing these values are priorities that stress secular, materialistic, and individualistic lifestyles linked to highly industrialized settings (Martin and Martin, 1978). Urbanization, however, is not the only process that promotes value changes that are antithetical to an extended family structure Upward economic mobility

46

also serves to promote such a value change. This is one reason why some researchers believe that once a family member gains middle class status, it is extremely difficult for that person to remain integrally connected to the rest of the extended network.

Take, for example, the middle class emphasis on individualism: the extended family network tends to discourage this trait in its members because it may undermine the mutual support system so crucial to the network. Paradoxically, it is this support from the network that enables many of its members to progress to middle and upper middle class status in the first place. Thus, the upwardly mobile family member is faced with a dilemma. In order to maintain middle class status, he/she must focus on personal economic sustenance to the relative neglect of extended family members; yet reciprocity is expected, for it was most probably the economic support of the family that helped him or her to obtain the present position.

A resolution to this conflict involves some give and take from both parties. First, the extended network may need to consider loosening its reins on individual family members and seek to modify norms of reciprocity when they become too rigid. If a family member or a sub-extended family grouping gains greater material wealth, they should not be expected to support the whole network. On the part of the upwardly mobile family member, remembering the cultural heritage and benefits of interconnectedness may temper the desire to become totally independent of the family.

Changes in Government Policies and Assistance Programs

Finally, among the most important external factors impacting the extended family presently and in years to come are the government support programs, such as Social Security and Aid to Families with Dependent Children. If we consider that a significant number of extended families are being aided by these programs, then we have cause for alarm when observing severe funding cutbacks. As commendable and effective as the mutual support of the extended family network happens to be, alone it is incapable of overcoming the financial stress placed on lower income families by Reaganomics (Zollar, 1985). Clearly, some additional economic support is needed to help many of these families survive.

Although increased funding for government welfare programs is necessary, it is insufficient to resolve the financial struggles currently overwhelming the poverty-stricken members in extended networks. Current welfare policies must be altered to become more sensitive to the needs and the dignity of poor families. These policies must be revamped in order to overcome their self-defeating structures. They must be restructured to work with the strengths of extended families, instead of against them.

For purposes of illustration, consider the current increase in abortions—not among young, unmarried Black mothers, but among married Black women (Edelman, 1987). This trend is in direct contradiction to the high regard the Black extended family has for mothering and children, as well as the anti-abortion attitudes commonly held. To understand this unfortunate turn of events, it is necessary to acknowledge the fact that a majority of Black married women are employed outside the home and contribute a significant amount to the extended family income. To lose the wife's income due to a pregnancy leave of absence places a severe strain on the family income, a strain that may plummet the family far below poverty level. While Black extended families are willing to absorb additional family members, it is usually impossible to do so at the expense of a working member's salary.

In fact, to their credit, the extended family network does an outstanding job of absorbing 90 percent of the Black children born out of wedlock via the informal adoption process (Hill, 1977). This is one of the primary reasons why many unmarried, unemployed Black females are able to keep their children: as long as there is some way the network can help to support these youngsters, they are loved and cared for. Additionally, these women are most likely receiving some government aid and their term of pregnancy does not necessitate a reduction in income, because they are not employed. On the other hand, Black employed married women understand the need to maintain their income and increasingly view abortion as a way to stay in the work force and support the network financially. Indeed, it can be concluded that welfare policies seem to encourage the unemployment of young, unwed mothers while simultaneously punishing married, working women for having additional children.

A final case in point concerns the policies of the Aid for Families with Dependent Children (AFDC) program with respect to Black males. In almost 40 percent of the states in the United States, an unemployed father must leave the home before the children are eligible for financial support from AFDC (Edelman, 1987). Even the simplest of minds can understand the heinous contribution such a policy makes toward the destruction of Black marriages. Not only does it encourage marital separation and divorce, but it also provides positive incentives for unwed Black parents not to marry. These are just a few of the more poignant examples of how potentially helpful government assistance programs are plagued by agendas that encourage their failure and subsequently harm many Black families in the process.

What can be done to prevent financially struggling extended family networks from collapsing, and to encourage the more economically stable families to progress further? The following suggestions are echoes of recommendations already presented elsewhere by concerned social researchers.

First, we must exploit the existing strengths of the extended network. Because the Black extended family is inclined to absorb its "illegitimate" offspring, federal subsidizing of informal adoptions could help to further reduce the number of Black children placed in adoption agencies. Robert Hill aptly notes that "child welfare has not made a heavy investment in maintaining families, but in maintaining children away from their families. Adoption policies have been dictated more by concerns [to satisfy] the desires of families in need of children than the desires of children in need of families" (Hill, 1977, p. 14). Because there is such a priority placed on children by Black extended families and a reluctance to place elderly family members in nursing homes, Hill recommends that child welfare programs converge with programs for the elderly to form creative support services for both groups. In this manner, multigenerational families are kept intact and are economically benefitted by remaining interconnected.

Secondly, a solution proposed by Edelman (1987) with regard to the working poor also applies to the extended families within their ranks. The proposal, simply stated, is that by raising the minimum wage and creating more training and employment opportunities, more extended family members will be able to become less dependent on welfare and more self-sustaining. Increasing the employment rate for more family members also results in a mutual aid system among extended families that will be more equitable and less demanding of the more upwardly mobile family members. These members, in turn, will be more likely to want to remain attached to the family.

CHALLENGES TO THE BLACK CHURCH

From a Christian perspective, the foundation of extendedness is rooted in the Scriptures. The Old Testament patriarchs all belonged to extended networks and the New Testament church is replete with examples of families consisting of multigenerational members. The mutual support system so crucial a component of Black extended families can be traced to a biblical mandate explicated by the Apostle Paul: "If anyone does not provide for his relatives, and especially for his immediate family, he has denied the faith and is worse than an unbeliever" (1 Tim. 5:8 NIV). Thus, in its values and composition, the Black extended family models a normative biblical family structure perhaps more closely than any other family unit.

It is with this thesis in mind that a final suggestion is made: Extended family networks would do well to revitalize ties between themselves and the Black church. The relationship between these two dynamic institutions has been ongoing, but secularized values embraced by younger family members have weakened the interdependence existing between them (Martin and Martin, 1978). Despite this trend, elderly Black adults still maintain close ties to local Black churches and receive a significant amount of informal support from church members in the form of advice and encouragement, prayer, and help during sickness (Taylor and Chatters, 1986).

It is no wonder that J. D. Roberts claims in his book, *Roots of a Black Future: Family and Church*, that ". . . the Black church is often much like an extended family of care, sharing, and fellowship. It is a place where one belongs, is affirmed, and finds acceptance" (Roberts 1980, p. 117). While Roberts maintains that the ministry of the Black church to families is in its sustaining and guiding role, he also warns that the failure of Black churches to execute these responsibilities "appropriately and urgently to families will hasten its own death" (p. 132). According to Martin and Martin (1978), the demise of the Black church has already occurred in some urban settings. I will hasten to add that unless the Black extended family seeks to remain an integral part of the church, it will find its own moral and spiritual foundations in a state of progressive decay. It is up to both the Black church and Black families to make concerted efforts to rekindle a vibrant symbiotic relationship.

SUMMARY

The Black extended family system, a network that transcends socioeconomic, biological kinship, and geographic boundaries, is a well-established component of Black culture. It has a prestigious history grounded in African heritage, many desirable strengths, and a few weaknesses that can be rectified. The future of this resilient family form depends on sensitive policy makers, committed social institutions, and individual family members dedicated to the perseverance of the ideals and norms of the Black extended structure of the past.

References

Al Frauqi, L. (1978). An Extended Family Model from Islamic Culture. *Journal of Comparative Family Studies* 9:243–256.

Allen, W. R. (1978). The Search for Applicable Theories of Black Family Life. *Journal of Marriage and the Family* 40:117–130.

Anderson, K. L., and Allen, W. (1984). Correlates of Extended Household Structure. *Phylon* 2:144–157.

Aschenbrenner, J. (1974). Extended Families among Black Americans. *Journal of Comparative Family Studies* 4:257–268.

————. (1975). *Lifelines: Black Families in Chicago*. New York: Holt, Rinehart, & Winston.

————. (1978). Continuities and Variations in Black Family Structure. In D. Shimkin; E. Shimkin; and D. Frate; eds., *The Extended Family in Black Societies*, 181–200. Chicago: Aldine.

Baughman, E. (1971). *Black Americans*. New York: Academic Press.

Beck, S. H., and Beck, R. W. (1984). The Formation of Extended Households during Middle Age. *Journal of Marriage and the Family* 46:277–285.

Billingsley, A. (1988). *Black Families in White America*. New York: Simon & Schuster.

Brookins, G. K. (1985). Black Children's Sex-role Ideologies and Occupational Choices in Families of Employed Mothers. In M. Spencer, G. Grookins, and W. Allen, eds., *Beginnings: The Social and Affective Development of Black Children*, (157–271). Hillsdale: Lawrence Erlbaum.

Chimezie, A. (1984). *Black Culture: Theory and Practice*. Shaker Heights: Keeble Press.

Dodson, J. (1981). Conceptualizations of Black Families. In H. McAdoo, ed., *Black Families*, 23–36. London: Sage.

DuBois, W. E. B. (1908). *The Negro American Family*. Atlanta: Atlanta University Press.

Edelman, M. (1987). *Families in Peril*. Cambridge: Harvard University Press.

Farley, R., and Allen, W. (1987). *The Color Line and the Quality of Life in America*. New York: Russell Sage Foundation.

Gutman, H. (1976). *The Black Family in Slavery and Freedom, 1750–1925*. New York: Random House.

Hall, E. J., and Ferree, M. (1986). Race Differences in Abortion Attitudes. *Public Opinion Quarterly* 50:193–207.

Hall, E. H., and King, G. C. (1982). Working with the Strengths of Black Families. *Child Welfare* 51:536–544.

Hays, W. C., and Mindel, C. H. (1973). Extended Kinship Relations in Black and White Families. *Journal of Marriage and the Family* 35:51–57.

Heiss, J. (1975). *The Case of the Black Family*. New York: Columbia University Press.

Hill, R. (1977). *Informal Adoptions among Black Families*. Washington, D.C.: National Urban League.

51

Hill, R., and Shackelford, L. (1986). The Black Extended Family Revisited. In R. Staples, ed., *The Black Family: Essays and Studies*, 194–200. Belmont, Calif.: Wadsworth.

Johnson, J. H. (1986). The Cure: Make Black Love and the Extended Family Concepts Priorities. *Ebony Magazine* (August):158–159.

Krech, S. (1982). Black Family Organization in the Nineteenth Century: an Ethnological Perspective. *Journal of Interdisciplinary History* 12:429–452.

Martin, E., and Martin, J. (1978). *The Black Extended Family*. Chicago: University of Chicago Press.

McAdoo, H. P. (1981). Patterns of Upward Mobility in Black Families. In H. McAdoo, ed., *Black Families*, 155–169. London: Sage.

Myers, H. F. (1982). Research on the Afro-American Family: a Critical Review. In B. Bass, G. Wyatt, and G. Powell, eds., *The Afro-American Family: Assessment, Treatment, and Research Issues*, 35–68. New York: Grune & Stratton.

National Urban League. (1981). *The State of Black America, 1981*. Washington, D.C.: National Urban League.

Nobles, W. W. (1974). Africanity: Its Role in Black Families. *The Black Scholar* 5:10–17.

Obikeze, D. S. (1987). Education and the Extended Family Ideology: the Case of Nigeria. *Journal of Comparative Family Studies* 18:25–47.

Peters, M. F. (1988). Parenting in Black Families with Young Children. In H. McAdoo, ed., *Black Families: A Historical Perspective* (2d ed.), 228–239. Beverly Hills: Sage.

Peters, M. F., and Massey, G. (1983). Mundane Extreme Environmental Stress in Family Stress Theories: the Case of Black Families in White America. In H. McCubbin, M. Sussman, and J. Patterson, eds., *Social Stress and the Family: Advances and Development in Family Stress Theory and Research*, 193–218. New York: Hawthorne.

Ploski, H. A., and Williams, J., eds. (1983). *The Negro Almanac: a Reference Work on the Afro-American* (4th ed.). New York: Bellwether.

Popence, D. (1987). Beyond the Nuclear Family: a Statistical Portrait of the Changing Family in Sweden. *Journal of Marriage and the Family* 49:173–183.

Reiss, I. L. (1976). *Family Systems in America* (2d ed.). Hinsdale, Ill.: Dryden.

Roberts, J. D. (1980). *Roots of a Black Future: Family and Church*. Philadelphia: Westminster.

Rokeach, M. (1968). *Beliefs, Attitudes, and Values*. San Francisco: Jossey-Bass.

Shimkin, D.; Louis, G.; and Frate, D. (1978). The Black Extended Family: Rural Institution/Urban Adaptation. In D. Shimkin, E. Shimkin, and D. Frate, eds., *The Extended Family in Black Societies* 25–147. Chicago: Aldine.

Skolnick, A., and Skolnick, J. (1986). *Family in Transition* (5th ed.). Boston: Little, Brown, & Co.

Stack, C. (1974). *All Our Kin*. New York: Harper and Row.

Sudarkasa, N. (1981). Interpreting the African Heritage in Afro-American Family Organization. In H. McAdoo, ed., *Black Families*, 37–53. London: Sage.

Tatum, B. (1987). *Assimilation Blues: Black Families in a White Community*. New York: Greenwood.

Taylor, R. J. (1986). Receipt of Support from Family among Black Americans: Demographic and Familial Differences. *Journal of Marriage and the Family* 48:67–77.

Taylor, R. J., and Chatters, L. (1986). Patterns of Informal Support to Elderly Black Adults: Family, Friends, and Church Members. *Social Work* 31 (6):432–438.

The Holy Bible: New International Version (1984). Grand Rapids: Zondervan.

Wolf, A. M. (1983). A Personal View of Black Inner-City Foster Families. *American Journal of Orthopsychiatry* 53 (1):144–151.

Zollar, A. C. (1985). *A Member of the Family*. Chicago: Nelson-Hall.

3

Single Female Parenting:
A Ministry Perspective

Sheila R. Staley

SHEILA RUTH STALEY is a counselor at Montgomery County Community College, Blue Bell, Pennsylvania. She is also a staff lecturer for Christian Research & Development, Inc., Philadelphia. Sheila has received training as a Marriage and Family Counselor from the Association of Marriage and Family Counseling (she is also a clinical member) and biblical counseling training from Christian Research & Development. She also attended Rosemont College and Antioch University, where she received a Bachelor of Arts degree in Art History and a Master of Education degree in Secondary Guidance and Counseling, respectively.

Sheila has written two books on the topic of single parenting, *Victorious Living as a Single Parent*, and a self-counseling workbook entitled *Mothers without Husbands*. She attends Christian Stronghold Baptist Church in Philadelphia, Pennsylvania, (her birthplace) where she was the former director of the single parent ministry. She is married to Kenneth Staley and they are the parents of three children, Tabbatha, Christina, and Harrison.

3

Single Female Parenting:
A Ministry Perspective

As we entered the 1990s, statistics showed that 54.5 percent of Black children under eighteen years of age lived in single-parent households. Of these homes, 51.1 percent are headed by females and 3.4 percent by males (U.S. Bureau of Census, 1990). Thus these households make up the largest percentage of Black families with children under eighteen years of age (see Figure 3.1). The problems and concerns of these households are as varied as the solutions presented by the larger society. But the concerns facing the Black single parent cannot be addressed until the underlying issues of isolation, alienation, depression, and hopelessness are resolved.

Social institutions have been largely unable to successfully address the issues of isolation, alienation, depression, and hopelessness. The solution to these problems also rests within the inner human spirit. For that reason, the Black church is a strategic institution through which many of these issues can be resolved. The Black church exists in the community along with single parent families and observes their daily struggle to survive as a family unit. That proximity promotes the possibility of meaningful ministry.

This chapter is written from a ministry perspective. I am not a single parent, but an individual who has ministered extensively in the community, attempting to communicate God's message of special love and hope to the single mother and her children. Please note that in this chapter, I often use single mother and single parent interchangeably. The information shared in this chapter has been adapted from two of my previous publications (Staley, 1981; 1986). It is used with permission from the publisher.

Living With:	1960	1970	1980	1989
Two Parents	67.0	58.5	42.2	38.0
Mother Only	19.9	29.5	43.9	51.1
Father Only	2.0	2.3	1.9	3.4
Other Relatives	9.6	8.7	10.7	6.7
Non-Relatives Only	1.5	1.0	1.3	0.8

Source: U.S. Bureau of Census (1990). Current Population Reports, Series, P-20, No. 445: Marital Status and Living Arrangements: March 1989. Washington, D.C.: U.S. Government Printing Office, p. 3.

Figure 3.1. Living Arrangements of Black Children Under 18 Years Old (Percent Distribution)

The goals of this chapter are twofold: (1) to provide encouragement and practical suggestions to the single parent; and (2) to encourage the church and others to be more active in providing biblical instruction and support to this important and often neglected population. In writing this chapter, it is recognized that there are single female parents who are effective in their role. Thus the suggestions contained herein are written for those who are having difficulties in this task and to those who wish to improve their parenting skills.

THE SINGLE MOTHER'S SITUATION

The rise of the Black, single parent, female-headed household during the eighties and the early nineties has had an unprecedented domino effect on the Black community. In 1965, only one out of four Black families was headed by a woman. Today, as noted earlier, more than 50 percent of all Black families are headed by women. It is predicted that by the year 2000, 70 percent of all Black families will be headed by single women. Matriarchal families comprise a larger percentage of the poor in present society. Some predict that these two facts will combine to cause Black women and children to outnumber their White counterparts among the new poor of the future (Whitman and Thornton, 1986).

What kind of life will they have? It has been amply documented that the poor suffer from more physical and socioeconomic problems than those with more educational and economic advantages. Proper education and training could qualify an individual for a well-paying job, as well as instill a sense of hope; lack of education and training causes the poverty cycle to repeat from one generation to the next.

When society focuses on the Black, single-parent, female-headed household, particularly in the inner city, it sees a despairing situation that offers little hope. It sees women struggling to provide for their families while experiencing loneliness, isolation, and depression. Many are looking for completion and fulfillment in their lives generally and with their men—men on whom the women and their children can depend. Instead, many single mothers find men who are overwhelmed with the issues related to their own survival as Black men. Unwilling to enter into a permanent commitment of marriage and family, the men and women typically drift in and out of relationships. In these situations, the children suffer the most. They are caught in the middle of a continuing cycle of poverty, isolation, and alienation, with little hope of escape.

This feeling of hopelessness often paralyzes the family, permitting apathy to set in. The motivation needed to change their circumstances too often evaporates.

Black leaders are constantly struggling to determine how to solve the problem. The larger society seems unwilling or unable to provide either hope or permanent solutions. Cutting back on social agencies and aid to dependent children will not help; however, neither will glutting our communities with such programs. Many of the solutions presented treat the symptoms—the problems exhibited in the behavior of the individual. They do not deal with the person within.

An individual's motivation and ability to produce effective, lasting change must come from within for there to be a real impact on his or her life. An individual is motivated to respond productively to life's complexities and crises when he or she believes that he or she can exert control over it; that there is a way to create an atmosphere that will enable him or her to reach full potential as a human being. When this hope is taken away, the motivation to progress also leaves.

As I minister and work within the Black community, I believe that this loss of hope is the core reason for despair, particularly in the single-parent family. In this society, a Black person's hope is often based on what can be seen. What one sees is a fast-moving, highly technical society of "haves and have-nots," competition, and racism. Many see themselves as having little possibility of the nation's material wealth, with little possibility of entering the mainstream of society to obtain

59

these things. Many of our grandmothers and great-grandmothers faced the challenge of being single parents with very little. However, the difference between their approach to the situation and that of the modern single parent is that our grandmothers had a substantiated hope, not an ordinary hope.

A substantiated hope is one that offers proof or evidence that you have placed your hope in a sure thing, a wish or desire supported by some confidence of its fulfillment. Our grandmothers weren't just hoping with no guarantee. They firmly placed their trust in God. Even when the odds were against them and circumstances in their lives were tragic, their faith carried them above their predicament. The outcome of their hope produced not material gain, but a deepening of their character. They called it faith.

> Now faith is the substance of things hoped for, the evidence of things not seen. (Heb. 11:1 NKJV)

The majority of single mothers today are fifty years old and younger. Many have rejected Christ, do not know the biblical truth of who he is, and have no understanding of the hope outlined in Hebrews 11:1. Of those single parents who have a personal relationship with Christ, many are unaware that God has outlined hope and encouragement for them and their children in his Word. The Bible has practical, godly solutions to the concerns of single parents. Single parents need to hear a clear message of salvation through Jesus Christ and to learn about the resources available to them in Christ Jesus. The church is a critical institution in carrying out this task.

GOD'S SPECIAL COMFORT AND HEALING

Faced with such a multitude of concerns, the single mother needs to realize she must be dependent on God for guidance in resolving her problems. The two needs that single mothers most often express are (1) for a loving, intimate companion, and (2) for someone to share the responsibility of parenting. God promises single mothers his special guidance and comfort in the raising of their children.

In Scripture, there is not a term for single parents; however, God's Word does make provision for a mother without a husband in its discussion of the widow. The term *widow* is used in the Old and New Testaments to describe women whose husbands are deceased. The terms *fatherless* and *widows* often are used together.

> You should not afflict any widow or fatherless child. If any afflict them in any way, and they cry at all to me, I will surely hear their cry. (Ex. 22:22–23 NKJV)

> Pure and undefiled religion before God the Father is this; to visit orphans and widows in their trouble, and to keep oneself unspotted from the world. (James 1:27 NKJV)

Where these terms appear together in Scripture, it is an implied challenge to the church and to individual believers to protect the unprotected. This is extended to women without the God-ordained protection of a husband, especially when children are present.

God will provide for the single mother's needs as her heavenly father, not as a substitute husband (Deut. 10:18; Prov. 15:25; Ps. 146:9). God desires a single parent to be complete and fulfilled as an individual in her present situation. He desires to be a partner with her as she endeavors to rear her children. Most of all, God desires that she and her children enjoy a rich and fulfilling life that only an intimate relationship with him can provide.

To experience the full benefits of an intimate relationship, an individual must be willing to give herself or himself to the other person. The single mother must realize that this same principle applies to her personal relationship with God. God wants 100 percent of that single parent—the physical, emotional, intellectual, social, as well as the spiritual aspect of her total being. She must be totally surrendered to Jesus Christ and must accept Christ as Lord and Savior.

With this decision, her relationship and position with God changes. She is now his daughter and a joint heir with Jesus Christ (John 1:12; Rom. 8:17). All of the resources of her heavenly Father are available to her (Col. 2:9–10). Her situation as a single parent will change as she is totally committed to allowing God to use her for his glory in her present situation (Gal. 2:20). God will direct her life (Ps. 37:23; Prov. 3:5–6). He will cause the single mother and her children to prosper (Ps. 84:11; Ps. 146:9). Finally—a great assurance in our troubled times—the single parent and her children are under God's personal protection (Jer. 29:11; Phil. 1:6).

The single mother is challenged in 1 Timothy 5:5–6 to trust God to meet her needs and the needs of her children, to pray for the strength to handle daily responsibilities, and not to live to fulfill her own desires when they are contrary to biblical principles. Her primary responsibility is to be a mother to her children. God in his creative plan never intended one individual to raise children. A parenting team of two was the original design. The effect of sin on family life can be seen in the various family configurations of today. Even the death of a spouse is ultimately a result of the curse of sin. God, however, in his love and mercy made provision for the single parent to be a complete parenting team. He has promised to be a "father to the fatherless" (Ps. 68:5). The single mother cannot be both mother and father. She need not try. She has the perfect father for her children in God, her Father.

The children of single parents must be reminded often of the special provision that God has made for them. The awareness of God's special love can provide a child with a solid foundation to develop a correct self-image. This knowledge of God's love should be nurtured through Bible studies of God as their Father. Failure to encourage growth in this area can produce children who are unable to love and accept themselves. Many of these children become underachievers and part of the underclass "poor."

The female parent should be diligent to train her children in God's principles for living. A scriptural example of strong female influence can be seen in the parenting of Timothy. In 2 Timothy 1:5, Timothy's mother, Eunice, and grandmother, Lois, made sure he was grounded in God's Word.

Single mothers should share the message of salvation with their children at as young an age as possible. Even if the mother's lifestyle has been immoral and thus inconsistent with God's Word, once she has asked for forgiveness and has made a personal commitment to Christ, she is forgiven and is seen by God as righteous in Christ. She should not be afraid or ashamed to face her children and to share her new relationship with Christ.

The healing process for the mother and her children begins when she asks their forgiveness for how she has offended or hurt them in the past. When a single mother humbles herself to approach her children in this manner, it awakens a desire in them to know the Christ who has made such a difference in their mother's life. Once the child makes a decision to accept Christ as Lord and Savior, the single mother must emphasize the responsibility they have to live according to God's Word, regardless of previous habits and lifestyle tolerated in the home. Establishing a consistent new lifestyle in Christ is often difficult. The single mother must keep in mind that God promises to be a father to the fatherless (Ps. 68:5), to supply wisdom for rearing her children (James 1:5), and to produce positive results from godly training (Prov. 22:6).

NURTURING THE CHILDREN

Many children from single-parent households experience their mother's rejection, anger, and frustration because they are a constant reminder of her previous bad relationship with their father, or of other troubled circumstances. The child in such an environment can be pushed out of the home and forced to look elsewhere for love and acceptance.

The Black male may find comfort and solace in a gang or in identification with a "street man," while many young girls attempt to find acceptance and love in an intimate relationship with a "man." As a result, their deepest need to be loved and accepted for themselves is left unsatisfied. They continue to drift.

It is essential for the Black single mother to accept and love her children just because they exist—unconditionally. In a society that constantly bombards Black children with negative images of what it means to be Black in America, home should be the one place where a child knows without a doubt that he or she is loved, accepted, and wanted.

Single parents need to be observers of their children, constantly encouraging them to develop their gifts, talents, and abilities. A child's strength can be developed by providing an environment that emphasizes home responsibilities, school activities, church involvement, enrichment programs, and privileges. The home environment should be structured to transform weaknesses into strengths. For example, a child who suffers from a physical limitation such as cerebral palsy should be provided opportunities to learn to cope with the limitations in order to experience a full life. In the spiritual realm, children should be taught to surrender their weaknesses to God to be used as strengths (Rom. 12:1–2). Thus a shy, introverted child can learn that God can use and has used various personalities to his glory. The total development of the child—physical, spiritual, emotional, intellectual, and social— must be the concern of the single parent (or any parent for that matter). In order to produce godly children, the foundation of their development must be the Word of God (Deut. 6:6–9).

Throughout the parenting process, single parents, like all parents, must be sure to encircle their children with love and discipline. The love must be expressed in both word and action. Often single parents, out of their own guilt, overindulge their children in material things and fail to discipline them. Beware of this pitfall. Children need a parent who is unafraid to do what is best in any situation. Single parents need to daily express their love and gratitude verbally for their children's presence in their lives. Children need to know that their efforts to assist at home and to be cooperative are appreciated.

It is not necessary for a single parent to be overly strict to insure her authority in the home. Her authority comes from God. Therefore, it is already insured. The children must be given loving discipline (Prov. 13:24; Eph. 6:4). They must be taught and trained to be obedient. Disobedient and uncontrollable children will be an unnecessary cause of stress.

Goals related to a child's total development should be clearly defined. Rules and standards are to be established. They should reflect God's principles for living and the family's goals. Home, school, and work responsibilities that are age-appropriate should be incorporated into the family's daily schedule. Rewards to motivate the children to carry out their responsibilities should be clearly outlined, as well as the punishment for any failure to obey rules or fulfill responsibilities. To minimize conflict and maximize cooperation, the single parent must provide opportunities for her children to express their opinions regarding the functioning of the home and the family. A weekly or bi-monthly family meeting is the best forum for such a discussion, with the mother as moderator. This process is extremely helpful to both the single mother and the children, regardless of their ages.

Parenting God's way is the most difficult challenge a single parent can face. One of the motivational goals for a Black single parent should be to halt, with her children, the replication of single-parent homes from one family unit. This can only be done by instilling new values in her children. In raising her children, the single mother must reinforce God's principles for living by word and deed. In that way, they will see that God's way is better.

THE FATHERS OF SINGLE-PARENT CHILDREN

In their search for love and companionship, many Black women have experienced several unmarried relationships that have resulted in children, thus creating single-parent households where the children have different fathers. In some cases, the father(s) is (are) no longer involved; in other cases, the father(s) may be living with the mother.

I will examine the latter situation, where the parents are living together unmarried, and its impact on the family. Regardless of today's standards, God clearly views this type of living arrangement as sin (1 Cor. 6:9–10, 18; 7:2). This living arrangement has a negative effect on all involved. It affects the children's relationship with God:

Children take [their] beliefs and values from what they see and experience. Instructing a child in a set of religious beliefs will not develop in the child a spiritual value system by which to live when there is a gap between what they have been told and what they observe in their home environment . . . These children often grow up to repeat the sins of their parents. They fail to experience God's blessings and comfort in their lives (Ex. 20:5–6; Ps. 37:28). . . . Many children, having grown up with the "live-in" mate of their parent, continue the vicious cycle of creating homes that lack the presence of both parents who are committed to a healthy marriage as well as rearing healthy children.

They live in an unstable home environment. There is not total commitment by the man to be the father of the children. All children are precious to God. He will judge any individual who harms children, especially fatherless children. Caution: children can be harmed physically, emotionally, spiritually, socially, and intellectually (Matt. 18:14; Ex. 22:22; Ps. 10:14). (Staley, 1986; pp. 18–19)

The impact on the single mother is just as great. Her relationship with God is affected. Because of her lifestyle, God is unable to fully bless and protect her as a mother without a husband. Being holy and just as well as the perfect father, God may permit her to experience hardships in her situation (Gal. 6:7). God's main goal is to bring her to repentance— back to him.

The single mother may also experience a lack of peace, a poor self-image, low self-esteem, emotional insecurity, guilt, and shame. To be restored to fellowship with God and to create a secure, stable home environment, the single mother must recognize that she is living in a sinful situation. She must be willing to take the necessary steps to correct the situation. Thus she must:

1. Confess her sins to God and ask for his forgiveness in the situation (Ps. 32:1, 2, 5; Isa. 55:6).
2. Ask him for wisdom and strength to make the necessary changes (Prov. 2:6).
3. Believe by faith that he has already begun to remove the barriers and to open up a way to a new lifestyle (Isa. 50:11).
4. Praise him for the already completed task (Ps. 86:12–13).
5. Begin to think and act in her daily life as a woman who has been restored to fellowship with God (Rom. 8:9–14).

God will provide the grace to change a lifestyle. However, the single mother must do her part. She should share her decision with someone who is able to give emotional, physical, and spiritual support.

This person may be her pastor, a relative, or a friend. She should make sure that she seeks wise, godly counsel on how to best dissolve the live-in situation. In many cases, legal counsel is necessary, especially if property or other assets are in joint ownership.

Finally, what type of relationship should the single mother and the children have with the father? The fact that he is the father must be respected. Negativism about the father to the children is discouraged. Children will discover any negative characteristics of the father on their own. The single mother should seek to share something positive about the father. (Remember, he was chosen at one point as an intimate companion.)

Children have a natural curiosity about their origins. Whenever possible, they need to know and to love both parents. Often an incorrect self-image develops in a child who lacks knowledge and understanding of his or her origin. If it is impossible for the child to know and experience a relationship with his or her father, the vacuum can be filled by teaching the child about the fatherhood of God as well as who he or she is in Christ. This can provide a perspective of human origin as it relates to eternity. Additionally, the children should be taught God's perspective on manhood through a biblical study of the men of Scripture. It is important for both sexes to be provided with godly male role models. These role models can be the father (whenever possible), a male relative, or godly men in the church and community.

The mother must prepare herself to deal with problems in her relationship with her children's father that could hinder her relationship with God and her children. Anger over wrongs done to her and bitterness over prolonged abuse and neglect can only hurt the single mother and her children emotionally and spiritually. The single mother should ask the Lord's forgiveness for her role in the wrongs done and be willing to forgive the father. She should also ask for wisdom, and seek counseling in resolving the problem.

Often the children have witnessed the upheavals between the mother and the father. They should be given an opportunity to discuss their concerns so that they don't blame themselves for the problem. The problems between the single mother and the father should not be used as an excuse to deny access to the father, though precautions should be taken if the mother fears for her children's safety.

In all her dealings with the father, the single mother should use wisdom. There should be a clear understanding between the parents regarding the father's responsibilities and rights. Custody, child support, and visitation should be clearly defined. Boundaries defining a single mother's personal and emotional involvement with the father should be set. She must remember that he knows her intimately—her strengths and her weaknesses.

God has called each single mother to purity (1 Cor. 7:34). She must fulfill her need for intimate companionship in a way that enables her to maintain a pure and holy life in behavior, attitude, and thought (1 Thess. 4:3–7). Some safeguards for the single mother in her relationship with the father include:

1. Do not have him visit at her home alone.
2. Do not visit him alone at his home.
3. Do not frequent old haunts with him that arouse sinful desires.
4. Do not turn to him when emotionally and spiritually low. PRAY! Read God's Word. Call a spiritual friend.

Beware of any attempts to use the children to rekindle old lifestyles. Example: A father, a former live-in partner, stays to comfort a concerned mother into the late hours because she is anxious about the rebellious behavior of a teenage son. The end result may be that the father doesn't leave until the morning, thus giving the appearance of wrongdoing to the son and the other children. This will create new problems rather than resolve old ones.

THE ROLE OF THE CHURCH

In the past, the Black extended family helped provide the support, encouragement, and protection necessary to keep the single parent household intact. With the breakdown of the traditional Black extended family and the rise of isolated family units, individuals normally active in sustaining the single parent are consumed with the pressures of their own survival. Often the single parent is isolated, and dependent on social services or her own devices for support. With the multitude of problems facing the single parent, she is greatly in need of assistance.

As previously mentioned in James 1:27, God has charged the church to care for the single parent and her children. The church has the message of salvation, comfort, and encouragement that the single parent needs to hear. The church is also equipped with the gifts and resources needed to undergird emotionally, spiritually, and financially the members of the body who are single parents. As this ministry is exercised, the church will become a beacon of light to single parents in the community.

In establishing a ministry to single parents, the local church should focus on meeting the needs of those single parents in their fellowship. When the community observes the church supporting their own, they will be drawn to that fellowship, thus creating within the community an oasis for God the Holy Spirit to prepare the hearts of single parents for salvation and growth.

The church can replace the missing "extended family" with a support network for single parents and their children. The model for a support network can be found in the Old and New Testaments. In the Mosaic law, provisions were made for widows and the fatherless (Ex. 22:22–24; Deut. 10:18; 14:28–29; 24:17–21). In the New Testament, Paul, a non-family member, adopted Timothy as his spiritual son (1 Tim. 1:2).

At Christian Stronghold Baptist Church in Philadelphia, Pennsylvania, where Rev. Willie Richardson is the pastor, a support network for single parent families was developed. The purpose of this network was threefold:

1. To establish within the church community a support system that would encourage and guide single parents in the establishment and maintenance of a family based on God's principles.
2. To create a support cluster among women who have children whose fathers are absent from the home, for the purpose of edification and teaching.
3. To establish support families to function as extended families for the purpose of edification, according to Hebrews 10:24.

In developing the ministry, it was important to connect with other ministries in the church that stressed spiritual growth and family development. These included Sunday school, Bible study, youth and children's ministry and watch care.

The support network for single-parent families consists of three levels. Level I is the training program or seminar that provides the foundation for the growth of the single parent. This training is followed-up with monthly or bi-monthly meetings for the single parent. Instruction and guidance are given on such topics as trusting God, God's special care for the fatherless, resolving bitterness, scheduling, financial planning, purity, dealing with male children, and establishing home rules and responsibilities. All the single parents are invited to participate in the ministry at this level. The seminars are usually open to the community.

Single parent clusters are organized at the second level. The clusters are organized according to geographic location. Ideally, no more than three families should be in a cluster. The clusters provide a vehicle for single parents to support one another in such areas as God's principles for living, babysitting, transportation, clothing exchange, and recreation and social activities. Financial needs are brought to the attention of the deacons or lay leader.

Each cluster is assigned a captain who is responsible to contact each member of the cluster to inquire about the family's well-being and other pressing needs. At Christian Stronghold, the cluster captains have been single parents. These single parents have provided strength and encouragement to other single parents who are struggling. However, being a single parent should not be a prerequisite. It is important that the captain be a woman—married or single—who is emotionally and spiritually mature and who applies God's principles to her daily life.

The third level is represented by support families. These families desire to be adopted extended families to the single parent families. The support family should believe that God is leading them to this ministry. They also should have the burden and time to assist single parent families. They should have demonstrated a knowledge of God's principles for a family and an ability to apply them. The support family assists the single parent in areas such as child-rearing and other home responsibilities.

Success in this ministry has been and will be evidenced by the changed life that results from a total commitment by the single mother to live a fully surrendered and committed life for Christ. The single parent ministry must be seen as an integral part of the church ministry in order to be effective. The church must be willing to meet the needs of this proliferating family unit. Within the Black community, it is an institution that can.

CONCLUSION

Many within and without the Black community are concerned with its survival into the twenty-first century as a positive contributor to society. Given the multitude of problems facing single-parent homes—the most common family unit in the Black community—it is mandatory that the church work with these families to provide them with hope, encouragement, and stability. The single mother must desire stability in her children and herself through a partnership with Christ and the church that can revolutionize her life.

It is extremely important for the single parent to be single-minded, focused on living a life in accordance with God's principles. Problems that previously appeared to be insurmountable then take on a different perspective. God can help the mother establish a stable home and rear her children. Through her, God will bless her children and all with whom she comes into contact. She will be seen as virtuous by others. Her children will rise up and call her blessed (Prov. 31:28).

Recommended Readings

Barnes, R., Jr. (1984). *Single Parenting: A Wilderness Journey.* Wheaton: Tyndale.
Bustanoby, A. (1985). *Being a Single Parent.* Grand Rapids: Zondervan.
Cook, J. (1977). *Now That I Believe.* Chicago: Moody.
Richardson, W. (1981). *Enjoying the Single Life.* Philadelphia: Christian Research & Development.
_____. (1984). *Thinking Right about Yourself.* Philadelphia: Christian Research & Development.
Rikers, G., and Swihart, J. (1984). *Making the Difference: Help for Single Parents with Teenagers.* Grand Rapids: Baker.

References

Staley, S. (1981). *Victorious Living as A Single Parent: A Seminar.* Philadelphia: Christian Research & Development.
_____. (1986). *Self-Counseling Workbook for Mothers Without Husbands.* Philadelphia: Christian Research & Development.
The Holy Bible: New King James Version. (1985). Nashville: Nelson.
U.S. Bureau of Census. (1990). Current Population Reports, Series P-20, No. 445. *Marital Status and Living Arrangements*: March 1989. Washington, D.C.: U.S. Government Printing Office.
Whitman, D. and Thornton, J. (March 17, 1986). A Nation Apart (Black Underclass: Special Section). *U.S. News and World Report*, 100.

4

Black Inner-City Teenagers

Carolyn B. Thompson-Wallace

CAROLYN THOMPSON-WALLACE is the Director of the International Youth Organization (IYO) based in Newark, New Jersey, and attends Redeeming Love Christian Center. Carolyn has extensive experience in working with inner-city youth. She was born in Jersey City, New Jersey, and grew up in Newark. Carolyn attended Southside High School (now Malcolm X Shabbazz). She is married to James Wallace and they have five children, Haywood, Stephen, Wanda, David, and Vincent.

4

Black Inner-City Teenagers

The ideas in this chapter concerning Black teenagers come primarily from my experience, rather than from the reading of literature or from academic research. I have been involved with adolescents for some thirty-five years as a parent, grandparent, Christian, manager in the for-profit sector of the economy, aide to an elected City Councilperson, and volunteer worker with a community-generated recreational program for young people.

The varied roles I have occupied represent the key institutions of society—the family, the church, the economy, the body politic, and the supportive community—and have culminated in the position I now occupy as the Executive Director of the International Youth Organization (IYO). IYO is a nonprofit, community-based organization that develops and administers programs dedicated to the positive growth and development of the youth of Newark and their families.

Because they reside in Newark, the adolescents I know best can be fairly characterized as inner-city youth. I do not claim any deep knowledge of Black teenagers in more middle class environments. No doubt as adolescents, these teenagers have the same developmental tasks to accomplish as inner-city adolescents. That is, all are faced with giving up childhood dependency roles and becoming autonomous adults. They are in the process of creating adult identities, and they have to learn to distinguish media fiction from social reality.

The origin of IYO, which my husband and I formed in 1970, started as a thirteen-person precision drill team. We had a very clear design for this organization. It was intended to provide healthy, after-school activities for the teenage children of tenants in a building where I worked for the management

73

Designed, however, is really too fancy a word, since it carries a connotation of social planning that we simply did not have. At that time, the IYO was simply a supportive community response to what we saw. It was very obvious to us that a significant number of young Blacks seemed to have nothing constructive to do, and as adults from the community, we believed that this was harmful to their future. We simply organized something for them to do. We further hoped to contribute to the community's goal of sending more Black young people to college. One might say that we created a small juvenile delinquency prevention program.

After many ups and downs, that simple drill team has evolved (with the neighborhood's needs) to a point where we now offer a varied educational, counseling, recreational, and training program for adolescents and their families.

How do I explain our growth and our success in dealing with teenage problems by creating the drill team? We had no doubts as to the need for order and mutual respect. Thus, the program we offered was structured and extremely disciplined, rather than permissive. It was, in effect, a peer group for young people with strong adult direction. We knew the ingredients needed to create that order and respect. Opening an evening of drill with prayer helped set the tone for an effective evening. Parental cooperation and assistance were also necessary—and forthcoming.

THE INNER CITY: A CURRENT ANALYSIS

The critical context for our program was a Black community in Newark, New Jersey. This community had substantial supportive traditions and high hopes for socializing their young even in the period just after the 1967 riots. Perhaps I idealize or romanticize the past, but in spite of low incomes, poor housing, and poor education, the Black community at one time observed and looked after its young people. All adults were aunts and uncles to the young people. The community unambiguously believed in structure as a survival strategy, and this structure was ultimately based on spiritual values.

I believe that it was this vital and adaptive community that made possible in the 1960s the successful elimination of legal racism. It also enabled us to survive Southern reconstruction, rural sharecropping, the great out-migration to the North, and our uneven entry into the urban industrial environment. It provided us not only with organization, but also gave us the moral high ground in the political struggles of the sixties.

I stress this once-supportive community context because I believe that sometime beginning in the seventies, it weakened and is now in danger of disappearing. Of course, a degree of maladaptive behavior in our communities always existed. However, encouraged by what seemed to be the permissiveness of the majority society, this behavior has come to dominate the inner city. To me, the distinctive nature of the adolescent problems of inner-city youth today comes from the peculiar environment that has replaced the once supportive community. The current inner-city environment is one that inhibits rather than facilitates the acquisition of social reality skills by young people. It seems to encourage an imitation of life rather than a focus on the real thing.

The physical aspects of the current environment are depressing. Youth are surrounded by empty lots, abandoned buildings, dirty streets, and vacant factories. The living conditions are so overcrowded that the hopelessness of the street scene invades the home and defeats attempts at good housekeeping. The society that youths know is dominated by the daily tragedies of real violence, real drugs, real jail, and even early death.

The result of these conditions is exemplified by a young man pleading to get his job back in a seafood restaurant by promising to be on time, though the real problem is the fact that he has been involved in several stabbings and the hassles of arrest. Another example is a young man who claimed he had never been to downtown Newark hotels and restaurants. He had been to nearby discos but had never noticed the mainstream adult institutions.

There is no doubt in my mind that a primary cause of this peculiar environment is the continued existence of day-to-day racial oppression. Racism is still a viable explanation for the inner-city situation.

It is important to understand that inner-city adolescents are very conscious that the majority society is hostile to them as they try to identify and develop their talents. Their actual social isolation from the majority society means that their information about the majority culture is more limited and distorted than that of young urban Blacks before the 1970s. Television is their primary source of information. With its two-dimensional escapes from reality, it does not help youth acquire a creative appreciation of their own situation.

EFFECTS OF THE INNER CITY ON TODAY'S YOUTH

This de facto segregation often produces a low estimation of self that may be more damaging than that revealed by earlier social scientists such as Clark (1965). The negative assessments of self may be masked by assertions and styles that, when unchallenged, sound confident and secure.

But this braggadocio is not challenged, and that is why self-esteem may be damaged even more severely than before. There are not enough adult "significant others" in the youths' environment to help create a positive self-image by example or by feedback. This may sound like a complicated way of saying that most inner-city young people are being raised by one parent. However, I mean much more than that.

Inner-city community life is impoverished by the relative paucity of day-to-day, block-by-block, examples of integrative adult behavior. The move of the new Black middle class (identified by Landry, 1987) away from the poor housing of the inner city has deprived inner-city youth of the models of successful socialization and integration that historically were part of the Black community. From the perspective of the inner city, this middle class migration looks and feels like abandonment.

A typical home I see in the inner city is a severely overcrowded three-bedroom apartment, housing ten children and four beaten-down adults. The housekeeping habits are unsanitary. The adults may be drug abusers and are likely to be unemployed. Some of the youth are school drop-outs and also drug abusers. One of the teenagers will likely be an unmarried mother. There are no study areas in this typical home and few learning tools. Some of the households will not even have pencils. The younger children are academically behind their grade levels. They may have moved three or four times. The conditions offer no privacy, no study time, nor any kind of regular schedule.

These low-income conditions mean not only poor nutrition, but also a lack of knowledge about basic household economics. Therefore, money cannot be saved, and investment in property cannot take place. There is an awareness, in a general way, of middle-class values, but nothing seems to produce the spunk required to defer immediate gratification.

Hence, the inner-city family as a socializing institution is in disarray. Edelman (1987) says that illegitimacy, marriage rates, single-parent households, and infant mortality are the end results of this disarray. But in different circumstances, these signs could be seen as coping strategies.

Much more fundamental though is that parents see their children as being out of control. They literally indicate that their children "won't listen." The parents, perhaps because of their own social choices, seem unable to be effective and authoritative with their own children. The peer group of the street corner and the media's depictions of reality undermine efforts by real adults to socialize the young.

The most bizarre outcome of this no-family situation concerns marriage and childbearing. Inner-city adolescents have separated marriage from childbearing. This is an extreme manifestation of the national trend among teenagers to separate marriage from sexuality.

Black teenagers' views on marriage are still quite traditional. Marriage is seen as a very serious commitment that is not to be taken lightly; it virtually has a sacramental meaning. Marriage also requires an economic ability to afford a "big" wedding. All this seems reasonably well related to tradition, although tinged with a fantasy element that has its roots in the media.

What is bizarre is that childbearing is not seen as at least equally solemn. It is not seen as something to be postponed until marriage. There is no doubt in my mind that many young, Black, inner-city adolescents are intent on having babies, or one might better say "live dolls." Dash (1989) correctly entitles his book on teenage pregnancy *When Children Want Children*.

I have found it impossible to make sense of the autonomous individualism of this choice to have babies. The bravado that child-parents spout is not persuasive. It seems plausible to me that a psychologist could see this as symbolic language. It may be an effort to affirm self-value in the face of a hostile environment. It may even be an effort to have a possession, an immediate "I want it," which is no different from wanting a car.

To adults and adult institutions, this would not make any social or adaptational sense. It seems to lack calculation, thoughtfulness, and the awareness of consequences. The inevitable intertwining of the young mother's life with the hated welfare system; the terrible personal strain between the mother's need to build her own future and her need to do the same for her child; the need to rationalize the nearly inevitable neglect of the child by both father and mother: all of this is self-destructive. Teenage childbearing to me is a sign, an indicator, that adults and community socializing are absent.

The socializing effects of work are also virtually absent. There are very few part-time jobs available for the young people we see at IYO. Recent College Board statistics indicate that 53 percent of prospective Black college students have worked part time, compared to 36 percent of whites (6.7 hours versus 8.2 hours). The availability of part-time work is even lower for the non-college-goers.

I wonder at times how street drug-selling is counted in published statistics. There is no doubt that irregular involvement in the drug

77

economy is available to young people. I know of young women whose desire for new Easter clothes led to a temporary involvement.

Most of the women do expect to work, are aiming to work, and perhaps have, as a result of the media, somewhat realistic ideas about entry points into the economy. Because they drop out of school less often, they have better scheduling habits than men. They certainly have, however, an unrealistic assessment of the strain that will exist between work and motherhood.

The men are more difficult to read. A common male approach to a career discussion is to assert that they are going to start at the top. This grandiosity at one level certainly is normal adolescent bravado, but its lack of any realism is troubling. At times, it seems to lead to the idea that if you can't start as the boss, then the only alternative is nothing. "If you are not the star, why play?" they seem to be saying.

Both males and females have what I call "attitude shells" that inhibit the remedial acquisition of employment skills. For the women, the attitude can be summarized as "I can do it for myself"; for the men, the attitude is "I don't need any help." While both attitudes are difficult to work with, the false pride of the men is far more frustrating.

Both genders are clear that they will not enter occupations that they consider menial. The fact that previous generations saw these same occupations as offering income and dignity, and that new immigrants to America do enter these occupations, does not motivate our children. It seems as if the omnipresent drug economy offers a "get rich quick" alternative that works against a healthy balance between aspiration and despair.

CHURCHES, SCHOOLS, AND OTHER AGENCIES

So far, I have reported the failures of the parents, the community, and the economy to successfully socialize young people in the inner city. What may be more surprising is the failure of religious institutions.

Within a four-block radius of the IYO facility, I can count numerous churches. I would say that very few of our inner-city youth have any serious connection with them. In fact, these churches often do not draw their membership from the neighborhood. There certainly are strong, church-going families in my neighborhood who are raising children successfully, but they are not the norm.

As socializing institutions, churches seem irrelevant to most inner-city youth. Civil behavior, a most obvious consequence of effective churches, is not evident. In fact, I have observed situations in which churches have had to call on others to control relatively minor, unruly street behavior. Young women are more likely to have connections to the church, but for young men, the church is too often seen as an institution for weak people and "sissies."

The church's perceived irrelevance is, I judge, at sharp variance with the traditions of Black history and culture in America. Some of the irrelevance probably reflects the crude materialism of contemporary young people in general. Some of it relates to a half-completed migration of some churches to the suburbs in an effort to follow their congregations. However, the problem seems deeper than this. A religious vacuum exists, and surprisingly, is not being filled. Even Islamic sects are not emerging to fill the vacuum, as was often the case in the past.

It is not surprising that governmental agencies also fail in their situation of *anomie*. The social service agencies and schools implicitly relied on a community context of strong parents, strong religious institutions, spiritual values, and hope. When these were in place, maladaptive behavior was the exception, not the rule, and it could be effectively corrected. But that is not the situation we have today.

The schools deserve particular note because, as institutions, they are assigned such a large segment of a child's life. They look as if they should be socializing agents. But in fact, as Woodson (1933) argues, they were never community-supporting. At best, they identified talent in an immigrant population, encouraged the process of upward mobility, and established a basic literacy level. At worst, they created distance between the child and the culture of the parents.

Today's schools have to do more in a more difficult social situation. Basic literacy is no longer adequate for our economy, and the inner-city school population is not the children of opportunity-seeking immigrants, but the people left behind. But because inner-city schools are still organized for a hopeful immigrant population, they are failing their actual students.

IYO AND ITS EFFECTS ON TEENAGERS

In an earlier section, I described the beginnings of IYO in 1970 as a small drill team. For over two decades, it has served approximately 6,000 persons.

Currently, we are in the process of formally evaluating its effectiveness. Based on my observations and the feedback of others, there is much to suggest that even a formal evaluation will agree with what we have seen. Feedback on effectiveness has come from parents, schools, funding agencies, and courts. The result is that we are not able to accept all referrals. Our current active clientele is approximately 2,000.

We have observed the following in alumni from our program:

1. A greater respect for and acceptance of discipline.
2. A better understanding of what education can do for a person. Many have gone on to obtain college degrees.
3. A greater recognition of the need for humanitarian roles. Many are now participating in such activities themselves.
4. A greater respect for the "gift of life." This is often seen in their childbearing patterns.
5. A greater respect for spiritual values and their importance, even if they have not accepted Jesus Christ as Lord and Savior.
6. A greater respect for the dignity and importance of work and the need to save for the future.

WHAT NEEDS TO BE DONE

What should our society be doing to reach our teenagers? First, we have to be angry about what is happening to our young. Without this anger and empathy, I doubt we will have the motivation to act or to spend the necessary resources. Clearly, our youth deserve to be saved. Money should not be a barrier.

Second, we need to make our public policy position clear. We must articulate that we are politically liberal in order to be socially conservative.

Third, I have no doubt that the most important thing is to rebuild our community institutions for this new era. We have to find a way to effectively mobilize middle class Black adults to be socializing agents in the inner city. May of them come to church in the city, and that may be one vehicle for organizing their talents.

Fourth, we have to redesign the schools, the churches, the social-service agencies, and the police in ways more appropriate to the actual inner-city situation. For example, Comer's vision (1980) of successful schools seems doable. The business community's genuine anxiety about the future work force can be effectively channeled to help combat the problem.

Fifth, I believe we need some sort of National Youth Corps to use the energy and talents of the idle young adults in the inner city.

Sixth, we need to support agencies and organizations that are effective in working with youth.

CONCLUSION

This chapter has briefly described one organization that is diligently working with inner-city youth. Additionally, a current analysis of the inner city is offered; the effects of the inner city on youth are outlined; the failures of churches, schools, and other agencies are mentioned; and the effects of IYO are described. Finally, a challenge as to what needs to be done is presented.

If the people in our society want to see Jesus, we need to begin again now.

References

Clark, K. B. (1965). *Dark Ghetto*. New York: Harper & Row.

Comer, J. P. (1980). *School Power: Implications of an Intervention Project*. New York: Free Press.

Dash, L. (1989). *When Children Want Children*. New York: Morrow.

Edelman, M. M. (1987). *Families in Peril: An Agenda for Social Change*. Cambridge: Harvard University Press.

Landry, B. (1987). *The New Black Middle Class*. Berkeley: University of California Press.

Woodson, C. G. (1933). *The Miseducation of the Negro*. Washington, D.C.: Associated Publisher Inc.

5

Improving and Strengthening Black Male-Female Relationships

Sherrill Burwell

SHERRILL BURWELL is employed as a children's social worker with the Department of Children's Services in Los Angeles, California, and is Director of Family Forum Ministries in Inglewood, California. She is married to William Burwell, Jr., and is a member of the First Berean Christian Church in Los Angeles, where she is the pastor's wife, Director of Music Ministries, and evangelism teacher. Sherrill has a Bachelor of Arts degree in psychology from Hampton University and a Master of Arts degree in marriage, family, and child counseling from Biola University, La Mirada, California. The Burwells have five children: Tony, Edith, Mia, Mandela, and Shabazz. Sherrill was born in Morehead City, North Carolina, and grew up in Raleigh, North Carolina.

5

Improving and Strengthening Black Male-Female Relationships

This chapter is for those who have experienced the emotional pain of broken relationships, those who continue to have relationship struggles, and those who want to improve their relationships. Singles (divorced, widowed, and never married) and couples alike will see themselves in the concepts and illustrations presented. All are encouraged to apply the principles to their unique experience.

The three major objectives of this chapter are: (1) to categorize relationship problems into a concrete and workable set; (2) to reframe what we typically view as problems by putting them in a different and positive perspective, thereby making more options available for conflict resolution; and (3) to offer solutions through the integration of some concepts from family-systems theory and biblical teachings.

To address these objectives, I begin by asking the question, "What is the problem?" I then reframe the problem using the concept of the "identified patient." Next, a challenge is offered to couples to restructure the thought processes that affect behavior and relationship dynamics by accepting God's design for human relationships. Later in the chapter, headship and submission, communication, conflict resolution, singles in relationships, and human sexuality are the topics for which solutions are offered.

WHAT'S THE PROBLEM?

Cazenave (1983) surveyed 155 middle-class Black men (class level was defined by occupational, family income, and educational levels), using questions that are summarized by the following propositions:

1. Black men perceive that Black women have too much control and power in their families.

2. Black men perceive that Black women have inadvertently helped to keep Black men down because of their low regard for them.

3. Black men perceive a serious deterioration of the relationships between Black men and Black women.

4. Black men perceive that Black women have more opportunities than Black men do today.

5. Lower-status Black men are more pessimistic about Black male-Black female relationships, and are more likely to view Black women as being responsible for relationship problems than are higher status Black men.

(p.343)

From the responses to these questions, it was found that "the majority of respondents . . . rejected the view that black women had too much control in the family; showed no clear consensus as to whether or not black women were at fault in keeping black men down; did not accept the view that there is growing distrust and hatred between black men and black women; and identified poor communication as the major problem affecting black male-female relationships" (p. 344). Mutual respect, competition, and sex outside of marriage were also cited as problem areas.

While the results of this study may not be generalizable to all, these are issues that continue to surface in family discussions, at social gatherings, and in the workplace. These are popular and controversial issues and are categorized in this chapter as poor communication, lack of mutual respect, competition, and premarital and extramarital sexual relations.

THE IDENTIFIED PATIENT

In family-systems theory (Satir, 1983), the concept of the identified patient suggests that when a family decides to seek help for a problem, there is generally one member who has been selected to be the scapegoat. This scapegoat, according to the family, is a problem, and if the scapegoat would change its behavior, the family could function normally. However, in reality, the scapegoat is not the central problem, but is only *symptomatic* (carries the symptom) of a larger problem within the family system.

For example, I am often faced with parents who want to send their teenage daughter to counseling because she's rebellious, withdrawn, and disobedient. In their view, she's the problem. However, when the parents participate in the counseling process, the family is confronted with the reality that the family marital system itself is in conflict, and that the daughter is reacting to the stress of having to co-exist in a poorly functioning family system. In this example, the daughter's freedom and healing will come only when she frees herself from the family labels, and begins to actively take responsibility for her own destructive behavior patterns.

By analogy, we all have at some time heard Black women accuse Black men of being a "problem" and vice versa. Specifically, we sometimes accuse each other of being stubborn, unfaithful, "full of ourselves," conceited, irresponsible, deceitful, noncommital, and unable to communicate. If we reframe this issue according to a family-systems approach, however, we see that *our problems are symptomatic of the problems of a larger society.*

For generations Black men and women have coexisted as a cultural minority without benefit of job or social equality, racial justice, or substantial alternatives for growth and development. We have reacted to this stress by displacing our anger and resentment onto each other, just as families do to the psychologically identified patient. It is here that the real challenge for change begins. In a wider and biblical context, " . . . our struggle is not against flesh [each other]. . .but against the rulers, against the powers, against the world forces of this darkness, against the spiritual forces of wickedness in the heavenly places" (Eph. 6:12 NASB).

The struggle in human relationships is not merely between men and women. The struggle ultimately is a result of our disobedience to the truths of God. As with the identified patient, any healing between Black males and females must follow a specific course: (1) reject the accusation that we are apathetic, argumentative, and irresponsible; (2) instead of blaming the (family) system, accept responsibility for any behavior or speech that causes conflict; (3) challenge control whenever it becomes humiliating and unproductive; and (4) repeatedly resist taking the blame for the malfunction. As the identified patient begins to find new ways to cope, the identified patient is less anxious, fearful, and hostile, and less likely to act out these emotions through withdrawal, angry communications, substance abuse, and flight and separation from the family.

THE CHALLENGE TO IMPROVING AND STRENGTHENING RELATIONSHIPS: TREATING THE PROBLEM

The root problem with human relationships is that we have deviated from God's order and design for the family system. Dysfunctional relationships are merely symptomatic of this deeper biblical problem, and for Black male-female relationships, the problem is further complicated by the stress of being part of a minority community. In this section, I will offer some ways to deal with the problem.

By definition, a challenge calls for special effort. In this context it calls for an examination of traditional roles, structures, and relationship boundaries, and an identification of new directions. The primary question to be answered is: Is the behavior biblical or is it traditional? All family systems have their traditions, ways of operating, and decision-making styles. Each of us learns a pattern of interaction and communication from the family system in which we are reared. Not all traditions, however, are biblical. Hence the real challenge is to reject those traditions in our relationships that are not biblical and accept God's redirection and teaching. This may be especially difficult, because to accept a challenge requires personal change, commitment, and accountability. It further requires taking an honest look at how we function and where we learned our behavioral patterns, and then setting out to change the part of our belief and value system that works against our present relationship goals.

THE CHALLENGE TO COUPLES

For married or engaged couples, it is important to have a clear concept of the biblical model for marriage to establish this model as the standard for relationships. Genesis 2:18–25 describes five basic elements of the first marriage instituted by God and provides a sound foundation for the marital union. These are:

1. **Companionship.** "It is not good for the man to be alone . . ." (2:18). This suggests that God is aware of our basic need for a partner and that he is the one who arranges for the "suitable" mate.

2. **Permanence** (2:24). Divorce and separation were not a part of the original design. Until sin there was no need to even entertain the idea. Divorce, therefore, is not a result of vague and generalized incompatibility and irreconcilable differences. It is the result of specific sins against God and each other.

3. **Severance** (2:24). When two people marry, they do not marry each other's families. Rather, they are to separate from families of origin

and "cleave" to each other. In doing so, they should confine their decision-making about child-rearing, house rules, and role assignments to their own marital unit. The advice of well-intentioned in-laws has been the source of countless marital conflicts.

4. **Unity** (2:24). Unity in a marriage implies that the couple has the same overall purpose and objectives for their lives. It implies neither uniformity nor total agreement, but oneness in purpose.

5. **Intimacy** (2:25). In this original state, they were both "naked and unashamed." There were no secrets, no hidden agendas, and no hesitancy about honest self-disclosure.

HEADSHIP AND SUBMISSION: ITS IMPORTANCE TO IMPROVING MARITAL RELATIONSHIPS

A structural approach to improving relationships in families involves reestablishing lines of authority so that each person is in proper relationship with respect to roles, power, boundaries, and control. Dysfunctional sets (personal reactions to each other in response to various stressors) tend to be repeated whenever conflict arises unless the relationship has been put into a more workable balance. Figure 5.1 illustrates my view of God's design for relationships as set out in 1 Corinthians 11:3 and Ephesians 5:18–33; 6:1–4. This model is the basis for the remainder of our discussion in this section.

In many instances, any discussion of headship and submission between couples becomes intense and requires an official referee. To most, headship means to give orders, boss, dictate, and rule, while submission is viewed as a pitiful existence of giving in, being ordered around, taken for granted, and saying yes when one really means no.

This improper understanding is not so much an indication of what we think of each other as it is an indication of what we think of God. God is not a dictator. He is not a chauvinist, and he has a high regard for both men and women—"for you are all one in Christ Jesus" (Gal. 3:28). Much of the female struggle for equal rights and power is a reaction to non-biblical, traditional thinking that a woman's abilities, contributions, and cognitive skills are inferior to a man's. The early church, carrying on the Hebrew tradition, regarded women as second-class citizens. Girls did not get the same education as boys, and women were said to be "light-minded" and not as adaptable to many occupations as were men (Edersheim, 1982). This same thinking was a part of the history and culture of the English immigrants to this country, whose principles reflected primarily a male attitude (Jordan, 1974).

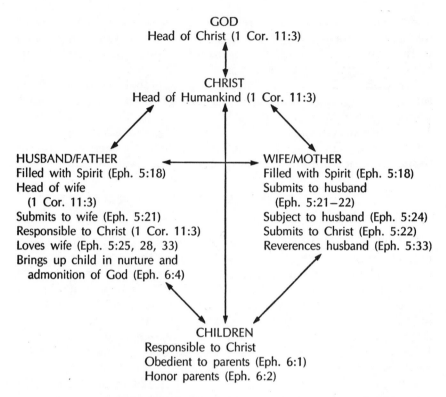

Figure 5.1. Biblical/structural Model for Male-female Relationships
(1 Cor. 11:3; Eph. 5:21–30; 6:1–4).

A study of Figure 5.1 and its accompanying Scripture references makes God's design palatable and appealing. Christ is the final authority in every Christian relationship. Headship in a two-parent family is a position given to the man by God and is parallel to the relationship between Christ and his bride, the church. This position is given to the husband regardless of his income, education, or job status. This fact does not imply female inferiority. For, as noted earlier, we are all one in Christ (Gal. 3:28).

To further expand on this biblical principle, imagine that Figure 5.1 represents a company (in this case, the family) where Christ is the owner, the husband is the manager, and the wife is the assistant manager. The image becomes one where the manager knows his staff, is interested in the growth of the company, assumes full responsibility for its operation, and delegates authority and tasks to the assistant manager based on skill, interest, and availability.

The manager is not in competition with the assistant because he is secure in his position; he respects her rights and opinions and knows that she plays an important part in the company's development. He keeps lines of communication open through frequent staff meetings. He readily accepts his assistant's counsel as long as it is consistent with the owner's rules. The manager is accountable for his decisions and sacrifices time and personal interests for the good of the company.

The assistant manager is also secure in her position and doesn't need to compete for the manager's position because she also respects the owner's policies and rules. She may not always agree with the manager, but they have mechanisms for handling disagreements and conflicts. She is comfortable in sharing her suggestions concerning the management of the company and is not upset when she is overruled. At day's end, the assistant manager can rest comfortably, knowing that the needs of the company have been met. Both employees (manager and assistant manager) are mutually supportive because they have the one purpose of pleasing and satisfying the owner.

In the example above, there is mutual esteem and unconditional love, which makes it possible to work together in spite of each other's differences and faults. Because of their good working relationship, the manager and assistant are able to negotiate roles and tasks and seldom find it necessary to bicker over who keeps the building clean, who sees that the car is maintained, or who makes deposits or signs checks. Their relationship is in balance, and, therefore, their roles are in balance.

COMMUNICATION: ITS ROLE IN RELATIONSHIPS

There are many reasons why couples find it difficult to talk through problems and resolve conflicts. Fears of rejection or of being misunderstood and ignored will quickly lead one to internalize anger, hostility, and hurt feelings. The longer emotions remain concealed, the more resentments build up so that when couples finally approach a sensitive subject, any hope for resolution is lost in arguments and blaming. We learn many dysfunctional communication patterns from parents and significant others who themselves may have had difficulty communicating. Poor communication patterns are many and varied, but a brief examination of three familiar and ineffective styles will teach us how to talk through issues by showing us *how not* to do it.

1. **The Double-Bind Message.** This concept is attributed to Bateson et al. (1956). It refers to a destructive style where any response to a question or statement is the wrong one. For example:

91

Male: Did you mail the check to the phone company?
Female: No, I didn't.
Male: Why not? I gave it to you two days ago.
Female: Yes, but you said you hadn't covered it at the bank yet.
Male: That's no reason not to mail it; it's already overdue.

In the above example, if the female had said, "Yes, I mailed it," the male response would have been, "Why? I told you I hadn't covered it yet." In such cases, not only is the person confused at the double message, but he or she is not allowed to comment on the inconsistency.

2. Mystification. Mystification (Laing, 1965) is a masking technique used to avoid confrontation by obscuring one's real feelings in order to maintain the status quo. If anger or hurt feelings are concealed, for example, one can avoid any possible open conflict and continue a surface appearance of the relationship being "okay."

3. Silence. Perhaps the most powerful and destructive tool one person can use on another in times of conflict when communication is appropriate is silence. Silence due to hostility, anger, etc. keeps the other party guessing about what one is thinking or feeling, frustrates attempts to force verbal expression, and relieves the self of any responsibility for the problem or its solution. Sexual interaction is frequently interrupted during these times and the relationship may suffer a major setback.

Clearly all three styles are to be avoided if one wants to develop a good relationship.

A SIX-STEP MODEL FOR CONFLICT RESOLUTION

Figure 5.2 is a model that can be used for working through sensitive issues. The model is especially helpful for relationship issues that involve intense anger, fear, and pain. This model presents the critical issue as the focal point (see inner circle) and assumes that the parties involved have agreed that the critical issue has become a problem. From there, one can proceed through the six steps, repeating the cycle as often as necessary each time a conflict surfaces.

Below is a step-by-step description of the model and an explanation of how to apply it to a problem.

Step 1: Pray and Establish the Process. Before beginning any discussion about a critical issue, we should pray and ask God for wisdom, clarity of thought, and emotional control. It is imperative that each person agree to be truthful about the issue and how he or she feels about it (John 8:32). Dishonesty and deceit are easy temptations to fall

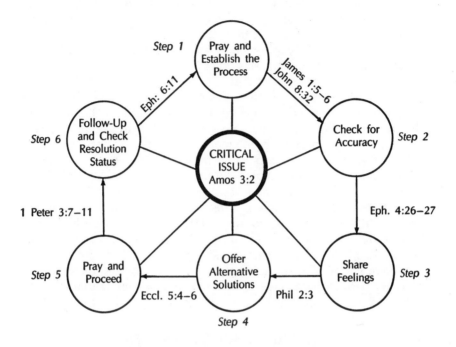

Figure 5.2. Effective Communication:
A Six-Step Model for Conflict Resolution.

into in times of conflict. Deceit, once discovered, often reveals a destructive layer of anger. A constructive process can be established by (1) identifying and agreeing on the exact issue to be discussed; (2) contracting to accept each other's feelings whether or not you share the same feelings about the issue; and (3) agreeing to discuss the issue for a consistent period of time until it is resolved, perhaps in family meetings once a week.

Step 2: Check for Accuracy. As each of you talk, be sure to confirm each other's recollections of events, time, people involved, and the impact of the event at the time it occurred. Often, misrepresentations of what was said or done are carried over from one issue to the next. Be certain that the information and perceptions shared by each of you are accurate by giving each other honest and clear feedback.

Step 3: Share Feelings. Share with each other specifically how you

93

felt about what happened. However, when emotions are high, feelings of anger, resentment, disappointment, and frustration can be easily misinterpreted as personal rejection. It's permissible to be angry (Eph. 4:26–27) as long as the expression of anger is aimed at correcting the situation and not punishing the other person.

Step 4: Offer Alternative Solutions. Every problem has at least one solution. Most problems have several solutions if we can be objective in our search. Selfishness and conceit (Phil. 2:3) should be abandoned in order to find alternative solutions to remedy the situation. Few problems, if any, have ever been created solely by one person, and no one person is individually responsible for the resolution. Look honestly at how each of you contributed to the problem. Bear each other's burden by forgiving faults and shortcomings (Gal. 6:2–4).

Step 5: Pray and Proceed. Pray and proceed to work on the solutions. In this step be careful not to make promises to each other or to God about what you intend to do unless you are committed to your promise. Don't let your speech cause you to sin (Eccl. 5:4–6).

Step 6: Follow-Up. In this final step, it is important to check with each other periodically to determine if the solutions are working and to identify what adjustments need to be made to resolve the conflict.

THE CHALLENGE TO SINGLES

Not everyone will marry; in fact, there is good biblical evidence that not everyone should be married (1 Cor. 7:8–9). Each of us can be a complete and whole person in Christ (Col. 2:10). If one wants to be married but is still single after praying and waiting, consider the following possibilities:

1. God could be calling you to a form of ministry that would be hindered by the restraints and responsibilities of a mate and a family (1 Cor. 7:32–34).

2. We frequently ask God to grant our requests according to his will, but then proceed to make decisions according to our will. For instance, it is possible that God has already put his person for you in your life, but you may have rejected God's choice because the person was too short, too low on income, too traditional, or in some other way below your requirements.

3. It may not be time for you to be married. It helps to view singleness as being for a period of time rather than for a lifetime. Unfortunately, the stigma of being single past the age of thirty (even younger in some cases) has caused many men and women to marry prematurely out of desperation and fear. Many have been so eager that

they have married unbelievers, placing themselves in clear opposition to God's command not to be unequally yoked (2 Cor. 6:14).

4. You may not have learned to be content with yourself and instead have placed unfair demands on someone else to make you happy. Good relationships are possible only when each person (a) respects him- or herself and the other partner; (b) has realistic expectations for the other partner; and (c) depends on God to prepare him- or herself for the relationship.

SEXUALITY: ITS ROLE IN RELATIONSHIPS

God instituted sex, and each person is a sexual being. To deny this fact is naïve, but failure to put our sexuality in proper perspective has been an overlooked source of trouble in many relationships. Because sex is only biblically sanctioned inside the institution of marriage (1 Cor. 7:2–9), the conflict in this area for the Christian rests with singles who engage in premarital sex and with married people who engage in extramarital sex.

My experience with the Christian community on this issue has been that the average Christian single does not consider the consequences of fornication except for unwanted pregnancy and disease. However, there are other ways that premarital and extramarital sex have an impact on the dynamics of a relationship.

Smedes (1984) makes a comment in response to the Apostle Paul's concern in this area. He states that "sexual intercourse signifies and seals a personal life-union" (p. 137). When two people engage in intercourse, they do something that binds them in a life partnership that the Hebrews called "one flesh" (Gen. 2:24).

Sex and the one-flesh doctrine might be compared to Bowlby's (1969) theory of attachment and separation between a baby and his or her mother. In the new life union, an attachment bond is formed to one person, and any disruption in this bond can cause emotional trauma for the baby. By analogy, God intended Christian marriage as a permanent bonding between two reborn Christians, and created sexual intercourse to confirm a lifelong union between the same two people. How many bonding experiences can one have without becoming confused, disappointed, or hurt when the union is disrupted by separation, divorce, or infidelity?

Couples who have been bonded to other partners before marriage often have difficulties that would have been avoided if they had remained abstinent. Four common difficulties are:

1. **Lack of Trust.** The old saying that "history repeats itself" is

95

appropriate. Jealousy and suspicion, however ill founded, are inevitable when couples know their mates have had other sexual partners.

2. **Performance Anxiety.** Unconscious mental processes can be controlling. Sexual competition with ghosts (former sexual partners) in a relationship can contribute to sexual dysfunctions.

3. **Guilt.** Guilt is ever-present with many singles who, after having been involved in a sexual relationship, have to repeatedly repent to God for the same sin. Guilt breeds low self-worth and self-punishment, and makes it difficult for us to change our behavior.

4. **Disillusionment.** Sex is far too often used as the way to joy. No matter how enjoyable the experience may be at the time, the feeling is only temporary. The reality of being lonely and unfulfilled soon sets us on yet another futile search.

However mysterious the bond created by sexual union, we know that God has reserved it for marriage and that the union parallels the relationship between Christ and the church (Eph. 5:31–32).

SUMMARY

In summary, relationships between Black males and females can be improved and strengthened by examining alternative ways of responding to the stress on our family systems, and by accepting the challenge to return our relationships to God's design and order. Use of a cognitive/behavioral approach that involves changing our traditional thinking about the family structure and then altering our behavior patterns will help couples and families to form a better foundation for relationships based on God's principles of trust, love, and commitment.

References

Bateson, G.; Jackson, D.D.; Haley, J.; and Weakland, J. H. (1956). Towards a Theory of Schizophrenia. *Behavioral Sciences* 1:251.

Bowlby, J. (1969). Psychoanalysis and Child Care. In J. D. Sutherland, ed., *Psychoanalysis and Contemporary Theory*. New York: Basic Books.

Cazenave, N.A. (1983). Black Male-Black Female Relationships: The Perceptions of 155 Middle-Class Black Men. *Family Relations* 32:341–350.

Edersheim, A. (1982). *Sketches of Jewish Social Life*. Grand Rapids: Eerdmans.

Jordan, W. D. (1974). *The White Man's Burden*. New York: Oxford.

Laing, R. D. (1965). Mystification, Confusion, and Conflict. In I. Boszormenyi-Nagy and J. L. Framo, eds., *Intensive Family Therapy: Theoretical and Practical Aspects*. New York: Harper and Row.

Master Study Bible, New American Standard (1981). Nashville: Holman.

Satir, V. M. (1983). *Conjoint Family Therapy* (Third Edition). Palo Alto: Science and Behavior Books.

Smedes, L. B. (1984). *Sex for Christians*. Grand Rapids: Eerdmans

6

The Role of the Home in the Spiritual Development of Black Children

Shirley Spencer June

SHIRLEY SPENCER JUNE grew up in her birthplace, Thomasville, Georgia. She received a Bachelor of Science degree in biology from Knoxville College and a Master of Science degree in Zoology from the University of Illinois (Champaign-Urbana). She also did a year of post-baccalaureate study (1966–67) in biology at Knox College. She is married to Lee N. June and they are the parents of twin boys, Stephen and Brian. Currently, Shirley is a homemaker, after working several years as a research assistant (electron microscopy) in a medical school. She is a member of the New Mt. Calvary Baptist Church in Lansing, Michigan and has been a Sunday school teacher and superintendent, as well as a youth worker.

6

The Role of the Home
in the Spiritual Development
of Black Children

> Unless the LORD builds the house,
> its builders labor in vain.
> Unless the LORD watches over the city,
> the watchmen stand guard in vain.
> Ps. 127:1 (NIV)

The home is a vital first environment for children. However, tremendous forces tug at its core, and some wonder how it will survive. Because the home, marriage, and family began in the mind of God the Creator (Gen. 1:27–28; 2:24; Ps. 127:3), efforts to remedy its ills must necessarily follow God's instructions if they are to succeed. Therefore this chapter will explore the role of the home in the spiritual development of Black children and how the home can impact the child for Christ in the early formative years.

Specifically, I will discuss (1) the case for the home, (2) the general challenge of parenting, (3) unique challenges to Black parents, (4) resources that can provide practical information and encouragement to parents seeking Christ-centered training for their children, and (5) suggestions to aid spiritual development of children in the home. To accomplish this task, I refer to various sources and draw on my experiences with children and parents in churches and schools as well as on my own experiences as a parent.

THE CASE FOR THE HOME: THE BIBLICAL MANDATE

I believe that the Bible mandates a role for the home in the spiritual development of children. Below I will comment on this mandate and its accompanying expectations.

Training is a responsibility of the home. To many, the ultimate responsibility for training children belongs unquestionably to parents. However, the erosion of family structures and the transfer of control from the home to outside agencies warrant our taking another look.

In Scripture, the mandate for training and development is given first and foremost to the home (Deut. 5:29; 6:1–3, 7–8; Prov. 1:7–9; Eph. 6:4). To Israel, God commanded that his laws and statutes be kept, and taught diligently to the children ". . . when you sit at home and when you walk along the road, when you lie down and when you get up" (Deut. 6:7 NIV). Their well-being, the well-being of their children, and their existence as a nation depended on it (Deut. 4:39–40). Biblically, parents are to teach, and children are to lay hold of the teaching they have received by letting it guide their lives.

For example, Proverbs 6:20–23 states:

> My son, keep your father's commands and do not forsake your mother's teaching. Bind them upon your heart forever; fasten them around your neck. When you walk, they will guide you; when you sleep, they will watch over you; when you awake, they will speak to you. For these commands are a lamp, this teaching is a light, . . . (NIV)

The Bible teaches that blessings abound for the individual, family, church, and nation that will dare to seek, obey, and line up with God's plans (Ps. 1:1–3; 103:17–18; 112:1–2). Of Abraham, father of the faithful, God said (Gen. 18:19), "For I have chosen him, so that he will direct his children and his household after him to keep the way of the LORD by doing what is right and just, so that the LORD will bring about for Abraham what he has promised him" (NIV). It follows then that God's best for individuals and families is thwarted when sin, rebellion, and disobedience prevail.

Are American heads-of-households willing and ready to reorder their lives to make training their children a top priority? Are African-American heads-of-households ready? Hopefully, the reader will decide (if he or she has not already) to make training in the home a priority so as to follow God's mandate and expectation in this regard.

Parents are to train so that the knowledge of God is passed to succeeding generations.

Psalm 78:1, 3–7 states:

O my people, hear my teaching; . . . [things] we have heard and known, [things] our fathers have told us. We will not hide them from their children; we will tell the next generation the praiseworthy deeds of the LORD, his power, and the wonders he has done. He decreed statutes for Jacob and established the law in Israel, which he commanded our forefathers to teach their children, so the next generation would know them, even the children yet to be born, and they in turn would tell their children. Then they would put their trust in God and would not forget his deeds but would keep his commands. (NIV)

Therefore those who know the way are expected to walk in it. They are to responsibly teach those born to them so that they might walk in it, as well as to diligently teach (make teaching a priority).

Fathers are expected to bring their children up "in the training and instruction of the Lord" (Eph. 6:4). A framework for parenting is thus established that includes (along with meeting the obvious needs of food, clothing, shelter, and protection) clearly communicating who God is, his nature, his works, provisions, and expectations in such a way that children can have hearts prepared to worship and reverence him. It is a joy when parents, grandparents, and great-grandparents can look over their generations and see that the knowledge of God is being passed on in line with biblical expectations.

Christian parents must decide to train biblically. Christian parents should and can make a conscious commitment to "parent biblically" from the earliest formative years of their children's home development. Doing so would entail a conscious surrendering of oneself to the Lordship of Jesus Christ, depending on his love, wisdom, and power working through us in fulfilling this God-given role, and accepting the Word of God as the authority in all matters of life and conduct. It further includes accepting the responsibility of being the primary agents in the training of our children as a calling from God, trusting the Holy Spirit to help us to train, and praying expectantly for our children.

A primary focus of training children is to establish early in them a view of God, the world, and their place in it that is consistent with what the Bible teaches. Because young children learn from various sources, a challenge facing the parent, then, is to show God's love, to establish God's principles, to model God's design for relationships in the home and in general conduct, and to believe and trust God's promises regarding their children.

Biblical training, to me, means to allow God's Word to influence every decision regarding our children's training. Such focused biblical training does not happen by accident. There must be a conscious decision to make it a priority. Remaining at home to train them, for instance, instead of immediately returning to work, is an option worth considering. Reading Scripture to them daily from infancy is highly recommended, and can become a treasured time for both the child and his or her parent or guardian. For the parent or grandparent who may have difficulty reading, the Scripture on cassette tapes might be a substitute.

The aim of this training is to make our children "wise for salvation"; that they might know God through Jesus Christ whom he has sent, and walk in his ways. "But as for you, continue in what you have learned and have become convinced of, because you know those from whom you learned it, and how from infancy you have known the holy Scriptures, which are able to make you wise for salvation through faith in Christ Jesus" (2 Tim. 3:14–15 NIV). While it may be difficult for some to make the decision to train and parent biblically through the home, God expects this of us and will give us the strength to accomplish the task.

Knowledge is to result in a change in behavior. The goal of biblical teaching is to engender an understanding that will result in reverential trust and obedience. Christian parents are also mandated to teach their children through precept and example. A New Testament parallel of the principle of parenting, for example, may be seen in Matthew 28:18–20 wherein Jesus instructed the disciples collectively to go into all the world and share the gospel, teaching the babes born unto him so that they too would grow to maturity and win and teach others.

The intent of Scripture is that knowledge is to result in positive action and commitment, rather than simply remain head knowledge without experience (Prov. 22:6). While avoiding negative lifestyles is good, avoidance cannot be considered, in and of itself, representative of spiritual commitment. Stanley (1986) describes the tendency of Christian parents to equate maintaining acceptable behavior norms with living a life for Jesus Christ. He noted that it is not enough to be concerned that our children "not do" this or that as a lifestyle; rather, the concern must be that our young people know Jesus Christ and are equipped and effective for him in their relationships with others. Ezzo and Ezzo (1987) have also related how scriptural training that ends in application has always been the biblical emphasis. Thus, as children grow as we impart to them spiritual knowledge, we will begin to see them incorporate this spiritual knowledge into their daily lives.

Training impacts a child's mental, physical, social, spiritual, and moral development. Just as Jesus grew in wisdom, stature, and in favor with God and humanity (Luke 2:52), parents through the home can help their children mature in those same areas. Training children only in selected areas would be like continually serving them only one part of a balanced meal, omitting the foods they don't like, and expecting their bodies to have all the nutrients necessary for proper growth and development. God has designed each of us as unique, complex individuals with specific requirements in each area of our lives. Thus, it is not enough to develop one area of a child's life to the neglect of the others if we are to achieve the biblical goal of wholeness and balance. This idea of wholeness and balance is also mirrored in the diversity of the body of Christ and the many functions of the various parts. There, too, one function does not negate the need for the others. Rather, only the proper functioning of all the parts results in a well-developed body.

With the enormous challenges of parenting, it becomes tempting to at least shift part of the home's responsibility to other sources. The demands can sometimes seem overwhelming, particularly in situations where stress and fragmentations in the family unit bring on additional difficulties and responsibilities. The erosion of support for the family in society, the fact that parents are tending to be younger or single (babies having babies), and economic pressures from difficulties in "making ends meet," are but a few factors that can compound an already complex job.

Of the organized efforts actually working to aid families, most seem to suffer from a benign neglect, if not deliberate exclusion, of a spiritual perspective. Thus, parents and the home can be the consistent voice of spiritual truth for their youngsters. Children need to be assisted in incorporating the view that they are made and loved by God, who has a purpose and value for everything he created, and that this is a surer, more enduring standard for judging their worth and behavior than can be found in the changing whims and norms of our culture. This is especially important in the midst of a culture where atheistic philosophies, traditions, and ideals are being legitimized. Nevertheless, in spite of these forces, if we train and parent biblically and consistently in the home, we will see our children grow over time in the mental, physical, social, and moral realms.

DEVELOPMENT AND FAMILY INFLUENCE

Critical to one's personal development is the formation of a positive self-concept. Researchers and writers say that this is an area in which parents (and thus the home) make a major impact. Some tell us that by the age of five or six, a child's views of personal identity and worth are already set, as are many personality traits.

Several writers have discussed the relationships between parenting styles and personality development (Hamachek, 1987; Meier, 1977), and parenting styles with certain behavioral responses in children (Dinkmeyer and McKay, 1982). Berkowitz (1964) and Hamachek (1987) both have noted the changes in accepted child-rearing patterns over time (these have gone from very strict to very permissive with gradations in between). These changes in accepted norms have led to different expectations for parents and their children. Meier (1977) and Meier and Meier (1981) describe several traits they feel characterize "mentally healthy" families: four of these are love, discipline, consistency, and example.

Hamachek listed four styles of parental interaction and the expected impact on the child's self-esteem: authoritarian (low self-esteem in the child), authoritative (high self-esteem and independent, socially responsible behavior in offspring), permissive (overly aggressive, immature, self-centered child) and harmonious (no distinct predictable pattern of behaviors). June and Fooks (1980) in a study conducted with Black professionals, confirmed the results of earlier researchers that parents are "key influencers" in the career choices their children make.

Studies have also been conducted on self-concept and self-esteem. Self-concept may be defined as a summary of those facts, opinions, and attitudes one carries about oneself, while self-esteem is the corresponding regard or evaluation of self based on those facts and opinions. Formation of self-concept and self-esteem starts at birth (Comer and Pouissant, 1975), can be damaged quite easily, and is shaped by interactions with significant adults and others with whom the child relates.

These studies serve to remind us that parents profoundly impact the lives of our children. Thus we need to make a most serious investment of our love, time, and commitment to train them during their formative years. Whether they grow up and choose to follow in our footsteps or go in paths of their own choosing, we still have an influence. Because we are also strong positive influences in the choices and career successes of our children, we need to make a concerted effort to make maximum use of that time when the foundations are being laid, when parents are most likely to spend the greatest amount of time with their children, and when children are most likely to want and welcome help and advice.

UNIQUE CHALLENGES TO PARENTS
OF BLACK YOUNGSTERS

In addition to the moral, spiritual, social, and physical challenges facing every parent, parents of Black youngsters have a larger task because of the racial issues in our society. However, while dealing with racial issues, we must also see the relevance of the gospel of Jesus Christ to our condition and life.

McCray (1987) emphasized the need for us to engage also in in-depth, comprehensive study of the Word for ourselves, and not just settle for "good preachin'" on Sunday morning or a Bible class during the week. He noted:

> At the age when your . . . mind is being challenged by the institutions of learning, at the time when you are seeking to get a diploma, and seeking to go on to perfect your learning and learning abilities, shouldn't you at the same time match or surpass this knowledge that you receive in the schools with the knowledge that you receive from studying God's Word? . . . We must know "What thus saith the Lord." (p. 29)

Helping youngsters develop in a society that often does not affirm who they are is an additional burden. The statistics that describe life and trends for the Black children and families in America are disturbing. These statistics suggest that families in general are vulnerable, but Black families typically struggle against more numerous, vicious, and relentless forces than do families in general.

To counter these negative forces, parents can focus on helping their children anticipate and interpret accurately and honestly the experiences they will face. Further, children can be helped to respond to these experiences in a way that fosters their positive development. This, however, is no small task because many of the problems Black families and children face in America today are the result of discriminatory practices that have been entrenched in American culture for many years (Comer, 1985; Comer and Pouissant, 1975; Hare and Hare, 1984; Kunjufu, 1983, 1984, 1986; Hale-Benson, 1987; Jacob, 1988). Much of this discrimination has been with deliberate, legal sanctions (Higgenbotham, 1978).

There are many common practices that continue to have a daily negative impact on masses of Black youngsters (Hale-Benson, 1987). These include educational testing or evaluative procedures that result in the mislabeling of Black youngsters, as well as the designing of whole educational programs without an understanding of, appreciation for, or desire to capitalize on the positive strengths or learning styles that exist within Black families.

In addition to the practices mentioned above, there are other factors that Black parents encounter. For example, there continues to be a disproportionate distribution of Blacks on the lower-economic level, where people bear extra burdens and confront excessive obstacles in their struggle just to meet basic survival needs. Many parents constantly confront the spiritual, economic, social, educational, and political policies and strategies that demean, miseducate, entrap, and even destroy Black youngsters. Because of these issues, Black parents can share information about these problems at a time when children can adequately understand and positively proceed. They can do it in a way that will not increase mental or social pressures, nor stir feelings of resentment and anger that are detrimental to the child. Fostering an appreciation of our own culture by acquainting youngsters with the rich heritage, contributions, and traditions of Black people is one additional antidote to these negative influences.

In many home environments, Black youngsters become adept at a style of interaction that may not be readily accepted by the larger society. A case in point is the use of language patterns (which may include "Black English") that help a child be successful at home but that work against him or her at school. While there is a long-standing debate over the pros and cons of speech patterns, it is often necessary for Blacks to modify their language style to function better in the broader society (see, for example, Jones, 1982). Black parents need to know that decisions and judgments are being made regarding their children, by educators and others, based on speech patterns. Parents must find out how these decisions and judgments are impacting their children's self-concepts and development.

RESOURCES

To help parents who take a biblical stand in training their children, I offer a brief listing of resources that could help in pursuing these goals. Because our children bring home report cards that indicate how well they have mastered the material presented to them during the previous "marking period," we as parents need materials to help us set and assess our goals for *our* "marking periods." This will help us know what our goals are, whether our goals are sound, and if our goals have been achieved.

The resources listed below contain many helpful insights and much practical advice for parents. Some resources raise issues that can help parents or prospective parents evaluate their own conceptual framework on parenting and make positive changes. While some were geared specifically toward issues affecting African-Americans, others discuss parenting generally.

Church and public libraries can be excellent sources of materials. Some information may be available through schools, though parents need to be aware that the goals, attitudes, and philosophies presented may differ from their own, and that selectivity on the part of the parent is therefore required.

1. *Growing Kids God's Way for No Excuse Parenting.* Gary and Anne Marie Ezzo. Twenty audio tapes and a workbook. Many topics covered, giving practical help in applying biblical principles in child-rearing. Available from Growing Families International, P.O. Box 8073, Northridge, CA 91327.

2. *God's Blueprint for the Christian Family* (1986). Anthony Evans. Six-part video series covering "Marriage: God's Style," "Roles in Marriage," "Parenting," "Sex in Marriage," "Divorce and Remarriage," and "Successful Singlehood." Produced by The Urban Alternative. Available from Renaissance Production, 759 N. Broadway, Pittman, NJ 08071.

3. *How to Protect the Family.* Charles Stanley. Six-part audio series, covering "How to Protect the Family, Parts 1 and 2," "Binding Satan," "Pulling Down Strongholds," "Hedge of Protection," and "My Prayer for You." Available from In Touch Ministries, P.O. Box 7900, Atlanta, GA 30357.

4. *How to Keep Your Kids on Your Team.* Charles and Andy Stanley. Six-part audio series. Topics: "Think Correctly," "Treat Them Correctly," "Equip and Challenge Them," "Teach Them Correctly," "Teach Them to Pray," and "Fulfilling our Roles." Order from In Touch Ministries, P.O. Box 7900, Atlanta, GA 30357.

5. *Child Training God's Way.* Gregg Harris. Two-part audio cassette series. Topics: "Training Grounds and House Rules" and "The Power of Companionship." Available from Creation Life Workshops, 180 S. E. Kane Road, Gresham, OR 97080.

6. *Bible Activity Workbook for Primaries* (1983). Marjorie Goodwin Garnes and Mardine McReynolds.

"Bible Story Time for Primaries" cassette tape. Joan Ganns.

Bible Activity Workbook for Juniors (1983) and cassette tape. Delores Jones. All present Bible stories with an emphasis on relating to the African-American child. Available from Christian Ed. Resources, Unlimited, Inc., Box 938, Midlothian, IL 60445.

7. *Self-counseling Workbook for Mothers Without Husbands* (1986).

Sheila Staley. Includes practical help in goal-setting and planning toward achieving a balanced life. Available from Christian Research and Development, 1822 68th Ave., Philadelphia, PA 19126.

8. *Lessons from History: A Celebration in Blackness* (1987). Jawanza Kunjufu. Geared toward older children; can be used by parents as resource for cultural awareness. Vocabulary and questions at end can help focus discussion. Available from African-American Images, 9204 Commercial Suite 308, Chicago, IL 60617.

9. *Parenting Isn't for Cowards* (1989). James Dobson. Waco, Tex.: Word Books. Focus on the Family has an extensive film and video-cassette series covering a variety of family and parenting issues. Available from Focus on the Family, Pomona, CA 91799.

10. *Emotions, Can You Trust Them?* (1981). James Dobson. Ventura: Regal Books. This book contains a checklist for assessing training goals.

11. *What the Bible Says About Teaching Babies* (1989). Carole Carner. This is a video accompanied by a manual and describes methods for training babies. It is available from Carole Carner Ministries, 14139 East 19th Place, Tulsa, OK 74108.

12. *The Great Dinosaur Mystery* (1987). Paul S. Taylor. El Cajon, Calif.: Master Books. This book provides some scientific evidence for creation.

13. *The Illustrated Origins Answer Book* (1989). Paul S. Taylor. Mesa, Ariz.: Films for Christ Association. Like the previous book, the author provides some scientific evidence for creation.

SUGGESTIONS TO AID SPIRITUAL DEVELOPMENT OF CHILDREN IN THE HOME

I have presented and discussed the Biblical mandate and expectations for the home, shared studies on development and family influence, discussed our unique challenges as Black parents, and presented some resources that can aid in the parenting process. Throughout, greater emphasis has been placed on the need for verbal communication of God's Word to children because that is one of the most neglected areas in many homes.

In this section, I will offer helps for aiding spiritual development of children through the home by making some additional suggestions in light of what has already been presented. Parents are encouraged to consistently incorporate these and/or other activities based on their unique situation.

Infancy Through Preschool

1. Pray for your children.
2. Read the bible to children beginning at birth, if not earlier. This has become one of the most valuable tips on parenting that I have ever received.
3. Expose children to written, audio and video materials, and games that help children know God.
4. Encourage children to read and memorize Scripture at an early age. Games of "competition" around memorization can be fun when created and played with parents. Rewards can be given for achieving certain goals.
5. *Take* children to Sunday school and church. There what they are learning at home can be reinforced.
6. Clearly present the plan of salvation and encourage them to receive Christ as their Savior and Lord.
7. Purchase materials (audio, video, written) that adequately present Christ.
8. Give them their own Bible, even before they learn to read. This can aid them in beginning to appreciate the Bible. Point out biblical characters who were Black. As they are learning to read, let them also read from the Bible.
9. Get children involved in Christian activities and reinforce this involvement through the home.
10. Teach them the biblical view of creation. Children can learn early to think of God through seeing the variety and beauty in what God has made: sunshine, moon and stars at night, flowers, trees, birds, pets, themselves, other children; and listening to different sounds in nature. They can be taught that the materials used to construct automobiles, streets, sidewalks, and buildings come from materials provided in nature that were originally created by God.

    The Institute for Creation Research has a wide selection of videos, books, and publications that would be useful to children and adults. These may be obtained through Master Books (P.O. Box 1606, El Cajon, CA 92022).
11. Monitor and limit children's TV viewing and listening to radio.
12. Let them *see* you praying, reading the Bible, and using biblical principles in your life.

Early School Years

1. Continue to do the things mentioned above. Some may need to be adjusted to be appropriate for this later age.
2. As they face issues in school, help them view and solve such issues from a biblical perspective.
3. Help to identify secular philosophies and how these often conflict with biblical views.
4. Help them recognize behaviors in themselves and in their peer group that are contrary to Scripture.
5. Spend time with them. They will see Christ through you.
6. As you do the above, don't be surprised that they will begin to pick out non-biblical behaviors in you. Children can more easily see their need to admit when they are wrong, and the need to repent, ask for, and receive forgiveness from God and others when they see that lived out in us.
7. Teach them to tithe their earnings.

CONCLUSION

The aim of this chapter has been to challenge parents and those who influence children to examine their perspective on parenting and child rearing; to make it consistent with God's perspective; and to put into place some reasonable goals, or checks to help us evaluate our efforts. Helpful resources have also been suggested.

Because children are gifts from the Lord (Ps. 127:3), parents are accountable to God for the nurture, management, and spiritual development of their children. Young people who have no time for God in their lives did not get that way overnight. The seeds of ignoring God are often planted and cultivated over a number of years and can begin in the home.

God's goal for children is the same as his goal for adults: to be conformed to the image of Jesus Christ. God's desire for children, as for us, is continual fellowship with him. Children need a solid background for answering questions like "Who am I?" and "Where do I fit?" Providing children with a strong image of who God is, and a sound basis for their self-worth as individuals and in relation to others, enables each one to see his or her need of the Savior, as well as to appreciate their unique mixture of gifts, talents, and abilities.

Children can learn to value what God has given each of them, rather than becoming rooted in a lifestyle of constantly comparing themselves to others. It is crucial to establish this foundation early, before the age when peer pressure and the need to conform become such powerful motivators. Our interactions and instruction should be such that these lessons seem not so much "taught" as "caught" by the child. Young people need to realize early that there is an alternative to the worldview popularized by the media through television, magazines, and radio.

Hopefully all parents will commit themselves to make teaching their children a priority. Scripture commands it, and conditions demand it.

References

Berkowitz, L. (1964). *The Development of Motives and Values in the Child*. New York: Basic Books.

Comer, J. P. (1985). Empowering Black Children's Educational Environments. In H. P. McAdoo and J. L. McAdoo, eds., *Black Children: Social, Educational and Parental Environments*. Beverly Hills: Sage.

Comer, J., and Pouissant, A. (1975). *Black Child Care*. New York: Pocket Books (Simon & Schuster).

Dinkmeyer, D., and McKay, G. (1982). *The Parent's Handbook: Systematic Training for Parents (STEP)*. Circle Pines, Minn.: American Guidance Service.

Ezzo, G., and Ezzo, A. (1987). *Growing Kids God's Way*. Ten-part video. Northridge, Calif.: Growing Families International.

Hale-Benson, J. (1987). *Black Children, Their Roots, Culture and Learning Styles*. Baltimore: Johns Hopkins.

Hamachek, D. E. (1987). *Encounters with the Self* (3d ed.). New York: Holt, Rinehart and Winston.

Hare, N., and Hare, J. (1984). *The Endangered Black Family: Coping with Unisexualization and the Coming Extinction of the Black Race*. San Francisco: Black Think Tank.

Higgenbotham, A. L., Jr. (1978). *In the Matter of Color: Race and the American Legal Process*. New York: Oxford University Press.

The Holy Bible: New International Version. (1984). Grand Rapids: Zondervan.

Jacob, J. E. (1988). Black America, 1987: An Overview. In J. Dewart, ed., *The State of Black America 1988*, 1–6. New York: National Urban League.

Jones, R. (1982). What's Wrong with Black English. *Newsweek C* (December) (26):7.

June, L., and Fooks, G. (1980). Key Influences on the Career Directions and Choices of Black University Professionals. *Journal of Non-white Concerns* 8:157–166.

Kunjufu, J. (1983). *Countering the Conspiracy to Destroy Black Boys*. Vol. 1. Chicago: Afro-Am Publishing Co.

_____. (1984). *Developing Positive Self-images and Discipline in Black Children*. Chicago: African American Images.

111

————. (1986). *Countering the Conspiracy to Destroy Black Boys*. Vol. 2. Chicago: African American Images.

McCray, W. A. (1987). *Black Folks and Christian Liberty: Be Christian, Be Black, Be Culturally and Socially Free*. (2d ed.). Chicago: Black Light Fellowship.

Meier, P. D. (1977). *Christian Child-rearing and Personality Development*. Grand Rapids: Baker.

Meier, P., and Meier, R. (1981). *Family Foundations: How to Have a Happy Home*. Grand Rapids: Baker.

Stanley, C., and Stanley, A. (1986). *How to Keep Your Kids on Your Team* (audio tapes, six-part series). Atlanta: In Touch Ministries.

The Role of the Church in the Educational Development of Black Children

Bonita Pope Curry

BONITA POPE CURRY is Associate Professor at the Counseling Center, Michigan State University, and also has a private practice. She received a Bachelor of Science degree in psychology from Denison University, and Master of Arts and Doctor of Philosophy degrees in counseling psychology from Southern Illinois University, Carbondale. Bonita was born and raised in Dayton, Ohio, and is married to Theodore Curry, II. They have one child, Victoria Briana. Bonita attends Friendship Baptist Church in Lansing, Michigan, and has worked in its counseling ministries.

7

The Role of the Church
in the Educational Development
of Black Children

What a precious resource the Black church has access to—and thus responsibility for—in the many Black children who participate in its various ministries! These children reap some of the most important benefits of the church's stewardship. Scripture makes it clear that children are to be ministered to and trained. For example:

> And thou shalt teach them diligently unto thy children, and shalt talk of them when thou sittest in thine house, and when thou walkest by the way, and when thou liest down, and when thou risest up. And thou shalt bind them for a sign upon thine hand, and they shall be as frontlets between thine eyes. (Deut. 6:7–8 NSRB)

> Train up a child in the way he should go: and when he is old, he will not depart from it. (Prov. 22:6 NSRB)

> And they brought unto him also infants, that he would touch them: but when his disciples saw it, they rebuked them. But Jesus called them unto him, and said, Permit little children to come unto me, and forbid them not: for of such is the kingdom of God. (Luke 18:15–16 NSRB)

The proper educational development of children is an essential task for the church. The church must join with the family to counteract any inaccurate, self-defeating, or damaging messages their children may receive from the schools, their peers, or the media. The church must also seek ways to integrate the Christian faith and Christian learning with secular education. In order to develop spiritual leaders who are able to effectively teach, counsel, or guide others, the church must actively promote the study and mastery of academic disciplines. The Black church is called on to continue to help produce political, economic, social, and educational leaders. While formal education is not in itself a sufficient element of Christian faith and belief, having educational tools better equips Christians to remain viable in a society that is increasingly complex and competitive. Reading, writing, mathematics, history, and other disciplines are essential not only for occupational success, but also for understanding and teaching the Bible, its principles, and Christian service (Paris, 1985).

In the past, we had the benefit of more extended-family and neighborhood networks that served to guide and nurture our children. Extended family members and others in the community were more actively involved in the lives of children and their social and educational development. But as family members become more mobile and scattered geographically, and as predominantly Black neighborhoods deteriorate to the point where children live among "undesirable elements," many of those supportive networks are no longer available.

The church, however, has remained a constant force in the lives of Black people. It therefore must strive to provide early, consistent, and relevant instruction to Black children. The church is where children are taught that Jesus loves them no matter what their skin color or socioeconomic status.

Many of our children never get a chance to be "innocent." They must face harsh realities at a tender age. It is in church that they are made to feel special, self-confident, and hopeful about their future. This chapter will address the challenge facing the Black church to make a critical, positive difference in the educational development of Black children.

THE EDUCATIONAL NEEDS OF BLACK CHILDREN

The educational status of American Black children is seen by many as a national emergency. On the average, nearly one-third of all Black high school students drop out before graduation. In some urban areas, the percentage is significantly higher. The Detroit chapter of the Michigan Association of Black Social Workers (1988) reported that in 1970, 8 percent of all jobs were available to high school drop-outs. It is projected that in the 1990s, only 3 percent of all jobs will be available to those without high school diplomas.

In the past decade, the number of Black students attending college has steadily fallen. The U.S. Bureau of Census (1990) reported that in 1988 only 29 percent of all Black high-school students went on to college. The fact that Black youth do not pursue post-secondary education in greater numbers is a severe problem that demands immediate attention.

While Black students make up 16 percent of the total enrollment of secondary students, they comprise 35 percent of those students categorized as educable mentally retarded and 27 percent of those categorized as trainable mentally retarded in our nation's schools (DBS Corporation, 1987). This could be due to the discriminatory nature of intelligence tests administered or to cultural differences between students and teachers. Despite the fact that there has been a reduction in the total number of children classified as educable mentally retarded, this has had relatively little impact on the ethnic disproportion (MacMillan, 1988).

It has been shown that Black students receive 30 percent of all suspensions and 31 percent of the corporal punishment rendered by school authorities. Also, Black students represent 27 percent of all students labeled with severe emotional impairment. In contrast, only 8 percent of students labeled gifted and talented are Black (DBS Corporation, 1987). Local and state school boards must be held accountable for the proper assessment and education of Black children. It is also critical that Black children have access to quality pre-school and early education programs, as well as vocational education and career development.

It has been said that the key to boosting the educational performance levels of Black students is for parents, teachers, and school administrators to form a coalition to improve academic achievement. Obviously, the church must be added to that coalition. This could be achieved by the church sponsoring its own tutorial and educational support programs geared toward preparing students for academic success and then interacting with parents, teachers, and school administrators. The church is an essential link in the chain of influences on a Black child's life. The Black church must reinforce and, in some instances, supplement the educational efforts of the school system. The responsibility for the educational development of the Black child lies with any segment of society that is concerned and equipped to make a positive impact. The Black church certainly qualifies as such.

HISTORICAL EDUCATIONAL EFFORTS

The Black church has always been actively involved in the educational and social development of Black people. Because Black Americans were not permitted access to formal education, the majority of Blacks were illiterate when slavery was abolished. The Black church immediately established schools to educate its people. The Black churches believed that the task of racial uplift, both educationally and morally, lay basically in the hands of Blacks themselves. Consequently, their schools became the prime examples of that viewpoint (Paris, 1985).

As the political gains of Reconstruction began to erode, Black denominational efforts to start schools of higher learning increased. Black ministers were convinced that education was the only way to insure survival with dignity. One reason for the desire that the masses be educated was a belief in the relationship between education and Christianity.

T. G. Steward, for example, suggested that Christians ought to learn to read and write as a part of their responsibilities as Christians. J. S. Flipper, an African American Episcopal (AME) leader, joined other ministers in maintaining that educated people made better Christians, because education helped them to understand the demands of Christianity more fully. Having an education let them develop their God-given mental abilities and their opportunities to understand God's dealings with the creation (Wheeler, 1986).

Various predominantly Black denominations were successful in establishing a number of colleges and universities. Approximately thirty of our historically Black private institutions of higher education are church-related. The Black churches were the birthplaces of Black schools and of other agencies that sought to promote the development of Black people (Nelson, Yokley, and Nelson, 1971).

CURRENT EDUCATIONAL EFFORTS IN THE BLACK CHURCH

The Black church has consistently been involved in all phases of Black life, especially its educational aspects. According to the National Council of Churches, more churches are engaged in early childhood development than any other American institution. Several church-sponsored educational programs were highlighted in an article by Poinsett (1988). They included Project SPIRIT, which stands for Strength, Perseverance, Imagination, Responsibility, Integrity, and Talent. This is a pilot program of after-school tutorials held at fifteen churches in three cities. This project has substantially improved the academic skills of six- to twelve-year-olds and made them more aware and proud of their cultural heritage. Project SPIRIT evolved out of the 1978 founding of the Congress of National Black Churches, which has also launched a national Anti-Drug Abuse Campaign to help Black youth combat drug abuse and the crime problems that result.

An adoption program, called "One Church, One Child," was launched in 1981 by Father George Clements. This program has spread to twenty-eight states and has resulted in the adoption of an estimated 7,000 Black foster children. Unified efforts by three Harlem Baptist churches and three community-based organizations have resulted in programs to foster youth leadership and empowerment. Similarly, Teen-Link: The Church Connection Project, a six-church program component of the Lincoln Community Health Center in Durham, North Carolina, promotes good health activities for teenagers. Project Interface, at Allen Temple Baptist Church in Washington, D.C., tutors youth in math, science, and computer literacy. For more than twenty years it has provided instruction for both elementary and high school students. In 1987, the church encouraged students to continue their education by awarding fifty-three college scholarships.

The Friendship Baptist Church in Lansing, Michigan, offers an "Academic Enrichment Program" that provides students with the opportunity to conduct hands-on science lessons, receive assistance in reading, math, and other academic subjects, learn about Black history, and practice computer skills directly related to classroom activities. Also, several thousand dollars in scholarship money are given out each year to college students attending the church. The Dixon United Methodist Church in Dayton, Ohio, has established a Youth Life Center that focuses on youth drug and alcohol abuse, peer pressure, teenage pregnancy, youth suicide prevention, and child abuse. It also provides sports activities and career development. In focusing on career development, participants are taught how to write job resumés, how to answer employment ads, and how to prepare and dress for job interviews.

The Emmanuel Baptist Church in Chicago has established Emmanuel Christian School, state certified for kindergarten through eighth grades. This spiritually-based school has a complete academic curriculum as well as courses in Spanish, physical education, music/band, and music enrichment.

Several churches have felt the need for programs that focus exclusively on the development of young Black males. They include the Black Youth Project at Shiloh Baptist Church in Washington, D.C. Through athletics, counseling, and academic tutoring, this project ministers to youths in Washington's "depressed" areas. Project IMAGE, a consortium of ten Chicago churches, seeks to strengthen the image, role, and presence of Black males in families, churches, schools, and communities through ecumenical, community-based programs that address the need for positive male influences among Black boys. Summerendipity, launched in 1986 at the Pilgrims' Hope Baptist Church in Los Angeles, counsels youth groups, teaches young people the evils of drug abuse and gang violence and the virtues of thoughtful career decisions, and generally helps them maximize their personal effectiveness.

Other youth activities sponsored by Black churches include cooperative YW– and YMCAs, Girl and Boy Scouts, youth ministries, recreational work, vacation Bible school, prenatal care, nutritional counseling for mothers and infants, and sexuality workshops for parents and their teenagers.

FUTURE CHALLENGES AND RECOMMENDATIONS

As the oldest and most influential institution controlled by the Black community, the Black church has a crucial educational and spiritual role to play in the development of Black youth. The church will inspire and encourage youth as its programs and ministries are culturally relevant and applicable to real life needs and issues. As can be seen, many Black churches are rising to the challenge effectively, and with a serious sense of commitment. They are providing a wide variety of needed services and reaching large numbers of Black youth.

These youths must also survive and thrive in a world outside the sanctity of the church. They are affected by the educational, political, economic, and social policies of secular structures. For that reason, the church must be actively involved with those structures to advocate for policies that are responsive to the needs of Black children. Chisholm (1978) also challenges the Black church to address the issue of economic resources and how they can be channeled to benefit Black children and youth. Nobles and Goddard (1985) state that if the authority of the church is God, and God created Black people, the church and its leadership should see the ecclesiastical support of Black programs and activities as consistent with God's creative design.

Several recommendations can be made to insure the continued positive impact of the Black church on the Black child.

1. It is important that Black children feel good about themselves in order to develop positive self-concepts. Churches can provide Sunday school, Bible school, and other church reading materials that portray Black people and Black family life in accurate and positive images. We should also work toward that goal in our children's textbooks and in the media. Urban Ministries of Chicago is one source of such materials.

2. Gainful employment provides financial independence as well as

120

self-esteem. Provide employment for Black youth in areas of mainte-nance, tutoring, nursery-school attendants, and other meaningful service needs of the church. This would also teach job responsibilities and employment socialization.

3. Youth need adults who are willing to spend quality time listening to their concerns and to give relevant guidance. Develop and implement mentoring programs to match youth with positive role models and adult companions within the church.

4. It is often necessary to supplement the efforts of public education to ensure that Black children receive an adequate foundation for higher education and training. Develop and maintain tutoring programs that will assist young people to achieve early academic success.

5. Quality child care is one of the most expensive items in a family's budget. Provide low-cost child care at the church facility for working parents.

6. The talents and affiliations of Black church members often go underutilized. The Black church should use all of its resources to ensure appropriate knowledge and receipt of public, tax-funded services. Develop a network of church members with professional or personal ties to organizations or agencies that are charged with providing services for children. Those members can serve as effective advocates for people most in need.

7. The Black church cannot afford to be passive when it comes to the education of its children. Require accountability for elected officials on state and local school boards. Also, churches should urge active parental involvement in Parent-Teacher Associations.

8. Black youth need relevant and straightforward information and guidance, especially from a Christian perspective. Churches should provide seminars and forums on topics of interest to the Christian adolescent. Topics could include substance abuse, sexuality, career planning, male-female relationships, relationships with parents, rela-tionships with non-Christian peers, political awareness, and spiritual struggles. The Church could provide the biblical rationale and founda-tion for all seminars and forums, as well as current and relevant examples of the issues.

CONCLUSION

Keniston (1977) states that "the system will continue to provide victims faster than we can salvage them until we move toward changing those deeper forces that are causing the damage." The crisis is apparent, and we must work purposefully to help Black children develop a positive sense of self and to acquire basic strengths and abilities.

It is critical that the church be actively involved in this process because the nature of some of those "deeper forces" goes beyond unconcerned politicians, indifferent school administrators, and negative peer influences. The church is a place where a child can develop the powerful weapons of prayer, fortitude, and faith. It is imperative that the Black church empower itself to prepare Black youth to meet future challenges with confidence and hope. The Black church has always played an extremely vital role in the lives of her people. She must continue to do so with new strategies for current concerns.

References

Chisholm, S. (1978). Black Religion and Education. In J. R. Washington, ed., *Black Religion and Public Policy.* University of Pennsylvania, Afro-American Studies Program symposium.

DBS Corporation. (1987). *Elementary and Secondary School Civil Rights Survey: National Summaries.* Washington, D.C.: Arlington, Va. Opportunity System, Inc.

Keniston, K. (1977). *All Our Children.* New York: Harcourt Brace Jovanovich.

MacMillan, D. L. (1988). "New EMRs," In G. A. Robinson, ed. *Best Practices in Mental Disabilities.* Vol. 2. Boston: Little and Brown.

Michigan Association of Black Social Workers, Inc. (1988). Detroit Chapter. Unpublished position papers.

Nelson, H. M.; Yokley, R. L.; and Nelson, A. K. (1971). *The Black Church in America.* New York: Basic Books, Inc.

Nobles, W. W., and Goddard, L. L. (1985). Black Family Life: A Theoretical and Policy Implication Literature Review. In A. R. Harvey, ed., *The Black Family—An Afro-centric Perspective.* New York: United Church of Christ Commission for Racial Justice.

Paris, P. J. (1985). *The Social Teaching of the Black Church.* Philadelphia: Fortress Press.

Poinsett, A. (1988). Black Churches' Youth-Oriented Programs. *Ebony* 63 (August): 10.

Scofield, C. I., ed. (1967). *The New Scofield Reference Bible.* New York: Oxford.

U.S. Bureau of Census (1990). Statistical abstract of the United States (110th Edition), P-20, No. 303, 1988. Washington, D.C.: U.S. Government Printing Office.

Wheeler, E. L. (1986). *Uplifting the Race: The Black Minister in the New South 1865–1902.* Benton: University Press of America.

8

Teaching Christian Values
Within the Black Family

Fred Lofton

FRED LOFTON is pastor of Metropolitan Baptist Church in Memphis, Tennessee, and past president of the Progressive National Baptist Convention, Inc. Two of his recent books are *Help Me Somebody* (1988) and *Our Help in Ages Past: Sermons from Morehouse* (1987), an edited work. Fred received his Bachelor of Arts and Bachelor of Divinity degrees at Morehouse College, the Master of Science degree in Education at the University of Southern California, and the Doctorate of Sacred Theology degree from Emory University. Fred is a widower and was married to Dorothy McKinnie. He grew up in Kinston, North Carolina, his birthplace.

8

Teaching Christian Values
Within the Black Family

The last decade of the twentieth century finds the Black family in crisis. There are those who think that there is no way for the Black family to survive as we approach the next century. Those who prognosticate its death point to some patterns that are admittedly frightening and disturbing. They point to the rise in divorce rates, the number of women who are heading Black families, the ever-increasing spiral of teenage pregnancies, and other disheartening statistics. They remind us of the high rates of unemployment among Black men, women, and teenagers, the lack of equal educational opportunities, drug abuse, and the cycle of Black-on-Black crime. These are just some of the pathologies that threaten the survival of the Black family.

But in spite of the doom and gloom, it is my contention that many of these problems can be solved if basic Christian values are taught in the homes of Black people. It has been stated that boys and girls who are brought up in Christian homes have less trouble adjusting to the demands of an exacting society. They have been given the values that undergird the Christian life, and find that there is a correlation between commitment and involvement in the Christian lifestyle and one's citizenship. That is, good Christians typically make good citizens.

"Train up a child in the way he should go: and when he is old, he will not depart from it." This admonition comes from Scripture (Prov. 22:6 KJV). The best teachers to train children in this way are found within the family unit.

We expect our children to grow up to be good citizens and good church members. Yet we expect other societal institutions such as the school and the church to shoulder the responsibility of helping our children to attain these goals. In reality, the responsibility for attaining these goals rests with the home, within the family. If God in his infinite wisdom saw fit to establish the family, surely we can work productively within its framework.

The concept of the family is firmly established in Scripture. The Bible affirms that the family is the unit that is the foundation for all other units or institutions. God established the family with Adam and Eve, the first man and woman. This occurred long before the tabernacle, the synagogue, the church, or any of the other institutions evolved.

Within the God-given Ten Commandments, three relate directly to family life:

> Honour thy father and thy mother: that thy days may be long upon the land which the LORD thy God giveth thee.
>
> Thou shalt not commit adultery.
>
> Thou shalt not covet thy neighbour's house, thou shalt not covet thy neighbour's wife, nor his manservant, nor his maidservant, nor his ox, nor his ass, nor any thing that is thy neighbour's. (Ex. 20:12, 14, 17 KJV)

In the New Testament, attention is also given to various phases of family life. Jesus relates to the family situation in his teachings. The story of the prodigal son in the Gospel According to Luke pointedly shows the role of love and forgiveness within the family unit. Instructions for husbands, wives, and children are also found in the writings of Paul, particularly in portions of 1 Corinthians, Ephesians, and Colossians. Cornelius, in the tenth chapter of the Acts, illustrates the role of the head of the household in leading the family in worship.

O. R. Johnston (1979) in his book, *Who Needs the Family?*, focuses on the unique role of the human family in this interesting excerpt:

> But what are the essential tasks of the family? Ultimately these stem from the constitution of humanity itself, and especially from the position of the infant child. There are basic needs of child-rearing and child-bearing that *must* be performed, otherwise humanity will perish. The human child is peculiarly helpless at birth, unlike many other living creatures. . . . The human child is not instinctually programmed. . . . Admittedly the human child has a complex brain and immense creative potential. But all the skills of living and surviving are *taught*. These things are transmitted by cultural channels. The child needs to learn them. . . . It is these essential needs of the child upon which the survival of the race depends, and which bring the importance of the family to the foreground. (p. 16)

Necessarily, then, parents and early care-givers within the family unit have the most important roles in transmitting the culture to children and passing on its values. What we say and do with, to, and for our children has a lasting influence. This idea is beautifully conveyed in these words from the pen of an unknown poet and quoted in Staton (1984):

> I took a piece of living clay
> And gently formed it day by day,
> And molded with my power and art
> A young child's soft and yielding heart.
>
> I came again when days were gone;
> It was a man I looked upon.
> He still that early impress wore,
> And I could change it never more. (p. 68).

Granted, the Black family is uniquely different from other families in America. It has had a turbulent history, beginning with the transportation of slaves to these shores. Nevertheless, it has survived. Surely only a deeply-rooted belief, faith, and trust in God could be the source of the resiliency, fortitude, and character it has shown.

When focusing on the teaching of Christian values in the Black family, the priority is not a debate over a Black theology; the primary thrust is in relation to biblical principles. However, this does not rule out direct references to the Black experience.

In every community there are basic concepts that are held dear, things that the particular group (and society at large) consider worthy of handing down to the next generation. These ideals become part of the culture and are deemed essential if the group is to survive and maintain its identity.

In the Christian community, certain values are considered ideal. They are characteristics that we wish to take on because they are the gifts and commands of God. Descriptions of most of these qualities can be found in the Bible. Some may not be stated explicitly in Scripture, but they are representative of the One in whose image we are made.

Thus the family becomes the agent for teaching its members to exhibit faith, hope, love, self-confidence, self-respect, self-esteem, self-pride, honesty, trust, and a fear of God.

In this chapter, we will briefly discuss the Scriptural mandate for teaching within the family. The development of Christian values will be encouraged. The Christian/spiritual values stressed will be faith, hope, self-esteem, and love. These are the values that have been an integral

127

part of teaching in the Black family from the days of slavery to the present time.

We acknowledge that changes have taken place in the Black family as it has been more thoroughly assimilated into the larger society. Because these changes are taking place and causing a decline in values once held in high regard, a challenge is now issued to the Black church.

Our attention will be focused in a general way on the educational task of the family, some changes that have occurred within it, and the challenge that comes to the church.

THE EDUCATIONAL TASK: ITS BIBLICAL BASIS

Moses gave the blueprint for the parents' educational task. Parents were instructed thus:

> And these words, which I command thee this day, shall be in thine heart: And thou shalt teach them diligently unto thy children, and shalt talk of them when thou sittest in thine house, and when thou walkest by the way, and when thou liest down, and when thou risest up. (Deut. 6:6, 7 KJV)

The Bible has no ambiguous statements concerning the duties of parents to children nor of children to parents. Parents are commanded to teach, love, and respect. Children are admonished to obey, honor, and love.

It was imperative that the Word of God be incorporated in the heart, and the heart be filled to the saturation point. Filling one's head has no priority, for what is in one's head will not necessarily fill the heart. The heart is the governor and center of life, the seat of the emotions, intellect, and will.

Values for the Christian family have their roots in the teachings set forth in God's Holy Word. The Bible is still the most reliable guide for family life. It contains truths that are solid, and truths that do not bend for situation ethics. In it are examples of all kinds of families with problems that have persisted down through the ages. The trek begins with the rivalry of Cain and Abel, the jealousies of the sons of Jacob, the single parenting of Hagar, on through the pages of the Old and New Testaments.

Christian parents must be well-grounded in the Word and prepared to pass on its teachings to their offspring. With the many and varied winds of false prophets, false doctrines, and cults of today, we can say that we are now at a spiritual point of life and death. We must allow God to direct and be Lord of our lives.

For the parent, teaching the truths of the faith and nurturing the child in them becomes a daily concern, not just a Sunday morning chore for the Sunday school teacher. The family becomes the cornerstone. Abatso and Abatso (1983) noted the following in regard to teaching values in the family.

> The Christian family has the primary responsibility of providing opportunities and encouraging the development of the following spiritual values which reflect God's nature: faith and confidence in God; loving submission to Him; social responsibility to others; a life purpose centered around God's plan for the individual and the world; a desire to seek the truth; fairness in all dealings; a commitment to high moral principles. (ch. 6, p. 2)

Throughout the Scriptures, examples of nurturing faith in the home can be found. Two examples stand out in the New Testament. Our Lord and Savior Jesus Christ was brought up in a religious home. His parents observed the religious practices of the day. No doubt the other members of Jesus' family were also influenced by the actions of Mary and Joseph. Another notable example is Timothy. In writing to him, Paul reminded Timothy of his early acquaintance with Holy Scriptures through the teachings of his grandmother Lois and his mother Eunice.

Just as the Israelites were commanded to teach their children diligently and the early Christians were admonished to pass their faith along to their children, the command is no less significant for us today. Each family must pass on to the next generation the family tree, the heritage, the traditions, and the causes for celebration. The Black family has a special mandate to do so because of past injustices and the failure to preserve much of our group culture. Lest we forget, Black people do have a "then," a "now," and a "tomorrow." History has a role in the life of many ethnic groups. The history of Black people is a rich one, definitely worthy of study and preservation.

"And now abideth faith, hope, charity, these three; but the greatest of these is charity" (1 Cor. 13:13 KJV). This was a conclusion Paul reached, and it can be a beginning, a cornerstone for the Black family to build on. For it is in believing, hoping, and loving that the family may possess the stamina and inspiration to pass on Christian values. The Black family must rediscover its roots and utilize the strengths that have enabled it to endure through the years. On a foundational level, this survival has been tied to the Black church and its spiritual traditions. There is no doubt that the Black family predates the Black church, but it was within the Black church that impetus was given to the yearnings of the souls of Black men and women to move boldly and prayerfully into the larger society.

VALUES TAUGHT

The slave forebears of the Black family possessed—and passed on—a faith that is one of the greatest gifts a child could ever receive. This God-inspired faith is more easily caught than taught. We recognize today the importance of passing on in tangible and intangible ways the faith we profess. As parents, we demonstrate our faith daily by knowing the truth, teaching the truth, walking the truth, and talking the truth. Our children are predisposed to respond in like manner. Their faith grows as they receive the loving spiritual care of Christian parents.

We often quote Hebrews 11:1 and consider it the most accurate biblical definition of faith. However, we must look closely at the depths of what is being said. Faith involves a total surrender of the heart, soul, and mind. It establishes meaning for our lives. It determines our course of action. It goes beyond intellectual and rational approaches. It involves a complete response to God and his faithfulness. For our children, our faith must be so strong that it becomes contagious.

As the faith was transmitted to the Hebrew children, to Timothy, and to others, so it should be passed on today. A modern Christian writer, Staton (1984), has wisely addressed this necessity:

> Little children need before them an example of faith in God and Jesus. They need someone to go with them to the service, not just to leave them at the door. They need someone to see them take part in the special programs. They need someone there when they sing for the first time in the choir. They need someone to sing "Jesus Loves Me" and "The B-I-B-L-E" with them. They need someone to tuck them in at night with a prayer. They need someone to take them to the youth meetings, encourage them to go to camp, and introduce them to Christian colleges, Bible Bowls, and youth conventions. They not only need a youth minister at the church; they also need one at home. (pp. 140–41)

Consequently, teaching values in isolation is difficult. While we care for one aspect of growth and development, others simultaneously receive care. Being at our children's side when they are involved in their activities provides the support they need to build self-confidence, self-pride, and trust in the larger world.

In a special issue of *EBONY* dealing with the Black family (August

1986), eight prominent Black Americans related stories of their families' influence on their lives. A common thread running through their anecdotes was that the family had been responsible for teaching them spiritual values by example and precept. The family had been supportive, loving, religious, inspiring, and insistent that the person do his or her best in whatever endeavor was undertaken.

The family unit instilled in these famous Americans a sense of hope and a deep desire to excel. Their experiences relate to these ideas (Martin and Martin, 1978):

> Child-rearing in black family tradition rested upon religious beliefs, strict discipline, respect for parental authority, and reliance on experience. The aged were nourished on a philosophy of hope, perseverance, and faith in God. By trusting in God, one could "make a way out of no way." No matter how big the problem, or how great the evil, nobody and nothing was bigger than God. God was close at hand, awaiting His children's call to intervene in their life and help them through troubled times. All they had to do was gather up the strength to persevere, do their best, and never lose hope that God would come and set everything right. (p. 49)

Hope was the mainstay of the slaves' existence. Their religion gave them hope that their lot would not always be that of a slave. They believed that someday their God would deliver them. This belief was expressed in their spirituals and through their emotion-filled worship services. They looked forward to a day when all men and women would be treated as equals and as children of God, free to enjoy all the blessings that a loving God provides. This is a hope that prevails today, as illustrated in this experience (Smith, 1985):

> The concept of the family as hopeful community was driven home in a class at Eastern Seminary on the black family. The discussion moved into the area of illegitimate births among teenagers and how many grandparents were becoming parents again by taking major responsibility in helping with the rearing of these grandchildren. A white woman in the class raised the issue of how despairing a situation this is. The black women in the class responded with a much different outlook. For each one, her position was that "We don't have time to be despairing. Our grandchildren need to be celebrated as ours whether they are branded illegitimate or not." This celebration of life is basic to African people. (p. 27)

We can place our hope in God to carry out his promises. We can be assured that if our hopes are grounded in him, he will sustain, direct, and carry us through illness, unemployment, death, other misfortunes—and even good times. Putting our hope in him gives us the confidence to press forward at all times. We can become participants in the blessings and goodness he has promised to be faithful. Our children need to know that this assurance is theirs to claim.

Self-discovery is vital to a person's spiritual development. When a person can identify him- or herself, that individual is well on the road to success in dealing with this world. And the more one discovers about God, the more one discovers about self.

During the turbulence of the sixties, Blacks began to look at themselves in more positive ways, and subsequently became less passive and more militant. Blacks had always instilled within their children a certain amount of pride, but because of the civil rights movement, they became very open and vocal about expressing pride in their Blackness.

An adage from the Igbos of Nigeria goes like this (Nwatu, 1987):

> Onye adikwana k'onu onye iloya kolu ya—nobody should let him-self/herself resemble the picture of him/her painted by his/her enemy. If this makes any meaning to the black family in America, in God's name let there be more sense of pride. (p. 39)

"I AM SOMEBODY!" The Reverend Jesse Jackson preached that slogan to Black youngsters to instill in them the idea that they should be proud of their worth and heritage. That idea was included in the teachings within the Black family unit, for it was generally within that unit that a child was encouraged to reach for the highest potential. Being created in the image of God gave the child invaluable worth.

When youth are nurtured in such a fashion, they come to realize who they are and whose they are and leave behind the unnecessary baggage of negativism. It is difficult to retain a negative self-image and at the same time forge ahead successfully.

It is vital that Black youth know and respect the rich heritage embodied in the traditions and customs of their group. When this happens, they become appreciative and responsible, and strive to achieve higher levels of self-acceptance. Thoughts of oneself, translated self-esteem or self-confidence, aid in accepting one's personal limitations. Such thoughts also help in accepting the assets and limitations of others.

Undergirding faith, hope, trust, self-esteem, and all other values transmitted should be love. Our children need to see love in action. They need to know that we love them as the Heavenly Father loves us. Our love should have no strings attached; we should not demand reciprocity. They need to know that we are always there and equally supportive in both good and difficult times. Withholding our love stifles—and may destroy—all that we have tried to instill in them.

As we discipline children and establish relationships with other family members, we must do so with the love of God in our hearts. The practice of the Golden Rule puts love in action. In order to love others, we must first love ourselves. Loving oneself enhances our capacity to reach out and embrace others. When we love ourselves, we are freed to love others. We are recipients of a boundless love of the Father. If we are to be like him, we must love not only in word, but in deed and in truth.

CHANGES IN THE FAMILY UNIT

We live in changing times, times that make no exceptions, even for the family. The Black family has been in a state of constant change, just as social conditions have been changing. It is no longer the same cohesive, extended family unit of yesterday. It has drifted into patterns much like the larger society around it. Aunts, uncles, cousins, and grandparents are no longer as close by to lend support. Family units have changed remarkably to accommodate a diversity of lifestyles— from extended family to nuclear family, from single parent and step-parent families to much smaller households, and other diverse arrangements.

The old values and behavioral standards are no longer upheld with the same reverence and fear. But even though these social changes are taking place, the Christian family lifestyle should remain constant and stable. The textbook for Christian living has not been amended or rewritten—the same truths still hold.

Families today have become more concerned with the accumulation of material goods, while ignoring the spiritual treasures to be gained. All too often the following teachings from the Gospel According to Matthew are ignored:

> Lay not up for yourselves treasures upon earth, where moth and rust doth corrupt, and where thieves break through and steal:
>
> But lay up for yourselves treasures in heaven . . .
>
> For where your treasure is, there will your heart be also.
>
> (Matt. 6:19, 20, 21 KJV)

The following are examples that point to the decline in spiritual values: increased reports of child abuse, more convenience abortions, more teenage runaways, higher rates of marital separation and divorce.

Children no longer have as much supervision in the home; many become latch-key kids—and the list goes on.

The Black family has suffered setbacks in this current decline. Many Black men are incarcerated; there is an alarming abundance of teen mothers, a disturbing lack of employment, and increasing Black-on-Black crime. Along with poverty and poor education, one root cause is the breakdown of value systems in the family unit. One positive way to alleviate this situation would be to make Bible study a priority. No schedule should be so full that there is no place for regular, consistent, and meaningful Bible study. From the Scriptures, one gains a knowledge of God that becomes the guideline for daily living.

Home should be a happy and welcoming place for the family. It is within the loving environment of the home that the family is made to feel secure. A bumper sticker carries this slogan: THE FAMILY THAT PRAYS TOGETHER STAYS TOGETHER. There is much wisdom there. Much can be gained through sharing, learning, and worship experiences, whether in Sunday school or in the formal worship service.

Above all, our lives should reflect Christ. It is through living the example he set forth that we can exert the greatest influence.

THE CHALLENGE

As American society has become more secularized, there has also been a dilution in the church. The breakdown of value systems within the family spills over into other areas of life. This is especially the case in our dealings with each other. One prime example is that we have become "suit-happy," shifting from a moral standard to a legal standard. We are not concerned so much with the ethics of a situation as we are with the loophole that our lawyer can find. Ethics, fair dealings, and the teachings of the Book are forgotten.

The Christian enjoys membership in a much larger unit than his or her individual family. One also has membership in a church family. For the Black family, the church is a viable force in all areas of life and a base of activity, whether spiritual, social, political, or economic. It is the one institution that has given unwavering support. For the Black family, the Black church and religion are a way of life, a sustaining force, and the glue that has held it together. It can and must be the force for the future.

With the upheaval and changes in society that the sixties and seventies brought, the church has a new mandate and a broader role. It must find new ways to deal with change yet still remain in accordance with biblical principles. Therefore, Christian education, and its role in the life of the church and the family, takes on added significance.

Of necessity, Christian education becomes very broad. The statement developed by the Protestant group in conjunction with the Cooperative Curriculum Project in the late 1950s and early 1960s encompasses this scope (Hanson, 1986):

> The goal of the church's educational ministry is that all persons be aware of God through God's self-disclosure, especially God's redeeming love as revealed in Jesus Christ, and, enabled by the Holy Spirit, respond in faith and love, that as new persons in Christ they may know who they are and what their human situation means, grow as children of God rooted in the Christian community, live in obedience to the will of God in every relationship, fulfill their common vocation in the world and abide in the Christian hope. (pp. 12–14)

A church that is committed to this goal can be one that will be family-centered, with God having primary emphasis. The emphasis then centers around developing the family, and not the church.

If we look at the church as described in 1 Corinthians 12:12–26, we see a body composed of many parts that work in harmony. The ingredients for that harmony are found in Galatians 5:22, 23: "But the fruit of the Spirit is love, joy, peace, longsuffering, gentleness, goodness, faith, meekness, temperance: against such there is no law" (KJV).

The cultivation of this fruit insures that the ministry of teaching Christian values within the church family will produce a bountiful harvest. Each member of the household becomes responsive to the other in a fertile way.

As a family, the church takes an interest in the individual families of the church. It identifies the makeup and needs of individuals. It establishes a priority of needs and effectively plans ways to meet those needs. Any venture demands wise and prayerful planning. The establishment of committees to study and evaluate the situation is a prudent first step. In current Christian education literature helpful guidelines, programs, and ideas may be found.

CONCLUSION

As a child matures, it is expected that he or she is ready to leave the security and protected environment of the family unit. The question then comes to that child and to the older generation, "Does he or she have the wherewithal to stand?" The degree of success or failure depends largely on the child's retention and utilization of the spiritual values and teachings shared during the formative years.

Through the good times and the bad times, if one has had the benefit of Christian orientation and nurture in the faith, one finds the strength to cope with whatever may come. Through the Christian's witness to society, the individual becomes the salt that flavors and preserves, and the light that leads. These resources were attained through the primary educator, the home where God was the ruler, guide, and teacher of the family.

References

Abatso, G., and Abatso, Y. (1983). *The Black Christian Family*. Chicago: Urban Ministries.

Hanson, G. W. (1986). *Foundations for the Teaching Church*. Valley Forge: Judson Press.

The Holy Bible, King James Version. (1975). Philadelphia: National Publishing.

Johnston, O. R. (1979). *Who Needs the Family?* Downers Grove: Intervarsity Press.

Martin, E. P., and Martin, J. (1978). *The Black Extended Family*. Chicago: The University of Chicago Press.

Nwatu, F. (1987). The African Family: A Model for Black Solidarity. *The Crisis* (November). Publication of The NAACP.

Smith, W. C. (1985). *The Church in the Life of the Black Family*. Valley Forge: Judson Press.

Staton, K. (1984). *Bible Keys for Today's Family*. Cincinnati: Standard Publishing Company.

"The Most Unforgettable Person in My Family: Eight Pay Tribute to Kin," *Ebony* (August 1986), 41, 102–6.

9

Pastoral Counseling
and Black Families

Lloyd C. Blue

LLOYD C. BLUE is president of Lloyd C. Blue Ministries, Inc., and pastor of the North Oakland Missionary Baptist Church in Oakland, California. He is nationally acclaimed for his lectures in the areas of personal evangelism, the ministry of the Holy Spirit, abundant Christian living, building disciples, church growth, family enrichment, pastoral management and counseling, the mechanics of expository preaching, and methods for a city- or state-wide revival meeting. Lloyd attended California Baptist College, received his Bachelor of Theology degree from the Institutional Baptist Theological Center, Houston Texas, a Master of Arts degree from Union University in Los Angeles, California, and a Doctor of Ministry degree from the University of Central America. A native of North Carolina, Lloyd is married to Tressie Blue. They have one son, Lloyd, Jr.

9

Pastoral Counseling
and Black Families

Pastoral counseling has been defined in various ways. For example, Capps (1980) defined it as consisting of the identification of the problem, the reconstruction of the problem, a diagnostic interpretation, and pastoral intervention. Wimberly (1989) defined it as a specialized area of pastoral care that focuses on the individual. Further, he stated that it must focus on the liberation of the personality from any belief in one's own powerlessness and is action-oriented. Adams (1970) indicated that pastoral counseling involves nouthetic confrontation (that is, confronting through teaching, reproving, correcting, or training). My definition of pastoral counseling is listening to the counselee until he or she reveals the principle of Scripture that is being violated. Secondly, it is sharing with the counselee the principle being violated and the way to walk in obedience to God's Word.

Henry Brandt (1967) wrote an article more than two decades ago on pastoral counseling that is still very applicable today. I have used his suggestions in my own ministry and will draw on them extensively in this chapter. Brandt noted that four things are important if the pastor is to be successful in counseling: (1) The pastor's concept of the Scripture; (2) The pastor's concept of humankind; (3) The pastor's character; and (4) The pastor's method of counseling.

In reference to the concept of Scripture, Brandt indicated that the pastor must see oneself as a specialist; that is, one who understands that being a pastor carries the responsibility of preaching, teaching, and counseling the truths of the Bible. The pastor must have an enduring love for the Word of God, a thorough knowledge of it, and a firm confidence that it is the sure guide for all. We must recognize that the

Bible detects our thoughts and motives; gives doctrine, reproof, correction, and instruction; and provides guidance for a happy and fruitful life (see, for example, Ps. 119:105; Heb. 4:12; 2 Tim. 3:16, 17). The pastor must believe, as noted by Harmon (1967) that the Christian also learns by experience, and that the Bible, welcomed into the heart, brings faith, peace, and triumph in one's life. If we neglect the Bible we will experience failure and sin.

In regard to the pastor's view or concept of humankind, it is essential to recognize and deal with the inner nature of the person—his or her mental, emotional, and spiritual conditions. Unfortunately, as noted by Brandt (1967), many pastors have been taught that psychological or emotional problems are outside their area of ministry. As a result of being told that these problems are deeply buried in the counselee's past life they feel that a clinically trained person must meet these needs. While some problems do require the aid of other professionals, there are many that the pastor can deal with.

Hurting people come from a variety of situations and circumstances (Brandt, 1967). They may have been mistreated, misunderstood, hated, rejected, and subjected to great pressures. Hurting people tend to respond to such treatment with rebellion, jealousy, anger, and an unforgiving spirit. While we cannot change our past, and the maltreatment by others may be beyond our control, this does not excuse our behavior. Biblically speaking, a person is responsible for those emotional responses and shortcomings that the Scriptures call the work of the flesh. (See, for example, John 15:4; Rom. 3:10, 11, 23; James 3:14, 16; 4:17; and Eph. 4:31.)

The third and fourth issues—character and the method of counseling—will be expanded on later.

God wants all to come to him (Matt. 11:28–30; John 1:12; and John 3:16). We must be willing and equipped in counseling to clearly communicate our love, as well as God's, for the counselee.

THE NEED FOR PASTORAL COUNSELING
IN THE BLACK FAMILY AND CHURCH

Some writers indicate (Oates, 1986), and studies show, that the church and the pastor are still the ones to whom people first turn for help. Therefore, pastors must recognize this and capitalize on our importance to the community. We, and the church, have a critical message of hope for those who are lost, as well as a message of more abundant living for those who are Christians. Both messages must be conveyed in the counseling situation.

Because Black families have few options in times of emotional need except the Black church, the church must be open to receive them, and the pastor must be competent to counsel in areas of human predicaments, as noted by Adams (1970). If the church and the pastor fail in this area of ministry, in my opinion it may very well lead to a further destruction of what we now know as the family.

Wimberly (1979, 1982, 1989) has written extensively in the area of pastoral care and counseling in the Black church community. In his writings, he has documented its importance in the Black community and has called for pastors to be better trained in its methods.

THE BIBLICAL BASIS FOR PASTORAL COUNSELING

The Bible presents many situations that involve the ministry of counseling and/or counseling-type situations. Therefore, when we examine some of the major passages dealing with counseling, we can see and understand the biblical ideas and principles for this ministry. As noted by Grunlan and Lambrides (1984), counseling is not a ministry of recent origin nor a new fad. Counseling situations are recorded in both the Old and New Testaments. Jesus Christ himself had an extensive counseling ministry that is clearly shown in the Gospels. God has worked through people in the ministry of counseling for centuries, and Jesus' style of counseling has been outlined by Carlson (1976) and McKenna (1977).

One can easily cite characters and passages from both the Old and New Testaments that involve counseling. Perhaps the most familiar in the Old Testament is the interaction between Moses and his father-in-law, Jethro (Ex. 18). Additionally, as noted by Grunlan, and Lambrides (1984), the book of Proverbs speaks often of the benefits of advice or counseling. For example, Proverbs 12:15 states that "a wise man listens to advice," and Proverbs 20:18 instructs, "Make plans by seeking advice." Likewise, in Psalm 55:13–14, David indicated how much he had enjoyed the counsel of a friend.

In the New Testament we find passages like Hebrews 4:12, which teaches us the power of God's Word; 2 Timothy 3:16–17 teaches us what the Word of God will do; and Matthew 28:18–20 shows us the power of the Word of God and outlines the Great Commission. For me, the most compelling of all New Testament passages for biblical counseling is the command to teach others all that we ourselves have learned (2 Tim. 2:2). There can be no doubt that the Bible has much more to say on this matter than I am highlighting here.

Personally, I can see no difference between pastoral counseling and

141

biblical counseling. They are both the same, for I can never think of counseling a person apart from teaching and presenting the Word of God. After all, the bottom line for pastors is making disciples and helping to move them toward full maturity in Christ.

CHARACTERISTICS OF AN EFFECTIVE PASTORAL COUNSELOR

As stated earlier, one's method of counseling is important.

Each pastor must develop a personal and distinctive way of counseling. But even so, the following factors are basic to effective counseling.

1. The pastor must be loving and compassionate. Brandt (1967) stated that the pastor must first and foremost love the counselee enough to present to him or her God's truths, regardless of what those truths may suggest. When we love the counselee, we must not force God's solution on them. We must always keep in mind that the counselee has the freedom of choice. They can reject or accept God's answer to their problem.

2. The pastor must identify the problem (Capps, 1980) and become convinced of it. The compassionate pastor will listen carefully before attempting to present to the counselee a biblical solution for the problem.

3. The pastor must demonstrate empathy (understanding of the counselee) and genuineness (sincerity and honesty).

4. The pastor must be an effective listener. Personally, I find that effective listening is one of the most difficult things to do. I am often tempted to go ahead of the counselee and present a ready-made solution to a problem before I have adequately listened. Grunlan and Lambrides (1984) list ten aspects of effective listening. According to them, effective listening:

> begins by indicating that one hears the other person's feelings and meanings.
>
> involves establishing eye contact and posture which clearly indicates that one is listening.
>
> involves attention to nonverbal clues such as the tone of voice, posture, gestures, and mannerisms.
>
> avoids nagging, criticizing, threatening, lecturing, and ridiculing.
>
> treats the other person as one would want to be treated.
>
> involves accepting the other person's feelings.

involves hearing the other person's feelings and meaning and stating these so the other person feels understood.

gives open responses that accurately state what the other person feels and means rather than closed responses which are judgmental or directive.

avoids responses that ignore the other person's feelings by communicating that one has not heard or understood.

lets the other person attempt to resolve his [or her] problems
(pp. 43–44)

It is just as important to listen effectively as it is to administer the solution. Effective listening is one step toward an effective solution. Listening is an art as well as a skill. Therefore, pastors must seek to improve both questioning and listening skills. We must read literature on techniques of listening, on empathy, and on interviewing. Then, as we gain experience in counseling, our skills will improve. Further, we need not be afraid to ask questions.

However, we need not listen to and explore endlessly the person's past. Listening to and an investigation of the past is helpful in understanding a person, but knowing the past doesn't change the present nor the future. Only the blood of Jesus can wipe away past sins. Counselees need to be assured and sometimes reassured of this fact (1 John 1:9).

5. The pastor should carefully lead the counselee to a biblical solution (Brandt, 1967). However, before this is done, we must be sure that we correctly understand the person's situation, and his or her attitudes and reactions in regard to the problem and the Bible. It would be a mistake to jump to a solution before one is sure of the exact nature of the problem. Often counselees will present an issue that is not their real problem at all. Therefore, as a counselor, be patient and continue interviewing and listening until you and the counselee can agree on the real problem. When an agreement is reached on the issue, one should gently, patiently, and lovingly offer God's answer. If the person is not a Christian, one should also present the plan of salvation. If the individual is a Christian, this is the time to teach how to be filled with the Holy Spirit and how to walk in his power.

Further action is up to the counselee. The counselee may or may not accept the biblical solutions. The person may want time to think about it, could become upset, or may return at a future time.

6. It is also critical that the pastor consult appropriate materials being written by Blacks, psychologists, and sociologists that will

broaden our understanding and be of great help in the counseling ministry.

7. An effective pastoral counselor will understand and draw on the power of the Holy Spirit (see also Adams, 1970). The Holy Spirit guides, teaches, and leads both the counselee and counselor if we allow him (see John 14 and 16). Without his aid, we will be ineffective.

8. Finally, the pastor must know when to make referrals. The next section will discuss the matter of referrals.

Making Referrals

Pastors, like others, need to be aware of their strengths and limitations. Therefore, at times, we will need to refer individuals to others. Referrals may be necessary for a number of reasons, including the following:

1. The individual is presenting an issue or problem that is beyond the counselor's capabilities.
2. The individual may desire to counsel with someone else.
3. The individual may be best served by another counselor.

Referrals may be made to another pastor, someone on one's own staff, or to another professional. In making a referral it is important that we know who the person is and the type of work they do. Both good and bad referrals reflect on us.

In the matter of a referral, one should keep in mind that the need to refer does not mean that we have failed to help. On the contrary, making an appropriate referral can aid the counseling process.

THE BENEFITS OF PASTORAL COUNSELING

The church and pastor who work hard to establish a pastoral counseling ministry will undoubtedly see at least some of the following:

1. Church growth that manifests itself spiritually, numerically, and financially.
2. Genuine fellowship (a mutual sharing one with another).
3. A deep respect for pastoral authority.
4. Greater male participation.
5. Faithfulness among young people.
6. A greater commitment to discipleship and evangelism.
7. A vision for world missions.

144

These are but a few benefits to expect in a church where biblically-based pastoral counseling is practiced.

ISSUES IN ESTABLISHING
A PASTORAL COUNSELING PROGRAM

Stigma. Most people would not want to be labeled as someone who has major problems or who cannot handle his or her own issues. The fear that one will be so labeled often keeps one from disclosing to the pastor and/or the counseling staff the issues that are affecting one's life. I do not view this, however, as an insurmountable problem. Once people realize that their "dirty laundry" will not be aired from the pulpit on Sunday nor gossiped through the community during the week, and that it is all right for everyone (including men) to engage in counseling, they will open up and share their innermost secrets.

Additionally, we can reduce some of the stigma by presenting counseling in a positive light. We can point out that the Bible tells us to confess our faults or sins one to another (James 5:16) and to bear or carry each other's burdens (Gal. 6:2). The pastor and staff must demonstrate trustworthiness, and nothing does it better than reaching out with compassion to build relationships with the families of the church, especially with the husbands and fathers. This is what makes Black male discipleship the foremost issue of our time. When husbands and fathers are being discipled, right relationships are being built and confessing faults becomes the order of the day.

Staff Credentials. I am sure that if we had our way as pastors, we would surround ourselves with professional counselors—doctrinally sound men and women with seminary degrees and a well-rounded understanding of how the Word of God applies to human needs. However, because, for the most part, this is not possible, it is very important that the pastor teach and train both clergy and laity to participate. This may sound as if it is asking too much. But it can never be too much, for again I call your attention to the Great Commission, which tells us to make disciples. As pastors, we must seek to multiply ourselves by training as many as possible to carry on the work of making disciples. It would be advisable for a pastor to go slow, training one or two counselors at a time to ensure their success.

Willie Richardson, the president and founder of Christian Research and Development, and the pastor of the Christian Stronghold Baptist Church of Philadelphia, Pennsylvania, has over many years developed staff and materials for both family counseling and discipling the Black male. Pastors who desire to begin a ministry of counseling should take advantage of what is offered by him. Pastor Richardson has an established track record in these areas and the evidence can be seen when the membership gathers at the Stronghold Church. I don't know of any other church that can claim to have a Sunday morning attendance that is approximately 49 percent male (in a gathering of some 2000 people). (See Richardson's chapter in this book for further suggestions on evangelizing the Black male.)

Secondly, I call attention to the Rev. E. K. Bailey, the president and founder of E. K. Bailey Ministries and pastor for the Concord Baptist Church in Dallas, Texas. Here again, one will see family counseling and male discipleship ministries in full bloom. I strongly suggest that contact be made with these pastors because they have so much to offer. My own ministry would not be what it is today without the assistance and the example of Pastors Richardson and Bailey.

Integration into Overall Church Program. Integrating the work of pastoral counseling into the overall ministry of the church will not be a problem for a church where fulfilling the Great Commission (Matt. 28:18–20) has been well established as a priority. The pastor must make the church aware that the priority of the church is making and maturing disciples. It must be clear that the work of evangelism is incomplete until the evangelized become evangelists. This being the case, the ministry of counseling must also vie for its place in any church program.

I have been doing expository preaching for some twenty years and I would not preach any other way even if I could. But I find that preaching from the pulpit on Sunday morning or teaching a small Bible class will never replace the value of one-on-one counseling. In the pulpit on Sunday morning, expository preaching (as vital as it is) is like standing in the pulpit with a water hose trying to fill up 2,000 cans. Needless to say, there will be a lot of water on the floor. But counseling is like taking a dipper in one hand and a can in the other and pouring the water directly into the can. When this type of vision is presented clearly, I do not feel that the pastor and church leadership will face any problems whatsoever integrating the great work of family counseling into the overall ministry of the church. I offer no dogmatic way to go about this, because each of us will have to work it out in our congregations according to our gifts and abilities.

HOW TO ESTABLISH A
PASTORAL COUNSELING PROGRAM

The Role of the Pastor

The role of the pastor in pastoral counseling is threefold: (1) counseling; (2) training others to counsel; and (3) overseeing the counseling ministry.

For pastors to be effective, we must first and foremost lead our own families to practice the Christian-family lifestyle. Our ministry as pastoral and family counselors will not be as effective as it should be in the congregation or the community if we are not practicing the principles we are teaching. (This is the issue of our character as mentioned in the introduction.) We must model for the husbands of our congregation what it means to be a loving leader of our family, and lead our wives to model for the wives what it means to be a biblical follower. Pastors must never take lightly the fact that all eyes are on them and their families. However, a word of caution is necessary at this point. That is, we must understand that our families are human like all others; they too are in a state of growth, gradually becoming what the Lord would have them to be. Therefore, motivation and dedication must be the key words in family development.

Second, the pastor must train others to counsel. Second Timothy 2:2 teaches that we are to teach faithful people who will in turn teach others to teach others, and so on. The work of counseling will fall far short of what it ought to be if the pastor tries to do it alone. The reason for this is because the Black pastor, by and large, does not have a ready pool of professional or lay people trained and equipped to assist. Therefore, we must select and train them ourselves.

Third, the pastor must be responsible for the oversight of the church—including its counseling staff (Acts 20:28). While the pastor will do well to have a competent assistant, one must never divorce oneself totally from the oversight of the staff.

The Role of Other Church Leaders

Presupposing that the other church leaders (deacons, stewards, etc.) are people carefully selected and trained for ministry as prescribed by Scripture, it has been my experience that they can best support the pastor by giving leadership for other ministries and programs of the church. It should never be supposed that because one is in a leadership-type position, one is automatically competent to counsel. No one, not

147

even ministers, should be given the responsibility of counseling without proving themselves to have the skills and spiritual gifts necessary to be effective.

The Role of the Congregation

The congregation must take a cooperative role (Heb. 13:17). It would be very difficult for pastors to establish a counseling ministry if the congregation refused to submit to proper authority. While this is true in all areas of ministry, it is especially true in the areas of pastoral and family counseling. The pastor must make the vision for counseling clear to the congregation and enlist their complete support. At the same time, however, pastors should make it clear that we are the ones responsible to direct and supervise the development of this ministry.

Selecting and Training a Staff

The pastor must select and train ministers and their spouses, lay couples, and others to participate in the ministry of counseling. The married staff must be people who are ruling their own homes well. By this I mean husbands and wives who are themselves practicing the Christian family lifestyle. This does not mean, however, that they have "arrived." It means that they are people who have grown, are growing, and have exemplified the spiritual gifts necessary to participate in this ministry. The pastor must also be sure that those selected are faithful, available, and teachable. Realize that each time they share with others, they are representing first, the Lord and second, the pastor. Therefore, the pastor must take extreme care in selecting those people who will work in this ministry.

In training the staff, the pastor must make sure that they understand the Scriptures and possess the basic characteristics of an effective counselor that have already been discussed. Workshops and seminars are often effective training vehicles. Such sessions may be done by the pastor with the aid of others already skilled in this area. Materials by Crabb (1975, 1977) can be extremely helpful in such training. In addition, I recommend the seminars offered by the Rev. Willie Richardson.

Scheduling, Office Hours, and Facilities

These will differ from congregation to congregation and from community to community. The pastor should be careful to schedule office hours and counseling sessions that are convenient for both the counselee and the counselor. It is extremely important that the facilities offer privacy. If the facilities are in a location where there is apt to be a steady flow of other people, persons in need of this ministry will shy away. Therefore, the pastor must work to make sure this does not happen.

Record-Keeping

Record-keeping cannot be overemphasized. The counselor may need to review the previous visit or visits before going into the next counseling session. The counselor will also need to know how many visits have been made in order to know when there should be a referral to another type of counseling or to a senior counselor. The number of visits will also give some idea of when counseling can be ended. There is no possible way to have an effective counseling ministry without appropriate records. Records, however, must be kept in a secure place.

Confidentiality

Confidentiality will either make or break a counseling ministry. When people are sharing their innermost secrets, thoughts, and feelings, they have a right to believe that the counselor will at no time, under any circumstance, divulge a single word. Here again, this is an area that cannot be overemphasized.

I am familiar with a case where a youth minister had counseled one of the young ladies of the church. Because this young lady was going on a youth outing with another church, he felt that he should share what he knew with the person in charge of the outing. While this was inappropriate, he did not further take into account the fact that the person in charge of the outing would share that information with the young lady's parent. Needless to say, a disastrous situation resulted and the pastor was held responsible for what took place. As pastors, we must very carefully keep ourselves and our staff aware of the importance of confidentiality.

Gaining Congregational Support

Before a pastor can "sell" this to the congregation, one must make sure that the congregation has a commitment to the fulfillment of the Great Commission. Counseling at its highest is making effective and mature disciples. Therefore, it must be viewed as a priority of the church's program. I find that in presenting a new concept, the pastor must be patient and begin by sharing the vision with committed individuals. Second, the vision must be shared with small groups, and third, with the church leadership. This should be done before presenting the vision or concept to the total congregation. Individuals will help small groups to understand, small groups will convince the leadership, and the leadership will assist the pastor in convincing the congregation.

I have used this approach for more than twenty-five years as a pastor and, at least for me, it has worked. In my opinion, to present such a concept to the total congregation without winning the support of key individuals, small groups, and the majority of the leadership is risking serious trouble for the pastor. My grandmother used to put it this way: "The longest way around is usually the safest way home."

CONCLUSION

Given what we are facing in our nation today—and that is the potential destruction of the family as we have known it—I do not see how we can hope to survive if the church of Jesus Christ does not take absolutely seriously the ministry of pastoral and family counseling.

Given the pressing needs of families and people in general, pastors must seek to fully equip themselves and their congregations in order to make use of the resource of pastoral counseling. I strongly encourage you to implement the suggestions presented and to consult the references at the close of this chapter to that end.

References

Adams, J. E. (1970). *Competent to Counsel*. Grand Rapids: Baker.

Brandt, H. R. (1967). *The Pastor and His Counseling Ministry*. Glen Ellyn, Ill.: Scripture Press.

Capps, D. (1980). *Pastoral Counseling and Preaching: A Quest for an Integrated Ministry*. Philadelphia: Westminster.

Carlson, D. E. (1976). Jesus' Style of Relating: The Search for a Biblical View of Counseling. In W. J. Donaldson, ed., *Research in Mental Health and Religious Behavior: An Introduction to Research in the Integration of Christianity and the Behavioral Sciences*, 318–330. Atlanta: Psychological Studies Institute.

Crabb, L. J., Jr. (1975). *Basic Principles of Biblical Counseling*. Grand Rapids: Zondervan.

———. (1977). *Effective Biblical Counseling*. Grand Rapids: Zondervan.

Grunlan, S., and Lambrides, D. (1984). *Healing Relationships: A Christian Manual for Lay Counseling* Camp Hill: Christian Publication.

Harmon, G. (1967). Evangelical Principles and Practices. *Christianity Today* 11:13.

The Holy Bible: New International Version. (1984). Grand Rapids: Zondervan.

McKenna, D. (1977). *The Psychology of Jesus: The Dynamics of Christian Wholeness,* 127–142. Waco: Word.

Oates, W. (1986). *The Presence of God in Pastoral Counseling.* Dallas: Word.

Wimberly, E. P. (1979). *Pastoral Care in the Black Church.* Nashville: Abingdon.

————. (1982). *Pastoral Counseling and Spiritual Values: A Black Point of View.* Nashville: Abingdon.

————. (1989). Pastoral Counseling and the Black Perspective. In G. S. Wilmore, ed., *African American Religious Studies.* Durham: Duke University Press.

10

Effective Marital Counseling with Black Couples

J. Derek McNeil

J. DEREK McNEIL was formerly a therapist in private practice in Pasadena, California, and Director of Ethnic Concerns at Fuller Theological Seminary. He has traveled nationally and internationally presenting workshops and seminars related to the Black family and marital issues. Derek graduated from Eastern College with a Bachelor of Science degree in psychology and from Fuller Theological Seminary with a Master of Divinity degree with a concentration in marriage and family therapy. Presently he is a doctoral student in counseling psychology at Northwestern University, having recently relocated to Chicago, Illinois. He is married to Brenda Salter McNeil. They have a son, Omari Immanuel. Derek was born and raised in Philadelphia, Pennsylvania.

10

Effective Marital Counseling
with Black Couples

With all of the transitions and social innovations of our culture, marriages—and especially Black marriages—are under assault. Changes in our society have reshaped the marital contract. Couples are having a difficult time knowing how to remain together.

Black marriages face these increased pressures at the same time that they are also losing their supports. It is clear that we must support the marital partnership if we are going to strengthen and stabilize Black families. The stresses are becoming more difficult to absorb into the marital dyad with the decreased availability of the extended family and other traditional social stabilizers.

The stress of a bad marriage drains the emotional resources of the family and leaves inadequate models for children. These children, in turn, must also learn to negotiate the pain introduced by the family conflict if they are to have successful marriages themselves. Failure here can easily lead to a cycle of disruptive households for generations to come.

Bad marriages are also contrary to the divine plan of God. Marriage is used as the biblical model to symbolize the relationship between Christ and the church. In Ephesians 5, husbands and wives are called to follow the example of Christ and the church in relating to one another.

The purpose of this chapter is to provide insights into the marital dyad that can assist counselors, clergy, or others in the helping professions to effectively intervene in the marital crises and conflicts of Black couples. It also provides an overview of what takes place in marital counseling. It may be helpful to the couple considering such counseling to have an overview of what to expect. This chapter will

(1) briefly look at the roles that Black men and women have played in marriage and the historical influence on the marital relationship; (2) review some theoretical views of marriage and its dysfunctions; and (3) give an overview of the counseling process and some possible interventions.

HISTORICAL ROLES OF MARRIAGE

The historical literature has focused on the stability of the Black marriage relationship and the roles that the spouses have taken within the family. Theorists and historians have been debating the issues of fidelity and stability in the Black family since slavery. Each time the plight of Black Americans comes to the forefront of national attention, a new series of studies are done on Black families, and different accusations are made. Accusations have primarily focused on the inadequacy of the Black family structure.

I believe that the historical issues of marital satisfaction and marital stability in Black families have reflected a clarity in role expectations. They also demonstrate the way these roles are shaped by the needs of the extended and nuclear families. The roles of each spouse have often been seen not merely in terms of the way one spouse supported another, but in terms of the supportive function for the rest of the extended family. In many Black marriages, the marital interaction has taken second place, at times, to the extended family's needs for survival and success.

Black marriages have always had to assume a great deal of responsibility and pressure because they have existed in the current ecological environment of American culture. Black family structure has taken on an adaptive form to deal with those ecological pressures. Specifically, Gutman (1976) suggests that Black households took on more of an extended nature in response to economic pressure.

The extended family had certain values and role delineations. Martin & Martin (1978) found that the role of the male in the extended family was to provide resources from the outside world to the family. Men were to provide the economic support, thereby stabilizing the family. Men gained negative labels if they were unwilling to work, thereby minimizing their value to the family unit. This put pressure on men who were unable to work, because employment became the families' standard for manhood. For men to stay and be valued and emotionally satisfied members of the family, they would have to meet the economic resource expectations of the wife and the family.

Historically, women were expected to provide internal stability to

156

the household, including the social networking and the care for the children. This sometimes included working outside the home to make sure "ends met." These roles appeared to have their origin in the extended families' need to survive economically; in turn, the extended families served as a support system to the marriages within them. The need for economic survival often overshadowed the need for emotional satisfaction with one's marital partner. Husbands were good husbands if they were able to support and care for their families; wives were good wives if they managed the household well and cared for the children. Though this stabilized the marriage, it did not necessarily mean that couples had good marital interaction. The expectations for a good marriage were tied to economic survival, stability, and marital fidelity, not necessarily emotional intimacy. Social conformity and economic reality kept some couples in a cooperative relationship, needing each other for the survival of the family, loving each other, but not always meeting emotional needs. The issues of economics and marital fidelity were the determining factors in marital satisfaction.

Presently, economics continues to play a major role in the marital stability and relational satisfaction of Black couples of all economic levels. As Black males experience greater unemployment or underemployment, they become more displaced from the family unit. They are not able to fulfill the traditional role of provider, and often experience a loss of esteem and a sense of inadequacy. This sometimes leads Black men to dominate and sexualize women to gain a sense of "manhood," thus triggering a negative labeling from Black females.

Other stresses typically arise in relationships when the female is in a better financial situation than the male. Educationally, Black women have increased their percentages in both college enrollments and graduations, whereas Black males have decreased in both categories. It is estimated that by the year 1992, there will be one million more female than male Black college graduates, thus creating a large pool of Black professional women with fewer professional Black men as potential mates.

This will lead to situations where women will marry men who are less educationally prepared to be successful in the marketplace. Such relationships also will displace the male, leading him to question his role and his value to his female counterpart. Some males will experience a loss of power and influence in the relationship, making them aware of the power issues in the relationship. This puts extra stress on the dyad, with the male trying to overcompensate for his perceived losses.

The danger of this scenario is that America is moving away from hard industry and toward service-oriented work. This will provide more opportunities for Black women, but will leave many Black men facing the possibility of permanent unemployment because of the decreased number of jobs available at their skill level. Socially, this raises important questions about how we must motivate Black men educationally and retrain those who have become underemployed.

This highlights the need for counselors to be aware of the "ecology" of Black couples. The ecology of the couple or family describes the relationship between the couple and their environment. What external forces or institutions interact with the couple and family and draw their attentions and resources away from the marital relationship? Often these forces will need to be addressed to allow the couple to focus on the relational problems of the dyad. It is also wise for the counselor to know which institutions support the survival of the family, empower it, and provide further nurture in lowering the family's stress.

Another expectation that has resulted from the great number of women entering the work force is that they are looking for men who can be more emotionally satisfying. With women becoming less dependent economically on men, Black women now look for other needs to be met as a measure of a good relationship. A major complaint from Black women is that men need to be more emotionally prepared to meet their needs. This complaint is not a new one, but it does take on new significance in present-day relationships.

This need or expectation has increased in intensity among women who lacked positive father figures in their family of origin. Some women have overcompensated for this and have decided that men are not really necessary to their happiness. Even when women are able to compensate for the absence of positive male figures in their lives, however, they often retain some bitterness or anger toward men.

Often these expectations are higher than men feel able to meet, given the fact that they are already trying to cope with the absence of clear male role models for themselves. If men have themselves lacked positive role models or satisfying relationships with their father figures, they may also have questions about their ability to be satisfying partners. This is often covered up with a defensiveness that exhibits itself in "machoism" or a defensive anger toward women. This puts Black men and women in a finger-pointing posture, with Black men wanting to return to the roles that gave them respect and comfort, and with Black women wanting more in their relationships with Black men. Whereas historically Black men and women joined together to survive and progress socially, they are presently in search of emotional fulfillment. These desires and expectations, when frustrated, lead to disillusionment and anger, increasing the probability of future relational failures.

The aforementioned expectations come from both society and the family of origin. These two in combination shape our view of what we feel marriage should be and what we expect it will be for us. These expectations are not always realistic or even fully known to us, but we bring these unconscious expectations and motivations to our relationships. This issue of expectation is important in order to understand marital satisfaction and will be discussed later in greater detail.

UNDERSTANDING THE MARRIAGE DYAD

It is important for the counselor to have a theoretical understanding of the marital dyad so that one does more than simply referee marital conflicts. It is inappropriate for a counselor to push a couple into our ideal mold of what a marriage relationship should be or to simply provide damage control. One's understanding of what is functional or dysfunctional in a marriage will dictate what counsel and support is given to the people who ask our assistance.

One often hears that opposites attract and that people who are different are drawn to each other. But it is also true that people who are attracted to each other are usually more alike than they are different. When we think of opposites that are attracted to each other, we think of their personalities and emotional styles and neglect to see how much a couple's lifestyles, socioeconomics, ethnicity, and cultural backgrounds are alike. So what appears to be more correct is that people who are alike are most likely to have a common attraction.

To fully understand a major aspect of attraction and mate selection, we must recognize that part of the process is unconscious. Much of the reasoning we use to choose a certain mate is beyond our immediate awareness. Usually we are still full of expectations about what the relationship will be for us and what needs it should meet. Some of the needs are the emotional cravings for love, nurture, security, and self-value. The more these needs went unfulfilled in our family of origin, the more we hope and sometimes fantasize, that marriage will bring their fulfillment.

For all of us, some of these expectations are not conscious, yet they remain a disappointment if not fulfilled. If they remain unfulfilled, we begin to resent the inability of our mate to meet them and the process of marital dissatisfaction begins. Often marriages will go on a long time with one or both spouses trying to figure out why their partner will not meet their needs in certain ways. The expectations that we bring to marriage are both known and unknown to us. It is the expectations that are unknown that cause problems in a marriage.

Psychiatrist Clifford Sager (1976) believes that we must discover the terms of the marital contract, spoken and unspoken, conscious and unconscious. These terms are the spouses' expectations—what each believes he/she will receive from the other. Sager suggests that there are three levels of awareness involved in the mate selection process. Level one consists of those issues in the relationship that are "conscious and verbalized." Each person is able to tell the other about their expectations and mutual exchange occurs. This might involve expressing future career goals, education goals, hobbies, likes and dislikes.

Level two consists of those things that are "conscious but not verbalized." This refers to each person's expectations, plans, beliefs, and fantasies. Often these are not verbalized because of the fear of rejection, shame, anticipation of anger from others, or inability to manage the vulnerability. Occasionally there are deceptions and conflicts of intimacy at this level, raising uncertainties about entering a more committed relationship.

Finally, there is level three, where things are going on inside us (intrapsychic) about which we have less awareness. This level consists of desires and needs that are often contradictory and unrealistic. They may be similar or in conflict with other needs going on at other levels. This is the area of power and control needs, closeness/distance issues, contradictory active-passive impulses, child/adult conflicts, gender identity conflicts, and so on. This is the most significant level because nonfulfillment of these unconscious expectations tends to evoke intense emotional reactions.

These reactions are often confusing and excessive to the situation. (It is not unusual that people are more aware of a partner's third-level needs than their own.) It is this third level that we will need to look at to understand how and why people are attracted to each other and also what it is that causes their conflict.

As noted earlier, it is those things in common that attract couples to each other. On level one, it is the similarities of the obvious and that which is expressed that allow us to establish rapport and reveal more of ourselves. On level two, it is also the realization that the other person has similar expectations or feelings about issues that allow us to become more verbal and trusting, leading to more self-disclosure. Consistently we are also attracted to people who have some of the same kinds of fears and concerns on the third level. Often we are able to see their issues and are drawn to them, not knowing it is because their issues are resonating within us as well.

Willi, a marital therapist, calls this unconscious drama collusion: "Collusion refers to an unconscious interplay of two or more partners which is concealed from both of them and which is based on similar unresolved central conflicts" (Willi, 1982, p. 55). In other words, we are attracted to someone who has the same unfinished business we have, or who is dealing with the same type of emotional struggle. We see our inner struggle as something we are attempting to conquer and look for support and help from a partner to fulfill needs unmet.

Often people marry expecting their partner to meet all their needs and to fill up some emotional area that is feeling empty. It is important to point out that we all have these feelings, but at different levels of intensity. The more intensely we are driven to meet unmet needs through another, the more skewed the relationship. As stated, these unmet needs are products of our family of origin and parental/marital relationship.

A good example of this is a couple I will refer to as David and Barbara. Barbara was from a home where her father abandoned the family when she was a little girl, leaving the mother and three children. Her mother never got over being left and leaned heavily on her children for emotional support. This meant Barbara had to take care of herself and be strong for her mother. Barbara, however, being a child herself, missed out on her mother's ability to nurture her sufficiently and never reconciled herself to why her father took off and left. Later, her father remarried and had other daughters, which further caused Barbara to feel rejected and unloved by him.

David also came from a disrupted family where he was raised by his paternal grandparents. He felt rejected by his parents, who were together but had a difficult marriage. He never felt close to anyone in his family, and felt like no one really cared for him.

David and Barbara married hoping that the other would meet their individual needs. Barbara was looking for security, acceptance, and a man to nurture her beyond her feelings of rejection by her father. David was also looking for a woman who could nurture him and help him feel loved and valuable. During courtship, they recognized some possible problems but they ignored them in the hope of securing a relationship that would be different from their parents' marriages.

After a few years of marriage, they recognized that they had developed a distance from each other. Barbara began taking on the role of an angry woman, pursuing David to get affection and experiencing rejection when he backed away. Barbara was frustrated because David

161

was expecting her to take care of him, because she was looking for someone to take care of her. David became the distancer, feeling impotent to meet Barbara's need for love and validation, and feeling misunderstood and rejected, much like a little boy.

The couple's relationship spiraled downward in their attempt to get out of each other what they needed. Both began blaming the other for the problems and seeing themselves as victims of the relationship. Each time David didn't respond in the way that Barbara thought he should, she experienced a sense of personal rejection. The pain of this was overwhelming for her because it reopened the memory of her first rejection by her father. David experienced Barbara as a dangerous threat to his self-value when she became angry. Because he could not read her moods, he had to withdraw from her to stay at a safe distance. This left him feeling inadequate to meet her needs and unable to get close enough to receive any nurture from her.

Neither spouse knew how to escape the cycle of frustration and anger that they had created. The unmet needs that the couple brought into the relationship created more problems than were resolved by the marriage. In this relationship as in most others, both spouses had unfinished business left over from their families of origin that made problem solving in the present more difficult when these issues remained unverbalized and beyond awareness. The more extensive the unfinished business, the greater the potential for marital conflict.

Another important way to view couples is to see the individual partners as part of a family system. Like any other system, each person has his or her own role to play, and each affects the roles of the others. The marriage is a subsystem of the larger whole of the extended family. Based on the needs of the family, its emotional style, and the personal styles of its members, roles develop. These roles, and the degree of influence the unit has on its members, are a matter of emotional style shaped by the family's history.

The marital unit is influenced by the extended family. This can be to its detriment as well as to its benefit. Black families have historically been more extended in structure than the families of other peoples. For the counselor, it is necessary to know how much influence the extended family has on the marital relationship and to develop a sense of whether this influence is positive or negative.

The marital unit also has its own emotional style. It is created by both partners from their own experiences, especially within their families. If long-term change is to occur, each spouse must change. There is no such thing as unilateral change in effective marital therapy. In other words, if one partner changes, both have to change for the change to be lasting. No matter how much like a victim a spouse may look or claim to be, the counselor must encourage this person to see him- or herself as an active or passive participant in the conflict. The counselor must understand how both spouses set up the situation and why they are unwilling to change. The key point is that a counselor is not trying to change a *person*, but an unhealthy system of relating that is created by both spouses.

THE THERAPEUTIC PROCESS

It is helpful to think of a therapy process in phases: a beginning, a middle, and a termination phase. This helps the counselor to work on specific tasks at each stage and to monitor the work the couple is doing. These phases overlap and are not always distinct.

Beginning Phase. The first stage is particularly important because rapport is established and the foundation is laid for the work that will be done in the future. I try to acknowledge and validate any difficulty a couple is having, helping them to verbalize how hard it is being in therapy. Though there are other tasks that one will want to accomplish in the first phase, it is most important to establish a good relationship with clear boundaries and positive regard for both spouses. Many couples will not return to counseling if they have not made some safe connection with the counselor. In my experience, this is the first critical area, particularly for men. Some Black men will be uncomfortable with the vulnerability of the process and will choose not to continue. Black men are wary of asking for help and acknowledging weaknesses, both of which are implicit in the counseling process.

Because Black people have not historically chosen in great numbers to use professional counselors, some will come into counseling one step away from divorce. Often they are resolved to end the relationship, coming either to receive a miracle or to absolve guilt. The counselor becomes a mediator in this situation, helping the couple to make decisions about their relationship and lower their hostility for each other. The job for the counselor is to provide hope that there are other options and that the counselor is either equipped to help them or can refer them to someone who is.

Another obstacle for Black clients is that they seem to be socialized to adapt to the pain in their lives. Coming to counseling implies an inability to handle their own problems. This can make clients feel extremely uncomfortable with the amount of information that the counselor requests. The counselor must be sensitive to these issues as ones that are inhibiting for the clients. One way to help clients relax and to increase your credibility with them is to help a couple solve some problem in a way that is measurable and attainable. This will usually involve a situation that frustrates them. An early success with a specific problem often will assure clients that the counselor can be helpful and that the process can be productive.

The second task in this phase is assessment and though it begins in this phase, it continues throughout the entire process. Assessment involves the analysis of marital dysfunction. There are three key areas to focus on in assessing the couple—the marital relationship itself, the family system, and the functional and emotional wellness of each spouse. Marital problems and conflict can have their origin in any of these three areas.

In evaluating the marital relationship, one is looking for communication patterns, power distribution, intimacy issues, and emotional triangles. The issue most important to understand is the triangles that affect the marital dyad. Triangles are relationships that the spouses enter into to disperse the tension of the unsatisfactory marriage. They may include relationships with children, in-laws, or extramarital liaisons that allow the couple to avoid dealing directly and honestly with their spouse.

"The function of the third person in the marital triangle is to allow stability without change, to dilute the tension between the couple, and to create a displaced issue around which the husband and wife can organize their conflict" (Guerin, Fay, Burden, and Kautto, 1987, p. 63). Triangles are a part of human relational patterns and play some part in almost all relational conflicts. If the triangles in a relationship are not discovered, the couple may progress, but they will eventually slip back or get stuck in the counseling process with no lasting change.

A common triangle in marital relationships is formed when one spouse brings his or her parent into the marital dyad by maintaining a closer relationship with that parent than with the spouse. This leaves the spouse competing against the in-law for the attention and time of the partner. I believe this is why the Bible says one must "leave" and "cleave" (Gen. 2:24)—that couples may "become one flesh."

Another common triad is formed when a parent overidentifies with his or her children and invests all his or her energies into the parenting role, making the child the way relational needs are met. (This may be the same parent who is the third party in the previous example, thus indicating that two marriages are in trouble.) Helping couples understand their triangles allows them to see the relational pulls that aggravate stress and inhibit their ability to resolve issues in the relationship.

The second area of evaluation is the family system and the family systems from which the spouses came. When two people marry, it is the joining of two family systems that attempt to become one. Each family has their own rules, style, and idiosyncrasies that the spouses then bring to the new marriage. If couples are unable to mesh their backgrounds, there can be lasting tension. Also, if families have a history of marital problems or family stress, the new couple might very well bring some of these tensions into their new relationship. The counselor can use this information to give the couple insight into their values and ideals about marriage.

In the last area, the counselor must assess the emotional health and resources of each spouse. This is an attempt to evaluate whether the individual spouses have the emotional equipment to have a viable relationship. Sometimes personal wounds must be addressed before an individual can focus on what is needed to have a good relationship. To some extent, this needs to occur with every couple, but some couples are simply unable to move at all until their individual needs are addressed. Unclear thinking and unrealistic fantasies that individuals are unwilling or unable to give up signal some deeper emotional issues.

The assessment stage is a phase of information gathering that helps the couple see the scope of their relationship issues. With the help of the counselor, the couple can choose the direction and the themes that need work. The counselor should be listening for patterns, roles, and themes of the relationship, and areas that give the couple trouble. What is the temperature of the relationship (hot or cold)? Who distances and who pursues in conflicts? What is the couple's ability or inability to hear each other's views, to empathize and not interrupt? What is the couple's capacity to work through their conflicts and to solve problems? The counselor is trying to judge the severity of their marital dysfunction and choose the direction of the intervention. The counselor must also decide if their skill level is adequate to cope with the level of dysfunction their marriage evidences.

During the first session I usually have each spouse tell how they got to be here, making sure not to allow the other spouse to interrupt. It is important to let each person tell his or her own story and his or her view of what the problems are. This process allows couples to move away from focusing on their rigid, combative roles and to begin to listen to each other without the pressure and need to defend. The counselor can also take this opportunity to model empathic listening for the other spouse.

Middle Phase. The middle phase begins when there is an adequate working environment in which the couple and the counselor can begin to actively address the marital themes that hinder the relationship. In the initial phase the goals are to, as accurately as possible, get a picture of what the couple's "dance" is; what they do to each other to keep the relationship unfulfilling; and what themes they individually bring from their family of origin that hinder their interaction. These themes will probably run through such issues as money, sex, extended family, and communication. The therapist takes on the role of a re-educator about the couple's marital process, applying insight when appropriate to the issues they raise.

In the middle phase, there is a greater focus on revealing themes for the purpose of change, or to make choices to change. By this time the counselor should have a general idea of what areas will need to be addressed if the couple is to feel hope and a desire for change. The counselor must address the double messages and the behaviors that hinder change, helping the couple to see how their relating patterns leave them stuck.

The best combination for change is insight and behavioral exercises that get the couple to break relational habits. I try to help the couple see what they are doing and then assign them homework to address it. If couples have problems doing the assignments, I must explore what they find threatening about changing.

The counselor will be asking for more work from the couple to move past their defensiveness and to begin to self-focus. By self-focus I mean that each spouse begins to face individual responsibility in the relational conflict. The relationship with the counselor should be "good enough" for the counselor to be able to confront the spouses on their personal issues and their limited view of the relationship. The counselor must take responsibility to hold the couple accountable to do the work necessary for relational change.

The unwillingness or inability of a couple or an individual to self-focus signals the level of resistance to change. It also means that the couple or individual is in a defensive posture, either sensitized or numbed to criticism or rejection. They are unable to easily raise painful emotions that are stimulated by introspection. When a couple is stuck in this way, one will often get a lot of blaming and victim/villain dialogue.

Self-focusing is necessary for progress in the relationship. Partners must be willing to move away from their defensive, blaming postures to see that there are things within themselves that contribute to the poor relationship. They can then see that there are things within their own relational styles that connect with their partner's relational style, causing roadblocks for both. Self-focusing is essential for the progress of the therapy and is the key issue at this stage. There are numerous reasons why an individual will be resistant at this point, but the counselor can use the assessment data given earlier to persuade the couple of the need for such activity and to gain the leverage needed to break down any resistance.

Couples often become resistant because they feel threatened or fearful of negative exposure. They may have themes that they find difficult to face. Sometimes these issues are too painful or too threatening. The counselor must avoid attacking the spouse who appears to be more blocked and to think in terms of supporting them to openness and self-focusing. The counselor must also avoid assuming that the spouse who appears most resistant is the only villain. The interaction of the spouses may make it a risk for either individual to self-disclose. Usually both spouses are taking on roles that make it difficult for the other to disclose.

If one individual feels really stuck, I will sometimes ask that person to come in for sessions alone to help them look at their issues separately. This will often allow them to feel less threatened by their spouse's presence and reveal more information about their blockage. When this is done, it is important for the counselor to clarify the boundaries of confidentiality. If the spouse reveals things that are important to the movement of the relationship, I would encourage that person to reveal it to their spouse. But it is the spouse's choice and responsibility to reveal this information.

Termination. Another area of importance is determining when the process is over. One must look for the time when the couple have changed their relationship to a point where they are not likely to have a relapse. This does not mean that all the issues will have been resolved. This does mean that they have some tools to resolve these issues themselves. One of the most valuable tools is that of communication skills. Communication skills will give them a deeper understanding of how their relational expectations, family of origin, and emotional well-being affect the stability of the relationship.

Black clients are more likely to terminate the therapy prematurely even when they have had a good experience. Some leave because they are concerned about becoming dependent on the process. Others leave because the relationship is getting better and they no longer feel the original pain. This usually means that they have changed some things in their relationship and have lowered their marital stress. It does not mean that the relationship is out of the woods and that they will not slip back into old habits. Still others will leave because they view the therapy as stuck and the counselor as ineffective when the real problem is that they have effectively prevented the counselor from digging any deeper.

There really is no way to keep a couple in counseling after they have decided to leave, but one can inform them of concerns and then keep an open door. If a couple terminates prematurely, it is often after the initial phase and before the middle phase, where more intense work on their part is required. Either the counselor did not know how to get past the couple's resistance, or they were unwilling to work on their difficult issues.

I prefer to close out the counseling process reviewing the history of successes and frustrations, and attempting to help the couple see the significant crossroads of their counseling sessions. It is also important to prepare them for the future problems that they will have to deal with to keep growing together. I remind them of the tools they have acquired and the work they will need to do to maintain their progress.

CONCLUSION

Counseling must be more than giving advice to couples and telling them they need to change. It requires a commitment to enter into the couple's relationship and help them wrestle with the patterns that are not easily changed. The goal of a couple's therapy is not to create the ideal relationship, but to develop tools to help a couple work through their issues together. Tools such as communication, conflict resolution, and interpersonal management skills build a hope, trust, and fairness essential to the growth of the relationship. This creates a desired fidelity in the relationship that encourages the spouses to a committed choice to love each other.

When trust and safety in a relationship have broken down, committed love comes under assault. This commitment to love is more than the feelings of love; it is a choice to bond beyond the feelings. It is in this commitedness that the relationship can nurture and enhance the feelings and allow the couple to work through the tough issues that any two people bring to a relationship.

The Bible views marriage as a significant institution. For many, counseling may be needed to help resolve issues and to learn to apply both psychological and biblical principles.

Those interested in further information on marital counseling are encouraged to read Boyd-Franklin, 1989; Carter and McGoldrich, 1980, 1988; Hines and Boyd-Franklin, 1982; Jacobs and Gurman, 1986; Klimek, 1976; McGoldrich and Gerson, 1985; Nichols, 1987; Pinder-hughes, 1982; and Stack, 1974. While these works are not specifically referenced in this chapter, they were consulted. Additionally, I drew from one of my earlier papers (McNeil, 1986).

References

Boyd-Franklin, N. (1989). *Black Families in Therapy: A Multisystems Approach.* New York: Guilford Press.

Carter, B., and McGoldrich, M., eds. (1980). *The Family Life Cycle.* New York: Gardner Press.

————. (1988). *The Changing Family Life Cycle* (2d ed.). New York: Gardner Press.

Guerin, P.; Fay, L.; Burden, S.; and Kautto, J. (1987). *The Evaluation and Treatment of Marital Conflict.* New York: Basic Books, Inc.

Gutman, H. (1976). *The Black Family in Slavery and Freedom 1750–1925.* New York: Vintage Books.

Hines, P. M., and Boyd-Franklin, N. (1982). Black Families. In M. McGoldrick; J. Pearce; and J. Giordano, eds., *Ethnicity and Family Therapy.* New York: Guilford Press.

Jacobs, N., and Gurman, A., eds. (1986). *Clinical Handbook of Marital Therapy.* New York: Guilford Press.

Klimek, D. (1976). *Beneath Mate Selection and Marriage.* New York: Brunner/Mazel.

New American Standard Bible (1973). The Lockman Foundation. La Habra, Calif.: Foundation Press.

Martin, E. P., and Martin, J. M. (1978). *The Black Extended Family.* Chicago: University of Chicago Press.

McGoldrick, M., and Gerson, R. (1985). *Genograms in Family Assessments.* New York and London: Norton and Co.

McNeil, J. D. (1986). *Life Cycles of Black Families—Literature Review.* Unpublished research paper, Pasadena.

Nichols, M. (1987). *The Self in the System.* New York: Brunner/Mazel.

Pinderhughes, E. (1982). Afro-American Families and the Victim System. In M. McGoldrick; J. Pearce; and J. Giordano, eds., *Ethnicity and Family Therapy,* New York: Guilford.

Sager, C. (1976). *Marriage Contracts and Couple Therapy.* New York: Brunner/Mazel.

Stack, C. (1974). *All Our Kin.* New York: Harper and Row.

Willi, J. (1982). *Couples In Collusion.* New York and London: Jason Aronson.

Sexual Abuse: Its Impact on the Child and the Family

Joan A. Ganns

JOAN A. GANNS is a family therapist who recently relocated to Tampa, Florida, and is involved in consultation, seminars, and private practice. Prior to her counseling career, she had been an elementary and secondary school teacher. Joan has a Bachelor of Science degree from Eastern Illinois University, a Master of Science degree in Education from the University of Illinois (Urbana-Champaign), and a Master of Arts in Psychology degree from Trinity Evangelical Divinity School, Deerfield, Illinois. Joan grew up in Chicago, Illinois. She and her late husband, Joseph Ganns, have three children: Lawrence James, Kimberly, and Karin. She has been active in church as a teacher and was recently a member of Paradise Temple Church in Chicago.

11

Sexual Abuse: Its Impact on the Child and the Family

To imagine that we might abuse someone we cherish might at first seem unthinkable. Yet our children, those in our communities, churches, and families, are being raped of their innocence, trust, and protection. All too often, this results in a life that is marred physically, emotionally, and spiritually.

To define child sexual abuse, to explore its causes and effects, and to discover appropriate ways of treatment and prevention is one of the greatest challenges and opportunities facing the family. Facing the ravages of sexual abuse is not a challenge, however, that most of us welcome. We are repulsed that it even exists. There is a tendency to deny its existence. We may also ask the question that, if it does exist, what can be done about it?

As responsible adults, we must educate ourselves, our neighbors, and our children to wage war in one of the deadliest psychological, physical, and spiritual battles waged on the family. To those of us who know Christ, his love compels us to seek his truth where there is denial; to apply his light to the evil of sin; to offer his comfort for shame and his forgiveness for guilt; to provide treatment for offenders and victims; to engender the hope of prevention for those who have not been injured; and healing for those who have.

DEFINITION AND DYNAMICS OF SEXUAL ABUSE

The legal definitions of sexual abuse vary. The literature reflects an unclear definition because of the concern of some, such as Finkelhor (cited in Mayer, 1983), for the motivations of the offender, accidental occurrences, and an excessive concern for the child's body. Debate goes on as to whether real harm has been done to abused children. There is also a significant amount of political activity on the part of special interest groups that promote the legalization of sex with children. Such dangerous groups as the North American Man/Boy Love Association (N.A.M.B.L.A.) and the René Guyon Society, which endorses "sex before eight or else it's too late" (Mayer, 1985, p. 9), advocate child and child-adult sexual activity.

It is my firm belief that an enlightened people has as one of its cardinal values the protection of its children. Therefore, it will demonstrate great concern about the kinds of experiences to which children are subjected. To me, it is inconceivable that there would be legitimate instances of child-adult sex.

Thus the broad definition of child sexual abuse includes any sexual acts between an adult and a child. For the sake of clarification, a distinction will be made between intrusive and less intrusive acts, though each are abusive and impact the victim. Intrusive acts include oral-genital contact; anal or vaginal intercourse; digital (finger) penetration; sadomasochistic activity; soliciting or exploiting children for pornography (tapes, films, or photos); and selling children (prostitution). Less intrusive abuse includes fondling; masturbatory activities; abuser exposing self to children, watching victims undress, disrobing or nudity in front of children.

Another important distinction needed to understand the problem, its diagnosis, and treatment is whether the abuse took place within or outside of the family. Sometimes the perpetrator is a stranger, but it is more likely a friend or family member. When any blood or step-relative has sex with another family member, violently or not, it is considered incest. [Sgroi's (1982) definition of incest extends beyond close relatives to include "surrogate family members of a step-parent or extended family member" (common-law spouse or foster parents) (p. 10). Attempting to arrive at a more inclusive definition of child sexual abuse, the Child Abuse Treatment Act of 1974 defines relatedness as anyone responsible for the child's welfare. (Hampton, 1987).] When abuse takes place outside the family, it is usually termed molestation or rape if there has been intercourse.

The offender is male perhaps 90 percent of the time. Unlike the incest offender, the pedophile (one who receives his or her gratification from children) is not a member of the family. This person, often a trusted acquaintance, views children as objects, thus abusing their trust.

The child is called a victim because he or sne cannot possibly be in control, exercise free choice, or exert power in the context of the abuse. In spite of those who accuse youngsters of seductive and instigating behaviors, upon inquiry it is usually found that so-called cooperation has been won by the offender through the provision of affection, security, and gifts. Sometimes threats, fear, or violence is used to secure compliance, and "secrecy" is always part of the dynamic.

Because of the intense emotional and social dynamics that are a part of the incestuous family, special attention must be given to the phenomenon of incest. It is as ancient as the Old Testament and forbidden by even the most "primitive" peoples. The eighteenth, nineteenth, and twentieth chapters of Leviticus cite very clear prohibitions against intercourse with relatives, naming in-laws, stepparents, parents, siblings, stepsisters, stepbrothers, aunts, uncles, grandparents, grandchildren, and of course, children. Judgments against the people and the land were promised for disobedience to God's commands against prostitution, adultery, bestiality, and other such activities. Guilt clearly rested on the offender, and the punishment of childlessness or death could be inflicted.

In the New Testament church at Corinth, there was the scandal of a man having his father's wife. Paul decried such an offense and indicated that it was not even expected from heathens. The sentence handed down to the one guilty of incest was that he or she would be expelled from the church community and "handed over to Satan so his 'sensual body,' [flesh] may be destroyed and the spirit saved in the day of the Lord" (see 1 Cor. 5:5).

PREVALENCE OF CHILD SEXUAL ABUSE

Just how prevalent is child sexual abuse? At least 22 percent of all Americans have been victims of child sexual abuse, although one-third of the victims told no one and lived with the secret well into adulthood, according to Timnick (1985). Adams-Tucker and Adams (1984) pointed out that of the 60 million children under eighteen years of age, one in four to one in three girls are sexually victimized by the time they reach their eighteenth birthday. Rogers and Terry (1984) focused on boys and estimated that "one-fourth of all victims of sexual assault or molestation are boys" (p. 91).

How prevalent is child sexual abuse in Black families? In the past, a color-blind approach was taken in research and clinical findings. As a result, there are few studies dealing with the relationship between race and child abuse. The available data are only for the "caught" cases. Existing data should be carefully examined to ascertain the reporting

175

process used, and to detect the researchers' attitudes toward children and ethnic groups. Attempts to delineate relationships between family violence and race have yielded mixed results. Hampton (1987) and Gil (1970) found that families who were reported for abuse were drawn disproportionately from the less educated, the poor, and ethnic minorities. Black children were over-represented as victims of child abuse.

In conclusion, researchers Pierce and Pierce (1984) note that "although several well known studies of sexual abuse have included racial minorities in their studies, none have looked at these groups individually" (p. 9). Therefore the existing statistics are imprecise.

Lest the reader think that Christians are exempt from this problem, a survey conducted by the Graduate School of Psychology at Fuller Theological Seminary (Peters, 1986) indicates otherwise. Pastors and Christian counselors found that out of 981 cases, 90 percent of the reported victims were female. Fathers and stepfathers were the most common offenders. In 64 percent of the cases, incest began when the child was between seven and thirteen years of age. Sixty percent of the cases were repeat incidents spanning a year or more. In nearly half of the cases, more than one child in the family had been molested.

How reliable is such reporting? It is the consensus of public and private reporting agencies that statistics are much lower than actual incidence of abuse for several reasons. One reason is that sexual abuse is often reported under the broad category of child abuse. Another reason is that police reports are often inadequate because cases given directly to prosecutors may not be reported, and non-forcible attacks are not always included in the count.

Unfortunately, many who are mandated to report abuse fail to do so. Many professionals are not trained to notice the symptoms of abuse. Others lack faith in the services of the judicial system, deciding that they can do a better job. Some physicians fail to give genital exams, believing them to be traumatic, so these cases are not reported as sex abuse. The victim and the family are often reluctant to report, choosing rather to suffer. There is the fear of family disruption, guilt, shame, and ambivalence concerning the "betrayal" of the offender.

Statistics relating to the sexual abuse of boys are often under-reported, due to the stereotypic view that males should be self-reliant and not frightened of sex. There are also fewer detectable symptoms with the abused male.

It is believed that the reporting of child sexual abuse has been uneven among social classes. Lower socioeconomic groups are more likely to become a part of the legal system, whereas upper and middle classes are more likely to deal with it privately, thereby keeping knowledge of the abuse from the reporting agencies.

The statistics that we do have should dispel certain myths forever, such as: intercourse between adults and children is rare; sexual abuse is always accompanied by physical force; boys are almost never victims; most abusers are unknown to the children; and only poor minorities experience child sexual abuse. None of these statements are true.

The statistics now available undoubtedly reflect the increase in awareness, the increase in free sexual expression in our culture, and the resulting epidemic of occurrences of child sexual abuse.

WARNING SIGNS OF SEXUAL ABUSE

What are the warning signs of sexual abuse? There are some behaviors and physical complaints that are common, but not limited, to sexual abuse. These are:

1. A new fear of being around those formerly trusted, especially men or boys.
2. Clinging, excessive crying.
3. Change of habits: sleeping, eating, playing, moods.
4. Unusual hyperactivity, change in personality.
5. Age-inappropriate sexual activity, excessive masturbation, putting objects in or on genitals.
6. Reluctance to go home after school.
7. Extreme fear of showers or bathrooms (the site of abuse).
8. Extreme agitation about being touched.
9. Sexual themes in art and play, or stories.
10. Deterioration in school performance.
11. Regressive behavior: bed-wetting, thumb sucking, nail biting.

The following are signs common in an older child (grade school and above) who has been abused:

1. Obsession with cleanliness.
2. Early pregnancy (refuses to disclose father).
3. Conflictual relationships, especially with Mom and siblings.
4. Role reversal (little mother type).
5. Sexualized behavior: seductive dress, language.
6. Refusal to undress for physical education or examinations.
7. Running away, truancy.
8. Promiscuity.
9. Alcohol or drug dependency.

10. Preference for older friends.
11. Extremely withdrawn or extremely aggressive behavior.
12. Complains excessively of various illnesses.
13. Extreme fantasizing (multiple personalities, psychotic).
14. Diagnosed behavior-disordered or learning-disabled (with expressive disorder).
15. Possession of extra money, gifts without explanations.
16. Poor hygiene.
17. Layers of clothing worn, as if to hide under them.
18. Suicide attempts, self-mutilation.
19. Extreme compliance or defiance.
20. Extreme self-consciousness.
21. Constant fear or anxiety.
22. Prostitution.

The following are often physical warning signs (Hulefeld, 1988):

1. Sexually transmitted diseases.
2. Unusual offensive odors.
3. Chronic urinary infections; bed-wetting despite medical help.
4. Rectal infections and bleeding.
5. Unexplained sores in the throat.
6. Throat problems (gagging, etc.).
7. Complaints regarding the genital area.
8. Chronic "high" stomachaches, with no medical explanation.
9. Abortions.
10. Bloody, stained underwear.
11. Pregnancy.

PERSONALITY TRAITS AND VULNERABILITY
TO SEXUAL ABUSE

What are some of the personality traits that make one susceptible to abuse? What are some of the indicators that a family may be at risk? What kinds of environmental stimuli are conducive to inappropriate sexual activity? Though there are some physical and emotional conditions that are generally present when there has been abuse, caution must be exercised because the presence of any one of them is not conclusive evidence that abuse is indeed present. However, typical traits or characteristics include the following:

1. **Isolation.** Usually an abusive family has few social outlets and little support from others. Lacking in social and communication skills, the ability to get one's needs met and solve problems may also be

limited. These families are often rigid in their structure, and the important code of "secrecy" maintains the isolation. A family that is so dependent on each other is also a very stressed family, sometimes seeking relief by having sex with each other (incest).

2. **Marital disharmony.** Very often the couple is not meeting each other's emotional or sexual needs. There may be some incompatibility, anger, fear, or unresolved issues from their past. One partner may be "over adequate," and the other woefully inadequate; one may be very distant and the other over involved. Conflictual marital relationships tend to threaten the emotional health of each family member and raise the probability of sexual abuse occurring.

3. **Lifestyle of the family.** Today's family faces tremendous pressures, but the disorganization of the family, perhaps more than anything else, has very often left our children in an unprotected and precarious environment. Absent fathers, leaving a mother and children to fend for themselves; working mothers (especially those working at night and leaving the children in the care of the father or baby-sitters); and daughters who function as "little mothers" are all configurations in which the children may be underprotected and potentially harmed.

A child sensing discord and the possible disintegration of the family is vulnerable in that he or she is often assigned, consciously or unconsciously, to keep the family together. She or he may already be experiencing neglect and rejection, so a fear of abandonment and loss are heightened. If this needy child rightfully searches for affection, the offender can rationalize that it is "right" to provide the victim with attention and affection.

The mother characteristically has some strong emotional needs. She may have a poor self-image, feeling inadequate and emotionally immature with some sexual hang-ups. Especially unfortunate for the family is the passive or dependent mother who feels that she is without the power, skills, and security she needs to rescue her child from injury. Perhaps she was abused herself. Butler (1968) noted that depression and withdrawal are common among these women.

McDonald (1971) believes that the mother's jealousy over the daughter's sexual development results in a breakdown of mother-daughter relationships, setting the daughter up for possible sexual abuse. Zaphiris (1978) characterized the mother in this incestuous triad as cold and frigid. For quite a long time, there has been the strong belief that many mothers have known about the abuse and even, at least unconsciously, "arranged" it. Many mothers, however, claim total surprise when faced with disclosure of the abuse.

4. **Offender-Father.** Abusers are found in every social class,

179

profession, geographical location, and ethnic group. Some attend church; others don't. The offender may appear to be a good, hard-working, and law-abiding citizen. However, upon investigation, the offender is really a dysfunctioning individual. Gottlieb (1980) believes that the incestuous father is insecure and so dependent on his family that, while he may experience sexual incompatibility with his wife, he cannot risk sexual relationships outside the family. If his wife is unavailable to meet his needs, instead of solving his problems appropriately, he may express his anger toward her by abusing their child.

Peters (1986) says that the abuser cannot distinguish between love and sex, so he is able to rationalize his behavior. Being socially inadequate, he may retreat to pornography or pedophilic acts. He often has poor impulse control, low frustration tolerance, and desires immediate gratification. Alcohol or other chemicals may be used to lower an abuser's inhibitions. He may have poor self-esteem, which is compensated for by exerting power over his victim. He, too, might have been a victim himself.

5. **Family crisis.** There are some situations that are so stressful that family members regress into infantile behavior that is not characteristic of them. Some crisis situations that might produce this include illness, unemployment, physical handicap, and overcrowded living conditions.

6. **Perversion of sexuality.** The failure to deal with our "sexuality" may well be a cause of increased sexual acting-out behaviors. What has been the family's attitude toward sexuality? Is accurate information about sex shared appropriately? Is physical affection shown? Is there a proper view of the human body? Is there a lot of anxiety about sex? Are the discussions about sex loaded with taboos?

7. **Sexualized interrelationships.** Family members may be accustomed to gratifying one another's desires with little or no thought to the impact of such behavior. Too often, sexual power plays are made, roles tested, and attractiveness used to woo family members rather than those outside the family. Seductive behaviors are learned and encouraged by the music, dress, language, and leisure activities of the family. The indiscriminate use of television, videos, and print can keep sexual energy fired up.

8. **Boundaries.** Is the privacy of each family member respected—including that of the children? Are the sexual roles clear between father, mother, and children? Is adult sexual behavior clearly distinguished from the child's behavior? Are sleeping arrangements appropriate (each having his or her own bed, and parents and children sleeping in separate rooms)? Appropriate boundaries significantly

reduce the possibility of sexual triangles. There are no marked role reversals, individual personalities are cherished, and differences accepted.

HIGH-RISK CHILDREN

Children in the following situations are at high risk for abuse:

1. Those in day care or with sitters (especially male).
2. Those who have had a parent leave the home.
3. Those in foster care or adoptive homes.
4. Children of chemical- and alcohol-dependent parents.
5. Those who spend lengthy hours before the television.
6. Latch key children.
7. Children who spend a lot of time alone.
8. Children whose mother works nights.
9. Those with overly harsh parents.
10. Psychologically abused children.
11. Unattached children (belonging to no one, little bonding).
12. Those receiving inconsistent discipline.
13. Those living in high-density housing.
14. Those whose parent was sexually abused.
15. Children living where the offender is yet in the home.
16. Young siblings of a victim.
17. Handicapped children.
18. Children living in crowded accommodations.
19. Children who loiter around convenience marts.
20. Children with low impulse control.
21. The "alone" child (not necessarily the only child).
22. Children of a mother with "uncommitted" boyfriends.
23. Those left in the care of the very young or aged.

SOLUTIONS

What is the fate of the abused child and his or her family? Are there ways to prevent the trauma of child sexual abuse? Is treatment available?

One solution is to build strong families. Strong families deeply value their children. As they do, they will have an intense commitment to creating and protecting the home. There must also be careful regard for the children of our neighborhood, city, state, and nation.

Another solution is to become acquainted with child protection agencies and their policies. We can work to simplify court procedures so as not to traumatize victims and their families. In addition, we can work for more stringent licensing procedures for day care centers and foster and adoptive homes.

Churches can play a crucial role in preventing sexual abuse. Some churches are already actively participating in prevention by providing day care centers and extended day care. Some churches are hosting family life education conferences, having regular midweek teaching to strengthen the family, conducting marriage enrichment weekends, and premarital counseling. They are also teaching about sexuality in a positive manner and looking for other creative ways to safeguard the sanctity of our families.

Some churches are pooling their resources to stop the multimillion-dollar pornography industry, by seeking to get the "smut" shops out of their communities, by refusing to bring x-rated video and cable stations into their homes, and by providing positive materials and activities in their place.

Another solution is to teach children how to protect themselves. While teaching is not a guarantee against abuse, it can help to reduce its incidence. Listed below are tips from the Mesa Police Department, the Anderson Security Agency, and the United Way:

1. Start teaching your children basic crime prevention.
2. Teach them not to accept rides, food, gifts, money from strangers.
3. Show them the safest route to and from school.
4. Know your children's playmates and where they play.
5. Instruct children to check with you before going anywhere.
6. Teach them areas of their bodies that no one touches, and that they have a right to say "no!"
7. Instruct your children to let you or a teacher know if they are being bothered by a stranger.
8. Make sure your child knows full name, address, and phone.
9. Instruct your child to report anything strange to the nearest public place, or yell for help.
10. Teach your child what to do when separated from you.
11. Do not allow a child to go to public rest rooms alone.
12. Do not allow your child to be released to anyone but someone designated by you.
13. Do not leave children unattended in cars, grocery carts, stores, or playgrounds.
14. Tell them never to enter a stranger's house.

The object of these interventions is not to scare children but to make them aware of possible dangers.

CONCLUSION

It is my plea that excellent professional treatment be secured for the victim and his or her family. The church would do well to make good use of its professionals. The unique skills of nurse, physician, social worker, counselor and pastoral staff are all needed to instruct children and parents in the prevention of child sexual abuse.

The extension of forgiveness to the offender is not enough! Child abuse is a compulsive and repetitive act and should be treated like chemical dependency. Secular treatment is preferable to no treatment. If treatment is omitted, the victim can suffer almost irreparable damage. However, with appropriate treatment, the survivor (adult victim) can experience restoration, even if no other family members are willing to face the abuse and receive help.

Jesus used children as models of trust and humility. Note these words of Jesus:

> . . . And any of you who welcomes a little child like this because you are mine, is welcoming me and caring for me. But if any of you causes one of these little ones who trust in me to lose his faith, it would be better . . . if he were thrown into the sea with a huge rock tied to his neck, he would be far better off than facing the punishment in store for those who harm these little children's souls. I am warning you! (Matthew 18:5–6; Luke 17:2–3 LB)

These verses outline traits that are needed to enter God's kingdom. Children desire to be with Jesus and to bring pleasure to him. Jesus did not abuse the needs of children for affection and love. When we are protective of children, we are fulfilling the calling of Christ, loving those he loves, touching them appropriately, and blessing them. According to Scripture, this is a way we can welcome Jesus and care for him. To protect children is to build a foundation of faith that can lead to salvation when the gospel message is received. Their hearts have been made ready because their trust has been handled judiciously, lovingly, and carefully.

References

Adams-Tucker, C., and Adams, P. (1984). Treatment of Sexually Abused Children. In J. Stuart and J. Greer, eds., *Victims of Sexual Aggression:*

Treatment of Children, Women and Men, 57–74. New York: Van Nostrand Reinhold.

Butler, S. (1978). *Conspiracy of Silence: The Trauma of Incest*. San Francisco: New Glide Publications.

Gil, D. G. (1970). *Violence against Children: Physical Abuse in United States*. Cambridge: Harvard University.

Gottlieb, B. (1980). Incest: Therapeutic Intervention in a Unique Form of Sexual Abuse. In C. G. Warner, ed., *Rape and Sexual Assault*. Germantown, Md.: An Aspen Publication, Aspen Systems Corporation.

Hampton, R. (1987). *Violence in the Black Family: Correlates and Consequences*. Lexington, Mass.: D. C. Heath & Co., Lexington Books.

Hulefeld, A. B. (1988). Warning Signs: A Handout. Oak Park, Ill.: Wholistic Health Center.

MacDonald, J. M. (1971). *Offenders and Their Victims*. Springfield, Ill.: Charles C. Thomas, Publishers.

Mayer, A. (1983). *Incest: A Treatment Manual for Therapy Victims, Spouses and Offenders*. Holmes Beach, Fla.: Learning Publications.

―――――. (1985). *Sexual Abuse: Causes, Consequences, and Treatment of Incestuous and Pedophilic Acts*. Holmes Beach, Fla.: Learning Publications.

Peters, D. B. (1986). *A Betrayal of Innocence*. Waco, Tex.: Word.

Pierce, R. R., and Pierce, L. (1984). Race as a Factor in the Sexual Abuse of Children. *Social Work Research and Abstracts* 20:9–14.

Rogers, C., and Terry, T. (1984). Clinical Interventions with Boy Victims of Sexual Abuse. In I. Stuart and S. Greer, eds., *Victims of Sexual Aggression: Treatment of Children, Women, and Men*. New York: Van Nostrand Reinhold.

Sgroi, S. (1982). *Handbook of Clinical Intervention in Child Sexual Abuse*. Lexington, Mass.: Lexington Books.

Taylor, K. (1971). *The Living Bible*. Wheaton, Ill.: Tyndale.

Timnick, L. (1985). 22% in Survey Were Child Abuse Victims. *Los Angeles Times* (August 25):1.

Zaphiris, A. G. (1978). *Incest: The Family with Two Known Victims*. Denver: The American Humane Association.

12

Sex and Sexuality Issues for Black Families and Churches

Lee N. June

LEE N. JUNE is a professor at Michigan State University and currently serves as Senior Advisor to the Provost for Racial, Ethnic, and Multicultural Issues. He is on leave as Director of the Counseling Center, a position he has held for eight and one half years. Lee has a Bachelor of Science degree from Tuskegee University, a Master of Education degree in Counseling, a Master of Arts degree in clinical psychology, and a Doctor of Philosophy degree in clinical psychology from the University of Illinois (Champaign-Urbana). He did post-baccalaureate study in psychology at Haverford College (1966–67) and was a special student during a sabbatical leave at the Duke University Divinity School (1981). Born and raised in Manning, South Carolina, Lee is married to Shirley Spencer June and they have twin boys, Brian and Stephen. He is a member of New Mount Calvary Baptist Church in Lansing, Michigan, where he is a deacon. Over the years he has served in his church in numerous capacities. He has written several articles in the area of counseling and career development.

12

Sex and Sexuality Issues
for Black Families and Churches

The purpose of this chapter is to examine aspects of sex and sexuality that are important to Black (African-American) Christian families and churches. Specifically, it will discuss why sex and sexuality are problematic for many Christians, how sex and sexuality are viewed biblically, important male and female sexuality differences and their implications for sexual relations, the challenges sex presents to the Black Christian family and church community, and the resources available on sex and sexuality.

Most would agree that sex is one of the most powerful (if not *the* most powerful) of the human drives and emotions. Illicit sexual involvements have caused numerous scandals and the downfall of major political and religious leaders. These have occurred throughout history. Bible readers will readily recall the role that improper sex played in the downfall of people such as Samson, David, and Solomon—just to name a few.

WHY SEX AND SEXUALITY ARE
PROBLEMATIC FOR MANY CHRISTIANS

Issues regarding sex and sexuality are problematic for many Christians for several reasons. These include the following:

1. Many do not fully understand what the Bible actually teaches regarding sex and sexuality. The result is that one is influenced more by society than by the Bible.

2. There is an absence of detailed, biblically based materials regarding sexuality. This is particularly the case in regard to materials

specifically oriented to the Black community. Unfortunately, there are no comprehensive books written from a Black perspective similar to books such as Wheat and Wheat's *Intended for Pleasure* (1977, 1981) and Penner and Penner's *The Gift of Sex* (1981) and *A Gift for All Ages* (1986).

3. When teaching is done, there is often an overemphasis on the don'ts of sex and sexuality. Hence the message conveyed is negative, even when this is not the intention.

4. Sexuality and spirituality are sometimes viewed as incompatible. Smedes (1976) discussed this issue in some detail under the heading of salvation and sexuality. The interested reader is referred to this chapter of his book.

BIBLICAL VIEW

While the Bible is not an explicit sex manual, it does set forth at least six principles regarding sex and sexuality.

1. Sex and sexuality are positive creations of God. Genesis 1:27 and 31 indicate that God created male and female as distinct beings, and that he felt *very good* about these creations. It is further noted in Genesis 2:25 that after the creation, Adam and his wife, Eve, were not ashamed of their naked state. This changed after their sin, but it nevertheless points to their comfortable acceptance of their physical nature.

2. One role of sexual relations is procreation. In Genesis 1:28 it is recorded, "And God blessed them, and God said unto them, 'Be fruitful and multiply, and fill the earth and subdue it . . .'" (NSRB). Genesis 4:1 states that "Adam knew Eve his wife; and she conceived, and bore Cain." It is through sexual relationships that the human race is replenished.

3. However, sex has a greater role than procreation. It is also intended for pleasure. Proverbs 5:18–19 points this out: "Let thy fountain be blessed and rejoice with the wife of thy youth. Let her be as the loving hind and pleasant roe; let her breasts satisfy thee at all times, and be thou ravished always with her love" (NSRB). The Song of Solomon cannot be read without clearly seeing the positive and enjoyable expressions of romantic love. First Corinthians 7:1–5 outlines the mutual responsibility for sexual enjoyment of husband and wife.

A major contribution of the books by Wheat and Wheat and Penner and Penner is their portrayal of sex and sexuality in a positive vein.

4. Sexual intercourse is to occur only within marriage. First Corinthians 7:9 delineates this principle.

5. Sexual intercourse outside of marriage is sinful. The above-mentioned Scripture speaks to this. This principle was also laid down in

188

the Ten Commandments, "Thou shall not commit adultery," (Exod. 20:14 KJV) and in 1 Thessalonians 4:3–5.

6. Not everyone will marry. This principle is outlined in 1 Corinthians 7:7–8 and Matthew 19:10–12. These Scriptures make it clear that there is nothing wrong with being single. However, if one is to remain single, one should live in this state according to biblical standards, abstaining from sexual intercourse.

Other treatments of the biblical view of sex and sexuality may be found in Collins (1988) and in Penner and Penner (1981, 1986).

DIFFERENCES IN MALE AND FEMALE SEXUALITY ISSUES

Researchers in the area of human sexuality have consistently called attention to the differences between males and females. Males and females often respond differently and report different needs. The Bible records that God made "man in his *own* image, in the image of God made he him; male and female created he them" (Gen. 1:27 NSRB). This passage indicates that while both males and females are created in God's image, there is a distinct human state of "maleness" and "femaleness."

Thus both males and females must learn about their own bodies as well as their spouse's. Young children, at the appropriate ages, also need such awareness. Adequate knowledge of sex and sexuality is necessary to improve relationships between males and females, to increase sensitivity between the sexes, to prepare a person for marriage, and to enhance sexual satisfaction in marriage. This knowledge is also necessary for younger people so that they understand their feelings and their physical and emotional development. Such knowledge is further necessary to remove the unhealthy mystery that is too often associated with sex and sexuality.

Unfortunately, few studies have been published that document the differences in attitudes, expectations, and preferences between Black Christian men and women. However, a few surveys on Blacks in general have been conducted. The available surveys, which tend to be published in magazines such as *Ebony* and *Essence*, and not written from a Christian perspective, suggest that men and women enjoy similar as well as different things as part of sexual relations.

For example, it has been reported in various sources that Black women consider the following important in sexual relations:

1. Talking.
2. Touching.

189

3. Extended foreplay.
4. Afterplay.
5. Feeling "loved" outside of the bedroom.
6. Being allowed to be the initiator.
7. Being cuddled, held, and romanced before and after love-making, thus eliminating the feeling of being a "receptacle" or having participated in a "bim bam, thank you, ma'am" brand of sex.

Edwards (1982) is one writer who has surveyed and discussed some of these issues for Black women.

Staples (1983) noted that even though Black males have been included in several historical studies, there have been no systematic analyses of any differences. His article reviewed the available data and summarized what is broadly known regarding the sexual desires of the Black male. He found that those surveyed desired:

1. Having the female occasionally be the initiator, thus eliminating a feeling of always having to do all the "work."
2. Having the female verbalize her desires.
3. A variety in sexual activities.
4. Different positions for sexual intercourse.

Staples covers a range of other topics, but they are beyond the scope of this chapter.

The above articles (Edwards, 1982; and Staples, 1983), while not based specifically on samplings of Black Christians, appear to have some application to the Black Christian community. However, the absence of comprehensive research on Christians regarding sex and sexuality is a major problem. Perhaps in the near future, such data will be forthcoming.

CHALLENGES AND SOLUTIONS FOR THE BLACK CHRISTIAN COMMUNITY

Because sex can be such a powerful drive and in the Bible is viewed positively, and because we are bombarded daily by messages of sex and sexuality, the Black church, the Black family, and the Christian community can do much more to educate its members about sexual issues. Below are several positive initiatives that can be taken:

1. There needs to be more teaching within the Black community regarding sex and sexuality. Churches can carry out a greater role in such programming. People who understand the biblical view and are

comfortable with the topic of sexuality should be trained to teach in this area. The family could also assume its responsibility for education and training in this regard through the home. Parents must become comfortable with their own sexuality and then be appropriately open and honest with their children. Wattleton and Keiffer (1988) have offered several suggestions on how to talk to children about sex.

2. Develop more biblically based resource materials that deal with sex and sexuality and that are oriented toward members of the Black Christian community. When this is done, it tends to enhance sensitivity to issues within the Black community. The next section will list some of the materials currently available. In developing such material, it must be in good taste but at the same time explicit enough to address critical issues directly. Materials that are available are few in number and tend to be in workshop formats, video and audiotapes, and/or are not very detailed.

3. Specific programming could be developed to reach young Black males and females. In such programming, the common stereotypes and myths about manhood, womanhood, and sexuality should be addressed.

To assist in this regard, one might draw from and have discussion groups on the content of articles published in *Ebony* (1983) and *Essence* (1989) while placing them in a Christian context.

For example, *Ebony* has published what have been considered constant and pervasive myths (several of which involve sexual issues) regarding Black men over many years. These myths are that Black men—

—Are naturally gifted athletes
—Cannot sustain stable relationships
—Are sexually superior
—Lack business ability
—Have no talent for science
—Are usually endowed physically
—Are lazy and shiftless
—Crave White women
—Are prone to be violent

Campbell (1989) wrote on myths of Black female sexuality and listed the following. These myths are that Black women—

—Physically mature faster
—Are more sensual and permissive
—Willingly have babies outside of marriage
—Have big buttocks and thighs

191

—Are more fertile than White women
—Use sex to gain material benefits
—In middle incomes are frigid
—Are better lovers
—Are more frequently than White women the victims of rape by
   White men and are more likely to be raped in general

Following each myth, both of these articles presented the realities of the situation.

An alternative approach to discussing myths and stereotypes is to have participants list what comes to mind when they think of "manhood," "womanhood," "Black male sexuality," and "Black female sexuality." This could be done by gender, followed by a discussion of similarities and differences in responses. One could also use the discussion to correct the myths and stereotypes mentioned.

4. Undertake programming and teaching that address the issues that are prevalent in the larger society, including abortion, sexual abuse, incest, premarital sex, masturbation, homosexuality, and acquired immuno-deficiency syndrome (AIDS).

To achieve this, one could use the expertise of Christians in local churches to conduct such programs. In the absence of church expertise, one could invite community resources that respect and understand Christian values.

5. Include teaching regarding sex and sexuality as an integral and routine part of church and family life. This could be done by using the opportunities that Sunday school and Bible study offer to explore sexual issues. One could also refer to incidents that the media offer to teach and discuss issues of sex. This would ultimately encourage young men and women to ask their questions and get answers within a Christian context, instead of through the media or from the streets.

6. When teaching and discussions take place, an atmosphere promoting appropriate open discussion must be encouraged. A model for maximizing the likelihood of open discussion is outlined below:

a. Select discussion leaders who have been trained and/or are experienced in facilitating discussions.
b. Divide participants into small groups. While this is not absolutely necessary, it can aid in engendering open discussions.
c. Divide participants according to age, and gear the content of the discussion accordingly.
d. Develop guidelines or ground rules for the group and get agreement on them prior to the discussion. For example, some guidelines may be that:

(1) One wants open discussion.
(2) Honest opinions are desired.
(3) All opinions will be respected.
(4) All participants will be respected.
(5) Views will be examined in light of Scripture.
(6) Confidentiality of views will be respected outside of the group.
e. The group leader must make sure that the agreed-upon guidelines are followed.

7. Given the similarities and differences between men and women discussed in the previous section, it follows that married couples need to discuss sexual issues to enhance their understanding of each other.

Figure 12.1 contains a questionnaire that could be used by married couples to enhance communication with each other on sexual issues. (A similar questionnaire, the Husband and Wife Sexual Inventory Sheet, has been developed by Richardson—1981a.)

Figure 12.1
Sexual Issues Within Marriage

1. I prefer sexual intercourse most often during the
____ a. morning.   ____ c. evening.
____ b. afternoon.   ____ d. other (specify) _____

2. The most enjoyable position for intercourse for me is
____ a. man above.   ____ d. side (face to face).
____ b. woman above.   ____ e. other (specify) _____
____ c. rear entry.

3. As to sexual matters, I want my wife/husband to be
____ a. always the initiator.   ____ c. never the initiator.
____ b. sometimes the   ____ d. other (specify) _____
     initiator.

4. I communicate to my husband/wife that I am in the mood for sex by
____ a. telling him/her.   ____ c. nonverbal cues (touch,
____ b. my manner of dress.   eye contact, etc.).
                            ____ d. other (specify) _____

5. What I know about sex, I learned primarily from
_____ a. mother.   _____ e. relatives.
_____ b. father.   _____ f. readings.
_____ c. brother.   _____ g. other (specify) _____
_____ d. sister.

6. Rank the following as to the purpose of sex (1 = most important, 2 = second most important, etc.):
_____ a. procreation (having   _____ c. expression of love.
       children).   _____ d. pleasure.
_____ b. relief of tension.   _____ e. other (specify) _____

7. I prefer sexual intercourse approximately _____ times per week.

8. All sexual behavior should end in intercourse.
_____ a. yes   _____ b. no

9. Birth control is the responsibility of the
_____ a. wife.   _____ c. husband and wife.
_____ b. husband.

10. Before intercourse, foreplay is
_____ a. very important.   _____ c. never important.
_____ b. somewhat important.   _____ d. other (specify) _____

11. My greatest deficiency in the area of sex is
_____ a. a knowledge of   _____ c. an inability to verbalize
       sexual anatomy.   my desires, unhappiness,
_____ b. a healthy respect for   etc.
       the differences   _____ d. other (specify) _____
       between males and
       females.

Each spouse can complete the questionnaire alone and then compare responses to determine where there are agreements and disagreements. The questionnaire is obviously not exhaustive. Married couples are therefore encouraged to add other categories that may be critical areas for their particular relationship.

As spouses complete the questionnaire, the areas of agreement and disagreement should be examined in light of Scripture and scriptural principles. However, if major disagreements occur that are not resolved and that interfere with the relationship, counseling is recommended.

The above questionnaire could also be used as a tool to facilitate discussions in appropriate groups.

RESOURCES AVAILABLE

Though not written for or from a Black perspective, the books by Wheat and Wheat (1977, 1981) and Penner and Penner (1981, 1986) are excellent general resource materials. From a more culturally specific perspective, the following materials are available.

1. *Tough Talk on Love, Sex and Dating.* (1985). This is a video presentation by Haman Cross, Jr. In it, he deals specifically with several of the issues that teenagers face. These issues are dealt with in a humorous yet hard-hitting fashion. The video may be ordered from Youth Encounter, P.O. Box 04706, Detroit, MI 48204.

2. *God's Blueprint for the Christian Family.* (1986). This is a six-part video presentation by Tony (Anthony) Evans and produced by The Urban Alternative. Topical areas are "Marriage: God's Style," "Roles in Marriage," "Parenting," "Divorce and Remarriage," "Sex in Marriage," and "Successful Singlehood." While all of the tapes have some reference to sexuality, the one entitled "Sex in Marriage" has the most direct application. These materials may be ordered from Renaissance Production, 759 N. Broadway, Pittman, NJ 08071. A manual accompanies the videos.

3. *Marriage Improvement Workbook (How to Practice Real Love, Changing Poor Communication, and Financial Victory; Series Book #1).* (1981a). This workbook by Willie Richardson is part of the national seminar on the Black family conducted by Christian Research and Development. The material is presented in a workshop format and may be ordered from Christian Research and Development, 1822 68th Avenue, Philadelphia, PA 19126.

4. *Enjoying the Single Life (Loneliness, Relationships with the Opposite Sex; Series Book #1).* (1981b). By Willie Richardson, this workbook is similar to the previous one, but focuses specifically on single people. It may be ordered from the address listed in #3.

5. *Enjoying the Single Life (A Manual for Christian Dating and Courtship; Series Book #2.* (1986). The manual by Haman Cross, Jr. covers areas of importance for people who are dating. The manual may be ordered from the address listed in #3.

6. *An Introduction to Maximum Sex* (1990). This is a six-part

audiotape (accompanied by a manual) by Haman and Roberta Cross. Six topics are covered: The Theology of Sex, The Sociology of Sex, The Biology of Sex, The Psychology of Sex, The Pathology of Sex, and The Technology of Sex. These materials were produced by Renaissance Productions and may be ordered from Network Unlimited, 308 E. Koenig Street, Wentzville, MO 63385.

CONCLUSION

The Black (African-American) Christian community (both church and family) can do much more to help correct and prevent many of the problems created by the lack of accurate information regarding sex and sexuality.

Christianity and the Black church continue to be prominent in the lives of Black people and the Black community. As churches and Christians carry out the task of "perfecting . . . the saints for the work of the ministry for the edifying of the body of Christ . . . " (Eph. 4:12 NSRB), there is the challenge to address the full range of issues affecting Christendom, including the areas of sex and sexuality. Given their importance and their potential to be positive or detrimental, one must do all that is possible to make sure that they are positive. This chapter has offered several suggestions and has presented various resources to assist in this task.

References

Campbell, B. M. (1989). Myths About Black Female Sexuality. *Essence*, **19** (12):71–72, 108, 113.

Collins, G. R. (1988). *Christian Counseling: A Comprehensive Guide, rev. ed.* Dallas: Word.

Cross, H., Jr. (1986). *Enjoying the Single Life: A Manual for Christian Dating and Courtship* (Series Book #2). Philadelphia: Christian Research and Development.

_____. (1985). *Tough Talk on Love, Sex, and Dating.* Detroit: Youth Encounter.

Cross, H., Jr., and Cross, R. (1990). *An Introduction to Maximum Sex.* Wentzville, Mo.: Network Unlimited.

Edwards, A. (1982). How You're Feeling. *Essence*, **13** (8):73–76.

Evans, A. (1986). *God's Blueprint for the Christian Family.* Pittman, N.J.: Renaissance Production.

Penner, C., and Penner, J. (1981). *The Gift of Sex: A Christian Guide to Sexual Fulfillment.* Waco: Word.

_____. (1986). *A Gift for All Ages: A Family Handbook on Sexuality.* Waco: Word.

Richardson, W. (1981a). *Marriage Improvement Workbook: How to Practice Real Love; Changing Poor Communication; Financial Victory* (Series Book #1). Philadelphia: Christian Research and Development.

_____. (1981b). *Enjoying the Single Life: Loneliness; Relationship with the Opposite Sex* (Series Book #1). Philadelphia: Christian Research and Development.

Scofield, C. I., ed. (1967). *The New Scofield Reference Bible.* New York: Oxford.

Smedes, L. B. (1976). *Sex for Christians.* Grand Rapids: Wm. B. Eerdmans.

Staples, R. (1983). Black Male Sexuality: Has It Changed? *Ebony,* 38 (10):104, 106, 108, 110.

The Ten Biggest Myths About Black Men (1983). *Ebony,* 38 (August):96, 98, 100.

Wattleton, F., and Keiffer, E. (1988). How to Talk to Your Child About Sex. *Ebony,* 43(5):60, 62, 64.

Wheat, E., and Wheat, G. (1977). *Intended for Pleasure: Sex Techniques and Sexual Fulfillment in Christian Marriage.* Old Tappan: Fleming H. Revell.

_____. (1981). *Intended for Pleasure: Sex Techniques and Sexual Fulfillment in Christian Marriage, rev. ed.* Old Tappan: Fleming H. Revell.

13

Drug Abuse and the Black Family: A Challenge to the Church

Michael R. Lyles

MICHAEL LYLES is currently the Medical Director of the Rapha Inpatient Unit at West Paces Ferry Hospital in Atlanta, Georgia, and has a
private practice in psychiatry with the Atlanta Counseling Center. He
received his Bachelor of Science and Doctor of Medicine degrees from
the University of Michigan and completed his psychiatric residency at
Duke University. Michael is a member of the Zion Baptist Church in
Roswell, Georgia, and currently is in charge of its drug program. He
also works with the children's church program. Born in Chicago,
Illinois, and raised in Spartanburg, South Carolina, he moved to
Detroit, Michigan, as a teenager. He is married to Marsha Washington
Lyles and they have two sons, Michael and Morgann.

13

Drug Abuse and the Black Family: A Challenge to the Church

It is impossible to consider the health of family life in America without discussing drug abuse. Recent studies have demonstrated that the abuse of alcohol and drugs has become the number one mental health problem in America. Approximately 15 million Americans have tried cocaine and that includes 16 percent of White adults and 12 percent of Black adults (Adams & Gfroerer, 1989). Over 50 percent of the young adult population has tried an illegal drug (Gold, 1988). Five million Americans are in need of treatment for drug abuse and addiction (Turner, 1988). Alcohol abuse and addiction continues as a major problem in our society (Kozel & Adams, 1986).

As a member of the Black community and a practicing psychiatrist, however, drug abuse means more than just statistics. I think of high school acquaintances, more talented than I, who never attended college because they damaged their brains with hallucinogens. I think of friends, patients, and loved ones who have lost their health, careers, savings, and severely damaged their relationships because of addiction to prescription drugs, cocaine, and alcohol. I think of talented young Black people who should be at the forefront of efforts to solve society's ills, but instead have wasted their talents at the end of a marijuana "joint." I think of children who have given up on life and assumed that they would never amount to anything because their parents esteemed "crack" as more important than they.

Writing this chapter was difficult because in doing so I have had to re-experience the pain involved in remembering the drug-shattered lives of many different individuals. However, I know that the battle for our families and against addiction begins with the weapons of correct facts and proper eduction—weapons that do not exist in many of our communities. To this end, this chapter is dedicated to helping the reader move beyond feelings and fears to understanding the nature of substance abuse and addiction and the treatment alternatives for those users, the people who love them.

Drugs are commonly used in our society, from a dose of caffeine (coffee) at breakfast to a dose of alcohol (wine) at dinner. Advertisements for nicotine (cigarettes) and nonprescription drugs for everything from headaches to hemorrhoids compete for our minds. Our society is very drug-conscious, but is not necessarily accurately informed regarding the facts about drugs. Many individuals associate drug abuse with the excessive use of "street" drugs such as crack cocaine. This is an incomplete definition, as drug *abuse* is determined by the *pattern* of drug use more than the *amount* or *type* of drug used. Thus a first task is to define what is meant by drug abuse and addiction.

DEFINITION OF DRUG ABUSE

Drug abuse occurs when a drug is repeatedly used in spite of the user's knowledge that the drug is causing a problem in his or her life. This problem may be social, such as a wife threatening to leave, or legal, such as losing one's license from driving under the influence of alcohol. It may be work-related, such as an employer suspending the cocaine abuser because of chronic lateness or absenteeism. The problem may be physical, such as the man with high blood pressure who continues to "snort" cocaine with his "friends" in spite of being told that it would elevate his blood pressure. Drug abuse is also defined by a pattern of use in situations that are physically dangerous, such as a worker operating dangerous equipment after smoking marijuana, or a truck driver using amphetamines on a routine basis to stay awake. These examples illustrate why it is not just the amount of drug used that defines abuse; a small amount of drug used in patterns also constitutes abuse.

It is possible to abuse any type of drug. There are people who abuse aspirin so badly that their stomach linings are injured and internal bleeding occurs. However, there are nine classes of drugs that are more commonly associated with abuse. These include (1) alcohol, (2) amphetamines (speed, some diet pills) and related compounds, (3) marijuana (cannabis, pot, weed, grass, Mary Jane, joint), (4) cocaine (coke, crack, rocks, base), (5) hallucinogens (LSD, mescaline, peyote, psilocybin, mushrooms), (6) inhalants (glue, gasoline), (7) opioids (heroin, narcotic analgesics, methadone), (8) phencyclidine

(PCP, angel dust), and (9) sedative/hypnotic (barbiturates, tranquilizers, and certain types of sleeping pills).

DEFINITION OF DRUG DEPENDENCY

Drug dependency can take two forms, physical and psychological. Physical dependency occurs in the individual who has abused drugs to the point that his or her body has adjusted to having the drug around. This usually requires frequent use, but not always. There are two common features of physical dependency. First, the individual develops a biological resistance or tolerance to the drug so that greater amounts are required to give the same effect. For example, the person who formerly would get a "buzz" after two beers now boasts that he or she can drink two six-packs and not feel a thing. This person has a big problem, for he or she has become physically tolerant of alcohol.

Second, physical dependency is characterized by the development of physical withdrawal symptoms when the use of the drug is suddenly stopped. The exact withdrawal symptoms will differ depending on the substance used, but will include nervousness, sweating, tremors, stomach pain, irritability, and increases in respiratory rate, blood pressure, temperature, and heart rate. These symptoms are more obvious after cessation of alcohol, opioids, and sedative/hypnotic drugs, and less of an obvious problem with cocaine, marijuana, and amphetamines. The length of time between the last use of the drug and the beginning of withdrawal symptoms is also highly variable, depending on the chemical personality of the drug. Physical withdrawal is quite serious as some drugs produce withdrawal states that include seizures, psychosis, and the potential for death. Delirium tremens (severe alcohol withdrawal or d.t.'s) for instance, can lead to death and is a medical emergency. Valium withdrawal can produce a psychotic reaction that looks identical to schizophrenia in many respects. Many addicted individuals recognize when withdrawal symptoms are occurring and will use their drug to self-treat. An example is the alcoholic who wakes up nervous and "shaky" in the morning and takes a drink to "calm my nerves."

When most people think of drug dependency, they think of the physically dependent individual in withdrawal. However, psychological dependency has gained increased attention as a major component of drug dependency (Nakken, 1988). Some have used the term addiction to refer to any psychological dependency, because the following elements can be applied to such addictive disorders as compulsive gambling, eating disorders, and sexual addictions.

Psychological dependency or addiction is similar to abuse in that the individual is repetitively using drugs in spite of the knowledge that the drugs are seriously hurting him or her. Thus, the individual tries to reduce or control their use but fails, and usually finds her- or himself using drugs more often and in larger amounts. An individual may also find him- or herself becoming preoccupied with the drug, thinking about using it, how to get it, where the money will come from, how to avoid getting caught, and actually using it. She or he may start withdrawing from family and friends to spend time alone or with "friends" who also use. This behavior is usually accompanied by "denial." That is, the addict denies having a problem and complains about others "blowing this out of proportion."

Some drugs produce a "craving" in the individual in which the person becomes so preoccupied with the drug that he or she can taste it and smell it and actually dreams about it. At this point, the drug has usually caused a significant change in the chemistry of the brain. Much research of late has described this in cocaine addiction, underlining why it is so difficult for some cocaine addicts to escape its grip (Wyatt, Karcum, Suddath, & Fawcett, 1988).

It is important to note that one can have a psychological dependency or addiction to a drug without having a physical addiction. In fact, it is common for addicts to deny having a problem because they are not physically dependent. Meanwhile, their lives are slowly deteriorating as the psychological dependency distracts them from their family, career, health, and spiritual development.

CAUSES OF ADDICTION

Many debates have centered on whether addiction is a medical/physical, psychological, or spiritual problem (Galizio & Maistro, 1985). The "disease model" of drug and alcohol addiction states that it is a combination of all of the above. There is compelling evidence that there is something different genetically about the way addicted and non-addicted individuals handle alcohol. Alcoholics, especially, seem to have a genetic "loading" that places them at risk for abusing alcohol (Goodwin, 1985). They really can't drink socially without it quickly getting out of control. Many researchers feel that there is something different about the alcoholic's brain, which leads to a lack of control. Critics of the disease model state that this releases the addict from taking responsibility for the problem. This, however, is not true. The addict is not to be held responsible for what he or she inherited, but the addict is responsible for what he or she does about it.

204

A further complication to the question of cause is added by the emergence of crack cocaine as the "drug of choice" by so many. This drug causes tremendous changes in the levels of certain chemicals in the brain after only one use. Repeated use can deplete the brain of one very important chemical, dopamine, subsequently causing the addict to crave more cocaine (Wyatt et al., 1988 and Gawin & Ellenwood, 1988).

This craving becomes so intense that laboratory mice in a state of dopamine depletion will use cocaine to the exclusion of food, water, sleep, and sex until they die. Humans addicted to crack cocaine follow a similar progression. With crack, the genetics do not have to be there for a problem to occur. The drug will create the problem without any assistance from heredity.

TREATMENT ISSUES—THE ADDICT

Treatment of the drug abuser or addict begins with a commitment to cease the use of *all* mood-altering drugs (Miller, 1987). The cocaine addict can't continue using marijuana, because this continues to place the addict psychologically in a pattern of using a drug to treat a feeling. Second, the individual will continue to encounter socially individuals who are selling marijuana and who will also try to get him or her back on cocaine (which is more profitable) by offering free samples. Third, under the influence of marijuana, one's ability to abstain from the cocaine will be much lower. One must break totally with drugs or it is a waste of time to discuss treatment.

For this reason, the initial phase of drug rehabilitation may need to occur in a drug-free environment, such as a hospital or half-way house. There, access to drugs can be eliminated long enough for the addict to go through withdrawal and craving attacks, and clear up his or her thinking enough to work on a rehabilitation program. The treatment of drug withdrawal with medications that correct the chemical and electrical (nervous) imbalances of withdrawal is called detoxification. This is often required for those with alcohol, tranquilizer, opiates, and cocaine dependencies before rehabilitation can begin.

Rational rehabilitation programs are based on the twelve-step program of Alcoholics Anonymous. This program approaches the different areas the addict needs to work on in a step-by-step approach. The initial steps help the addict confront his or her denial of the problem and admit to their powerlessness to control it.

Next the addict is encouraged to develop healthy coping mechanisms by developing spiritual resources with God, open, honest communications with others, and a heightened awareness of one's own problems and character faults. A resultant dependence on God will aid in the healing of these problems. The twelve steps of Alcoholics Anonymous have been adapted to other substances, including cocaine and narcotics. Recovering addicts are strongly encouraged to attend "meetings" with other recovering addicts who are at various stages of recovery from their addictions.

These meetings (Alcoholics Anonymous, Cocaine Anonymous, Narcotics Anonymous) are greenhouses in which the recovering addict can begin applying the twelve-step principles of recovery while receiving support and encouragement from others who share that commitment. Respectable inpatient programs expose addicts to the twelve-step principles of recovery and develop "aftercare" plans that will coordinate their transition into the "safety net" of those similarly recovering in the community (that is, the recovering community). This helps to prevent a relapse after discharge from the hospital.

Recovering addicts will often need counseling to help resolve their feelings of sadness, anger, grief, and embarrassment about the time wasted while abusing drugs. Rehabilitation may also include improving reading skills, finding a job, and teaching recreational skills, because most addicts have forgotten healthy ways of having fun.

Addicts have critical spiritual needs that demand attention if a drug-free lifestyle is to be maintained. Addicts need to understand how Christ can address their need for power, hope, honesty, lifestyle change, forgiveness, relationship-building, and submission. Thus, learning how to connect with God in order to improve self-esteem, resolve conflict, handle strong feelings, and develop healthy relationships is very important.

However, many addicts will deny that they have a problem. They will avoid treatment and get into a vicious cycle of abusing drugs to treat anger, shame, boredom, sadness, and grief, and then feel guilty for using. Often these individuals will not have healthy coping mechanisms for dealing with stress. Thus, the guilt, anger, sadness, and embarrassment of "using" actually places the addict at risk for using again to escape the pain (Nakken, 1988).

In a very real sense, the addiction starts to fuel itself; the individual can't "just say no" because the drug is screaming yes. The individual is in bondage at this point. Hence, what started as a genetic predisposition for abusing drugs has turned into a nightmare. The addict, at this point, is not responsible for one's genetics, but is responsible for facing the problem and seeking treatment. But whether addicts seek treatment or not, their families are always in need of help.

TREATMENT ISSUES—THE FAMILY

Often the family is more hurt than is the user by the addiction because they are dealing with the pain, anger, and embarrassment of the addiction while sober. They are hurting desperately while the addict is lost in an insane, addictive fog. This results in the family, adjusting to the addict in ways that often facilitate the addiction. This syndrome is called codependency or coaddiction (Beattie, 1987; Springle, 1990).

Codependency is the result of living in a family that is chronically in crisis over the effects of the addiction on the family. Repeated verbal arguments turn into a silent truce, or the all-too-frequent absence of a spouse for days at a time—usually after payday. Sexual problems develop as the spouse either loses interest in sex or cannot perform due to impotence or the inability to reach orgasm. Children and spouses learn to ignore their anger, embarrassment, shame, and confusion after living with the addiction for awhile. They prefer "to hear, see, or speak no evil," because what they say doesn't seem to make any apparent difference. This, however, results in family members becoming depressed and mistrustful of relationships because they have been hurt so badly by the addiction.

Some family members learn too well from the addict's pattern of "coping" and start running from their feelings with addictive behaviors themselves. For example, they may be driven to overachievement or the "hero syndrome," workaholism, promiscuity, overeating, compulsive bulimia, or the abuse of drugs or alcohol (Woititz, 1983 and Whitfield, 1987).

Twelve-step programs for families exist through Al-Anon, Cocanon, and Naranon. These resources are critical to the family in which the addict is in denial and refusing help. In addition, support groups for adult children of alcoholics are becoming more prevalent. For too long, the impact of addiction on the family has been ignored or minimized. However, this is rapidly changing.

CHALLENGE TO THE CHURCH

Recently, there have been several prime-time specials on drug abuse. In these programs, representatives from law enforcement, the media, medicine, and politics debated the potential contributions of each discipline in addressing this problem. Rarely, if ever, is a single pastor, Black or White, represented in such discussions, and the church is not mentioned. Several recovering addicts are interviewed, and again the church is not mentioned. All of these specials have focused on Black communities in particular, and the only mention of the Black church is usually an excerpt from the funeral of a person who has overdosed.

We are in the midst of a growing crisis in family life due to drug addiction. If the church of Christ is to fulfill her role as a healing agent in all communities, she must come out of her denial and admit that drug abuse is destroying and killing people within her walls also. A drug-free society will not occur until we have drug-free churches, with leadership committed to sobriety. Pastors cannot preach sobriety and then personally abuse alcohol. Deacons cannot frown on the teenager who became pregnant (while high on drugs) and then abuse prescription medications themselves. Sunday school teachers cannot buy suspected stolen merchandise and then criticize a pupil who was caught smoking crack at school. A drug-free church begins with a drug-free leadership that abstains from the use and sale of illicit drugs or any behavior associated with it.

Once a church is serious about fighting addiction, as evidenced by the commitment of the leadership, programs must be instituted. What follows is a list of possible interventions a church could offer.

1. Sponsor twelve-step support groups through secular organizations such as Alcoholics Anonymous, Cocaine Anonymous, Narcotics Anonymous and the family support groups of Al-Anon, Cocanon, and Naranon.
2. Sponsor more explicitly Christ-centered twelve-step support groups such as Alcoholics Victorious and the Overcomers.
3. Start Bible studies that focus on biblical answers to the needs of the addict.
4. Institute support groups for the adult children of alcoholics.
5. Develop a network of spiritual big brothers/sisters who can help the recovering addict learn how to study the Bible, develop a prayer life, participate in worship, and network with other Christians committed to sobriety.
6. Become active in holding elected officials and law enforcement agents accountable for their work in the surrounding community.
7. Provide financial assistance for addicts who are seeking help but lack resources.

Much of the church's opportunity lies in preventing members from using drugs in the first place. Many have described drug abuse as a symptom of the spiritual emptiness and hopelessness of many in our society. The church has the responsibility to describe how Christ relates to this need, with the following as possible approaches:

1. Teach parents how to model responsible behaviors financially, educationally, vocationally, sexually, and chemically, so that children will learn from example how to make responsible decisions.
2. Expand young people's horizons by involving them in organized groups such as Scouts, Junior Achievement, church athletic leagues, bowling leagues, and academic clubs (college-bound clubs) that help young people believe in a future and have hope.
3. Provide structured teaching about relationships, self-esteem, family relationships, dating, marriage, sexuality, and communication from a biblical point of view.
4. Provide big brother/big sister relationships for children of single parents.
5. Sponsor family recreational outings (picnics, talent shows, camping/fishing trips, etc.) that will help families learn how to have healthy fun.
6. Provide tutorial help for kids with academic problems.
7. Teach about the differences between healthy and dysfunctional families. Pray for dysfunctional families.
8. Discuss the influence of growing up in an addicted family with an adult child of an alcoholic during premarital counseling. Appropriate reading material should be provided at this time.
9. Develop networks to help members find jobs and learn how to succeed in those jobs.
10. Provide workshops on the relationship between acquired immune deficiency syndrome (AIDS) and drug abuse.

CONCLUSION

Family life is at a point of crisis in our society, with addiction a major threat. The perception by some that this is a Black problem is wrong and oversimplified. This chapter applies to any race or cultural group in our country today, because we are losing an entire generation to addiction. Many segments of our society, not just the church, will have to be involved if the war on drugs is to be won. However, the church needs to reflect God's concern and compassion for those in bondage by addressing the needs of the communities. Otherwise alcohol, cocaine, and methamphetamines will fill those needs.

References

Adams, E. H., and Gfroerer, J. C. (1988). Elevated Risk of Cocaine Use in Adults. *Psychiatric Annals* 18:523–527.

Beattie, M. (1987). *Codependent No More*. San Francisco: Hazelden.

Galizio, M., and Maistro, S. A. (1985). *Determinants of Substance Abuse*. New York: Plenum Press.

Gawin, F. H., and Ellinwood, E. H., Jr. (1988). Cocaine and Other Stimulants: Actions, Abuse, and Treatment. *New England Journal of Medicine* 318:1173–1182.

Gold, M. S. (1988). *The Facts about Drugs and Alcohol*. New York: Bantam.

Goodwin, D. W. (1985). Alcoholism and Genetics: The Sins of the Fathers. *Archives of General Psychiatry* 42:171–174.

Kozel, N. J., and Adams, E. H. (1986). Epidemiology of Drug Abuse: An Overview. *Science* 234:970–974.

Miller, N. S. (1987). A Primer of the Treatment Process for Alcoholism and Drug Addiction. *Psychiatry Letter* 7:30–37.

Nakken, C. (1988). *The Addictive Personality: Understanding Compulsion in our Lives*. San Francisco: Hazelden.

Springle, P. (1990). *Codependency: A Christian Perspective*. Houston: Rapha Publishing/Word.

Turner, E. C. (1988). The Cocaine Epidemic and Prevention of Future Drug Epidemics. *Psychiatric Annals* 18:507–512.

Whitfield, C. L. (1987). *Healing the Child Within*. Deerfield Beach, Fla.: Health Communications Inc.

Woititz, J. G. (1983). *Adult Children of Alcoholics*. Deerfield Beach, Fla.: Health Communications Inc.

Wyatt, R. J.; Karcum, F.; Suddath, R.; and Fawcett, R. (1988). Persistently Decreased Brain Dopamine Levels of Cocaine. *Journal of the American Medical Association* 259:2996.

Suggested Resources for Christian-Oriented Twelve-Step Bible Studies

The Twelve Steps for Christians (1928). Recovery Publications, 1201 Knoxville Street, San Diego, CA 92110.

Claire, W. (1982). *God Help Me Stop*. Books West, P.O. Box 27364, San Diego, CA 92128.

McGee, R. S. (1990). *Rapha's Twelve-step Program for Overcoming Chemical Dependency*. Houston: Rapha Publishing/Word.

14

Evangelizing Black Males: Critical Issues and How-Tos

Willie Richardson

WILLIE RICHARDSON is the pastor of Christian Stronghold Baptist Church in Philadelphia, Pennsylvania, and is also the president of Christian Research and Development (CRD) of Philadelphia. He is a graduate of Philadelphia College of the Bible and serves on numerous boards. CRD was founded in 1977 and is involved in developing the Christian family and church through seminars, conferences, retreats, and workshops. Willie has authored several workbooks. He is also the Founder-Director of Inner City Impact. Willie has a commitment to developing pastors as managers and has done so successfully with some 100 pastors. He was born in Florence, South Carolina, and is married to Patricia Richardson. They have four children: Gregory, Garin, Gwendolyn, and Gerald.

14

Evangelizing Black Males:
Critical Issues and How-Tos

Evangelism was never offered as optional for the individual Christian or for the church. God commands that we carry out what is called the Great Commission (Matt. 28:18–20). Because of the state of Black males today, we are in a crisis, and evangelism is more important than ever before. Some sociologists believe that the Black man faces extinction in the future if conditions and trends do not change.

The Black church is the only institution that has been consistently concerned about the issues affecting Black people since the time of slavery. It is the Black church that must provide leadership in carrying out the mandate to evangelize Black males.

Too many men are hopeless and desperate. They do not know in which direction to go, or they are going in various directions that are detrimental to themselves and others. There is an urgent need for Black males to hear a vital message of hope. The gospel message of the Lord Jesus Christ is that message of hope and salvation. When I make this statement, I am not speaking only of spiritual salvation. Included in the power of the gospel message is deliverance. This message must be carried to Black men instead of waiting for them to come to the church (note that in this chapter I often use "males" and "men" interchangeably).

UNDERSTANDING THE PROBLEM OF EVANGELISM

In order to be effective in evangelizing Black males, we must have a burden for them. It is not very difficult to have a burden for Black men if we look seriously at the trends and statistics. For instance, although

Black males make up about 6 percent of the general population, they comprise some 44 percent of the prison population. It should be noted that 96 percent of state prisoners and 93 percent of federal prisoners are males. Further, according to the United States Department of Justice and the Bureau of Justice statistics for May 1986, 72 percent of all males in state prisons are eighteen to thirty-four years of age. A similar pattern is true for federal prisons. Among prison inmates, slightly over half have never been married, and another 24 percent are divorced or separated (Flanagan and Maguire, 1990).

This situation has a direct impact on other problems in Black family life. There is a shortage of eligible men for Black women to marry. This is further evidenced by the fact that about 57 percent of prison inmates were raised primarily by one parent, or by other relatives. The Black male's life expectancy is lower than the White male's. He is more likely to be the victim of homicide. His unemployment rate is usually higher than that of other ethnic groups. Even when employed, he earns only 47 percent of the dollar White males earn. Reardon (1986), on the staff of the *Chicago Tribune*, stated:

> A multitude of local and national studies show that the more deeply a person is stuck in the underclass, the more likely he is to be a crime victim or a criminal.
>
> In addition, Black men are six times more likely than White men to go to prison at least once during their lives. In fact, one out of every fifty black men in the United States older than eighteen spent at least some time in prison during 1982 alone.
>
> The Illinois Criminal Justice Information Authority conducted a study of 12,872 homicides in Chicago over a seventeen-year period and found that 70 percent of the victims and 68 percent of the killers were Black.
>
> The poor have always been with us, but not the levels of violent crime that exist today in the ghettos of Chicago and the rest of America. (p. 44)

In considering the evangelization of Black men, we must also consider the conditions of Black youth. Nearly 80 percent of Black youth live in poverty (U.S. Bureau of Census, 1990). The Black high school drop-out rate is currently 40 to 60 percent, depending on the city and school. Some have estimated that 25 percent of the income of Black youth comes from crime. Fifty-one percent of Black children are being raised in fatherless homes (U.S. Bureau of Census, 1990); and one out of every six Black males will be arrested by the time he reaches age nineteen. Twenty-five percent of our children are being raised by high school drop-outs. Unemployment among Black youth between the ages of 16–19 is around 32 percent nationwide; however, this percentage is greater in some of our major cities (U.S. Bureau of Census, 1990).

Clearly, there are Black middle-class males who are doing better than in the statistics mentioned above, but there are problems that are common among Black men in general. For example, marriages and family life are deteriorating, homes are breaking up, divorce rates are high, and unmarried couples are living together and having children. All of these are growing trends. Also, some Black men simply cannot cope with life problems such as racism and family responsibility. These are some of the reasons that a growing number of men are becoming drug abusers and alcoholics.

More of us must have a burden to change the plight of Black males, but we must be burdened enough to evangelize them. There are some who believe that the Black church has never been involved in evangelism, but this is not true. The Black church, perhaps, has not done evangelism in the way that is prescribed by many White theologians and writers, but the Black church from its inception has been involved in evangelism. We must understand that basic evangelism is simply telling someone else about Jesus Christ, and, in turn, having that person profess faith in Jesus Christ as Lord. The Bible teaches that it is faith in Jesus Christ that saves a person. Many, over the years, have come to Christ simply because a church member invited them to church. They heard the preacher preach about the goodness of God and the miraculous power of Jesus Christ, and in the quietness of their hearts, they committed themselves to Christ. Even though this happens, the focus of the salvation message in the Black church needs to be sharpened. Many more people would come to Christ and become church members if the salvation message were clearer (see for example, Hinkle, 1973).

In my own case, I grew up in the church but was not a Christian. When I was eighteen years old, my aunt, who belonged to another church, challenged me to be saved. She, however, never told me *how* to be saved. She invited me to her church to "get the Holy Ghost." I was open to receiving Christ until her pastor accused me of committing a list of sins of which he thought all young people were guilty. I was insulted by his accusation and returned to the church in which I grew up. I don't think the pastor intended to insult me; he just didn't know how to give a clear presentation of how to receive Christ.

For the next three years, I asked Christians within my church and outside of my church, "What must I do to be saved?" I received such answers as "You must go to the mourners bench;" "You must get the

Holy Ghost;" "You must join the church" (I was already a member of a church, but not saved). No one ever answered my question clearly because in most of our churches, neither pastors nor church members have been taught how to lead a person to Christ.

After three years of inquiring about how to be saved, and because of my unhappy life, out of desperation one Tuesday morning in my bachelor's apartment, I fell on my knees and simply said, "I give my life to you, Lord; save me." God saved me in spite of the fact that no pastor or church member had ever evangelized me. A year or so later, in an evangelism class at the Philadelphia College of the Bible, I learned in a clear manner how I was saved. This personal experience has motivated me as a pastor to see that every member of the church is taught clearly how to lead a person to Christ.

PRESENTING THE GOSPEL MESSAGE TO BLACK MALES

When presenting the gospel message, it must be presented as a message of hope, and not a message of condemnation. Much of the materials used in evangelism today and much evangelistic preaching employ a message of condemnation. We must understand that the Black male is generally in an atmosphere of condemnation already. He may have already been told that he is not qualified to work, that he is too lazy to work, and that he doesn't have the intelligence that is equal to other men. He may have already been blamed for the Black family's situation and all of the crime in our community. He thus exists in an atmosphere of continual condemnation. Therefore, many men are turned off when they hear another message of condemnation. White (1984) describes the Black male's experience in our society in the following manner:

> In a society that placed a premium on decisive male leadership in the family, the Black male was portrayed as lacking the masculine sex role behaviors characterized by logical thinking, willingness to take responsibility for others, assertiveness, managerial skills, achievement orientation, and occupational mastery. The Black male in essence had been psychologically castrated and rendered ineffective by forces beyond his control. He is absent within the family circle and unable to provide leadership and command respect when he is present. After generations of being unable to achieve the ideal male role in the family and in American society, the Black male is likely to be inclined to compensate for his failure by pursuing roles such as the pimp, player, hustler, and sweet daddy, which are in conflict with the norms of the larger society. The appearance of these roles in male

behavior in the Black community, rather than being interpreted as a form of social protest, reinforces the majority culture stereotypes of Black males as irresponsible, lazy, shiftless, and sociopathic. (p. 61)

In the Bible, the only time Jesus condemned anyone was when they rejected the gospel message. Sometimes we begin the salvation message with a message of condemnation, but the gospel message, as I understand it, is a message of hope. It is a message of salvation. It is very clear in the Old Testament that when the salvation of the Lord is mentioned, it is referring to spiritual salvation, deliverance from physical danger, deliverance out of trouble, or deliverance from a problem. The spiritual deliverance of the gospel message is primary, but it also opens the way for God to move into these other areas that need deliverance. The Black male needs to hear a message that God loves him and has a better life on earth for him.

THE SALVATION MESSAGE
THAT BLACK MALES MUST HEAR

There are several key things that we must communicate to Black males. Among them are the following:

1. *God has a love attitude toward men.* If one does not reject God, he does not condemn us. Jesus came to seek and save the lost (Luke 19:10). God loves: "For God so loved the world, that he gave his only begotten Son, that whosoever believeth in him should not perish, but have everlasting life" (John 3:16 KJV). The gospel clearly is a message of love, and if we are going to evangelize Black men, we must make sure that they get this message of love, and not a message of condemnation.

2. *God desires to have a personal relationship with each man.* God created us so that he would have fellowship with us, and he wants to be personally involved in our life. God never intended man to be on his own, dealing with his problems, and trying to come up with solutions for them by himself. God has always wanted to be a partner. He did not create us, walk away, and leave us on our own. But as we would submit to him, God desired to have a relationship with us.

3. *There is sin that stands in the way of this relationship.* When God created us, he created us a little lower than the angels, and crowned us with glory and honor, but sin has marred that image. Sin started with our father Adam, who went his own way. Since then, we have also gone our own way. The Bible says, "All we like sheep have gone astray; we have turned every one to his own way; and the LORD hath laid on him the iniquity of us all" (Isa. 53:6 KJV). Therefore, the thing that

217

stands in the way of our having this fellowship, this personal relationship with God, is sin. God is concerned about sin because he is holy, totally righteous, just, and perfect (and therefore hates sin). Yet God loves us all. Therefore, we have a sin problem.

4. *There is something that can be done about the sin problem.* The Lord Jesus Christ has solved the sin problem. Our Holy God demands that sin be paid for. The Bible says, "The soul that sinneth, it shall die" (Ezek. 18:4 KJV). Sin calls for a sacrifice, a blood sacrifice. Before the foundation of the world, God came up with a plan that would solve the sin problem, help us recover the fellowship we had with him, and establish once again the relationship he has always wanted with us.

The Lord Jesus Christ came from heaven to earth, humbled himself, took on the body of a man, and died on the cross for our sins. All the wrong that we have done in the past, all the wrong that we are presently guilty of, and all the wrong that we may do in the future, Christ has paid for. Christ was our substitute on the cross. He paid the penalty of sin.

The Bible says, "The wages of sin is death." There is a physical death and a spiritual death. Therefore, we die physically and spiritually. Spiritual death is to spend eternity in hell, a place of eternal torment. But Christ solved that problem when he died on the cross for our sins. He then arose from the grave for our justification. Now we can come to God through Jesus Christ, the Son of God. We must be willing to accept the love of God, accept what God has done, and be willing to surrender our lives to God by faith in Christ.

5. *Black men can have a close relationship with God.* We have a responsibility to God as our Creator. God did create the salvation plan before the beginning of the world, but he also has a plan for our lives. He has a personal plan for each individual, and we have a responsibility to submit to God our Creator. We have the responsibility and opportunity to receive Jesus Christ by faith. We have the responsibility after receiving Christ to let God show us his personal plan for our lives. God reveals this through the study of the Scriptures, by the guidance of God the Holy Spirit, and through our walk with him.

EVANGELIZING BLACK MALES: THE ROLES
OF THE PASTOR, WIFE, CHURCH, AND OTHER MEN

Every church should have an organized evangelism ministry. By organized, I mean that there should be set times when members of the church actually do evangelism. It should be scheduled in the same way as the choir has a set time to rehearse and to sing on Sunday mornings.

There also needs to be a set time to teach and train the members of the church in doing evangelism. The church must have a trained group of people who actually are set apart to run this ministry. In a smaller church, the pastor should be the one who is giving direction to it. Even in the larger churches, evangelism should be a top priority for the pastor, although someone else may be appointed to run the evangelism ministry. However, all pastors should lead people to Christ by sharing their own faith as the opportunities arise. Other evangelism workers are often motivated when a person stands in church and testifies that the pastor personally led him or her to Christ.

Starting with the pastor, the church leadership must have a "made-up mind" that they are going to have an evangelism ministry. I have helped some churches get started in evangelism and then, later on, other things crowded it out of the pastor's priorities. I remember one church in particular in which the pastor had the evangelism ministry going on week after week, month after month, for a few years. The church grew numerically and spiritually. However, he later developed other priorities and drifted away from evangelism. As a result, the church stopped growing.

In training Christians to share their faith, we must use uncomplicated methods and simple materials that will enable those trained to train others. Materials such as Hyles' booklet, "Let's Go Soul Winning" (1962) and Lovett's booklet, "Soul Winning Made Easy" (1978), are easy to use. Also, there are Black evangelistic and follow-up materials such as "The Newborn Christian," written by Ron Ballard of Home Ministries (1982).

In order to reach men for Christ, we must train the married women in the church based on the promise in 1 Peter 3:1–6. I focus on the wife, not because she is the only one who can effectively evangelize her husband, but because she is an effective though often neglected vehicle. Thus we must train wives to reach their own husbands for Jesus Christ. We have many Christian women whose husbands are unchurched or don't attend church, and who have not received Jesus Christ as Lord and Savior. Though we learn from 1 Peter 3 that she is to win him by her behavior, the wife is also supposed to make a clear presentation to her husband as to how to be saved. The 1 Peter 3 passage puts more weight on the fact that he is going to see Christ in her; hence, there's a possibility that she can win him to Christ by her behavior. It is not that the married Christian wife has to do anything so unusual. She is merely to carry out her wifely duties as taught in the Bible, to express Christian love to her husband, and pray for him. For instance, in Ephesians 5, wives are told to treat their husbands with respect and to submit to their leadership. When it comes to submitting to the leadership of an unsaved husband, she is to submit to everything but sin. If the man wants to run the house a certain way, the Christian wife tries to support his leadership. She also tries to be his advisor, but not his boss. She is his counselor and thus lets him know if she thinks he's wrong, but she does it in a very submissive way. She must reverence her husband and also respect him.

Another area of critical concern is outlined in 1 Corinthians 7, where we are told that when a married woman or man is not meeting the sexual needs of the partner, they are in sin. We have learned from our counseling centers that many Christians, for one reason or another, are not meeting the sexual needs of their spouses. Some even refuse to sleep in the same bed. The Bible has more to say about the duties of spouses, but as I have counseled families in these areas, I find that this area can be a stumbling block to spouses' coming to Christ. Some even have a self-righteous attitude, saying that they shouldn't even have sex with their spouses because they are not saved, while they themselves are "holy." God will call us into judgment regarding the marriage vows we have taken, and 1 Corinthians 7 clearly teaches that each spouse should be carrying out his or her responsibility in this matter.

Another group in the church that should be trained are the men who are already members, whether this be one man or a few. Men respond better or perhaps more quickly when other men share their faith with them. All of us, men and women, should be sharing our faith with every man, woman, boy, and girl; but our focus here is how to evangelize Black males. I am simply saying that we must train men specifically to evangelize other men.

There should be a plan and a strategy. It should be on paper. For instance, the plan could be divided into winter and summer activities, depending on what part of the country one is in. Summertime gives outdoor opportunities that are not available during the winter. We have to be committed to evangelism because in the summer, the believers want to just relax and take it easy even when there are great opportunities present to lead men to Christ. I am not saying no vacations. What I am saying is that the whole church doesn't go on vacation for the entire summer.

In reaching males for Christ, we must also include youth ministries that are geared to reach teenage (and younger) boys to bring them into the church and keep them. Of course, if we reach children or teenagers for Christ, we will likewise have to go after their parents. We must reach their parents in order to preserve the young people.

OUTREACH

The mandate from the Lord is to go and make disciples. Thus, we must have outreach. We cannot simply wait for people to come to church; we must go to where the men are. We must go to their homes. We should sit down with the men being trained for evangelism and compile a list of those men who are known to be nonbelievers or unchurched. For instance, we can make a list of the men with whom we work who are not believers, neighbors who are not believers, and the people with whom we come in contact on a regular basis (like the gas station attendant, and the men in our barbershop). After we make the list, we can focus on some particular men by beginning to pray for them. The men who are going to do the evangelism should pray for one another and for the men on the list. The prayer must be that these men would come to know the Lord Jesus Christ.

We have to go where the men are. We need to go into the streets. We need to be able to talk to men on the street concerning the Lord, and we also need to stand outside the taverns, the bars, and private clubs as the men go in and out of these places. We need to have some men outside of such places who are willing to share their faith. In some instances, we can go inside and share our faith, but we must use good judgment and be very careful, especially because some men can be drawn back into sin simply by being in the places they used to frequent. We must go house to house; we must sit down and think and be imaginative; we must go before the Lord and let him give us ideas as to where and how we can reach men for Christ.

CONSERVATION (DISCIPLING)

The general pattern is that we can get men into the church, but they do not stay. The routine is that men come into the church and join, and then we expect things to happen automatically. We expect them to come, sit, and hear the preaching on Sunday morning and that's it. Once a man is converted and, as the Bible states, "moves . . . into the marvelous light of Christ" (see 1 Peter 2:9 KJV), the job is not finished. The man must be discipled. Discipling, in the context of evangelizing Black men, certainly is teaching the men the truths of the Bible so that they will clearly understand what salvation is and understand their spiritual benefits, but it is also much more.

I recommend that all churches have new member classes, that is, instruction that gives the new member the basics of the Christian life,

221

what is expected of them as good members of the church, and what we expect of them as Christians.

We also need discipleship groups in which one man will take time with another man or a few men (a Paul and Timothy type of relationship). The older church member must take the time with the new man. In discipling, we are teaching how one ought to walk and, at the same time, modeling what the Bible looks like in the life of a believer. We are told in the Bible that we are living epistles read by all men. Of course, that is the only thing some nonbelievers will ever see.

Inside the church, believers are models to one another. Therefore, we need men who are willing to disciple other men. We at Christian Research and Development have materials that have been developed for the sole purpose of evangelizing, discipling, and building up Black men once they get into the church (Richardson, 1985). When these men have finished our training material, they are to reach men outside of the church, bring them inside the church, and start the process over again (the principle of multiplication).

Discipling, as far as the Black male is concerned, includes dealing with life's problems and dealing with the problem of self-image. Black men have to be motivated to deal with life's problems. Black men must understand and be encouraged to believe in themselves. They must believe that, with the help of God, they can deal with things that they would not have considered before they met Jesus Christ.

Black men must be discipled to understand how to lead a family God's way. The Black man is too often criticized, told that he's not playing the proper role, and that he is not as involved in family life as he needs to be. But I have found in our training programs that once we have trained a man and let him know what he is supposed to do, most men respond in a positive way. Therefore, when I talk about discipling, I am not only talking about teaching Bible truths, but also about teaching how to implement the Scriptures into one's life. A man needs to learn how to deal with the problems of life, how to still have hope and not give up when he is unemployed, how to understand that he has a resource beyond himself in God when he cannot find a job, that God is concerned and still has a plan for his life, and that life will change for the better.

Another factor involved in discipleship is helping men come together to learn brotherhood: to learn that we truly can love one another and can be committed to one another; to learn that we can be loyal to one another; to see that there is someone, another man, who understands, to whom he can talk—a man who really cares and is willing to walk with him as a brother

Too often in our churches, the way our ministries are set up (or just the very atmosphere) puts men in competition with women in a negative way. For instance, some of our traditional activities, such as women's day and men's day for the purpose of raising funds, are often a put-down to the men. This is true because first of all, the women usually outnumber the men and will therefore raise more money. Even if there were the same amount of men and women in the church, women usually are more aggressive in carrying out these kinds of activities. The end result is that so often on women's day, the women are commended for what they have done and the pastor makes a statement such as "If only we had some men who would do something," or "If the men would do just half of what these women do!" This is clearly putting men down. That is one of the reasons men do not like to come to church.

CONCLUSION

The church must have a very encouraging atmosphere. We must encourage men publicly. We must encourage the women to help in this endeavor. If we are committed to reaching men for Christ and bringing more men into the church, that would certainly help us with our family problems. These men would become better family men, not only because they are now Christians, but because once they come into the church, we have established ways of conserving them, developing them, and building them up. They can be built up through the new members class, the discipleship ministry, and the time we are spending with them in order to conserve them. This will also result in more Christian men for Christian women to marry. Eventually it will have an impact on our country for Jesus Christ.

Black males are open to the gospel message. Our challenge is to become serious and systematic in reaching them with the message of Christ in a manner in which they can receive it.

References

Ballard, R. (1982). *The Newborn Christian*. Detroit: Home Ministries. (Address: 15360 Indiana, Detroit, MI 48328.)

Chicago Tribune staff. (1986). *Crime: The American Millstone*, 44. Chicago: Contemporary Books.

Flanagan, J. J., and Maguire, K., eds. (1990). *Sourcebook of Criminal Justice Statistics 1989*. U.S. Department of Justice, Bureau of Justice Statistics. Washington, D.C.: USGPO.

Lovett, C. S. (1978). *Soul Winning Made Easy.* Baldwin Park: Personal Christianity.

Hinkle, J. H. (1973). *Soul Winning in Black Churches.* Grand Rapids: Baker.

The Holy Bible, King James Version (1975). Philadelphia: National Publishing Co.

Hyles, J. (1962). *Let's Go Soul Winning.* Murfreesboro: Sword of the Lord Foundation.

Richardson, W. (1985). *Making Jesus King.* Men's Discipleship Ministry, Disciple's Workbook. Philadelphia: Christian Research and Development.

U.S. Bureau of the Census. *Statistical Abstracts of the United States* (1990)(110th ed.). Washington, D.C.: USGPO.

White, J. L. (1984). *The Psychology of Blacks.* Englewood Cliffs, N.J.: Prentice-Hall.

15

Principles of Money Management
for Black Families

Marvin Lynch and Jackie Lynch

MARVIN LYNCH and JACKIE LYNCH are husband and wife. Jackie was born in West Virginia and grew up in Detroit, Michigan. Marvin was born and raised in Lansing, Michigan. They are the parents of three children, David, Timothy, and Melody.

Jackie is a graduate of Eastern Michigan University with a Bachelor of Science degree in Sociology. Marvin is a graduate of Eastern Michigan University with a Bachelor of Science degree in Public Administration. Jackie is a Financial Aid Counselor in the Office of Student Financial Aid at the University of Iowa. Marvin is the Director of the Office of Personnel Services at the University of Iowa. They attend Parkview Evangelical Free Church in Iowa City. Both have conducted financial management workshops for conferences and church groups.

15

Principles of Money Management
for Black Families

Finances! When one hears that word, what comes to mind? Bills to pay? Debts owed? A budget? If finances were mentioned to 100 people, one would probably get 100 different answers. Finance is a subject that affects us daily because money is needed in order for us to function in society. It can cause much anxiety or bring much blessing.

The proper use of money is perhaps one of the least understood topics in our society. Yet thousands of families (Black families included) make financial decisions daily. Financial counselor Larry Burkett (1987), president of Christian Financial Concepts, states that money is "typically either the best area of communication in a marriage or the worst." Burkett (1978) estimated that 90 percent of all marital breakups can be attributed, at least partially, to financial tension in the home.

Christian leaders remind us of how important it is for believers to place themselves completely under the lordship of Jesus Christ. This is always an appropriate message to hear for those who know Jesus Christ as Lord as well as Savior (see Rom. 10:9). In obedience to GOD, Christians are to bring all areas of their lives under subjection to him. Yet for many, the area of personal or family finances regularly remains outside the control and influence of Jesus Christ. It appears that most Christians do tithe or contribute to the Lord's work in some way. However, when one considers the way in which finances are handled in a great number of Christian homes, it would appear that there is little regard for the way God says finances should be managed. Yet the Bible, God's inspired Word, is the most important source from which to draw financial advice.

THE BIBLICAL VIEW OF FINANCES

In an effort to explain how Christians can handle money in a biblical manner, we begin with God's thoughts on this matter. Most basic, yet most needed, is for Christians to mentally give up ownership of all possessions (and finances) to God as shown in Psalm 24:1. What one owns must not be viewed as one's own but the Lord's. Christians must come to the realization that they are stewards (caretakers) of what God has entrusted to them. It is then our responsibility to manage our material resources in a way that would please him. These principles are taught in Matthew 25:14–30.

Jesus gave several parables that clearly point out that Christians are not owners of their resources but rather stewards or managers. These parables offer clear principles about the attitude that must be adopted if one is going to be successful in money management. In the parable of the talents cited in Matthew 25:14–30, one sees evidence of how God wants his followers to think about money. (You are encouraged to read it with the understanding that the talents in the parable are material resources, even though the context would suggest that it goes well beyond a discussion of material goods.) In his book, *Your Finances in Changing Times*, Burkett (1975) states the following concerning this parable:

> This parable is prophetic in nature. It is given in the 25th chapter of Matthew, a chapter that deals with the second coming of Christ. It reveals many things:
>
> 1. God will entrust to us that which is within our own ability and not beyond it [each servant (steward) had a different number of talents].
>
> 2. God is the owner and has the right to recover what he has given us to manage (he expected an accounting of how the servants had handled their talents).
>
> 3. God thoroughly disapproves of slothfulness on our part (as in the case of the servant with one talent) and expects us to multiply the assets he leaves us, *not* just to maintain them. (p. 47)

Thus far, much emphasis has been placed on the attitudes needed to successfully manage financial affairs. Conversely, if we show discontent with what we have, a desire to "get rich quick," or are just plain greedy, then no amount of planning or budgeting (which will be discussed later) will help us honor God with our finances. Attitudes are the results of values that are promoted by the culture around us. For example, the choice of particular foods and styles of music are the result

228

Figure 15.1. Factors that influence our values.

of the influence of our cultural environment (see Figure 15.1). One may prefer certain types of foods because of their association with family traditions as well as because of their flavor. One may select a style of music on the basis of what one listened to while growing up, what the religious peer group sanctioned, what the media promoted, and so on. In much the same way, money values develop as we grow up and determine how financial affairs are managed. Money values are closely associated with feelings of security, acceptance, and personal resourcefulness.

ATTITUDES THAT HINDER
SUCCESSFUL MONEY MANAGEMENT

There are several attitudes that can hinder our ability to successfully manage our money. Greed, defined as always wanting more and never being satisfied with what one has, is an attitude that dominates much of society. It doesn't seem to matter whether there is a need for more or whether one can even afford it; some people seem to just want the biggest and the best. However, Jesus said, "Beware, and be on your guard against every form of greed; for not even when one has an abundance does his life consist of his possessions" (Luke 12:15 NASB).

Covetousness is another attitude that can cloud one's perspective regarding finances. Many Christians experience little success in managing their money because they desire what others have. Call it what you want—"keeping up with the Joneses" or "I've got to have the biggest and the best." This kind of attitude will only put you in financial bondage to material possessions. It has been said, "One reason why we're in debt is because our neighbors are always buying something we can't afford." One of the best remedies against covetousness is found in the book of Hebrews: "Let your conversation [lifestyle] be without covetousness; and be content with such things as ye have: for he hath said, I will never leave thee, nor forsake thee" (Heb. 13:5 KJV).

"Get rich quick" is the last attitude to be discussed. Unfortunately, this is a pervasive attitude in the Black community, perhaps because we as a people have suffered a great deal of economic loss. One can have a get-rich-quick attitude whether there is a lot of money or very little. The motivation behind this attitude is to make a lot of money—quickly— with very little effort. Activities such as gambling and playing the lottery fall into the category of get rich quick. In addition there are a host of other programs—many legitimate in themselves—that feed on this attitude, which all too often is found among Christians. Many people who get involved in such programs invest money in them that they can ill afford to lose. Many families have been wiped out financially because of a get-rich-quick attitude. They would have been wise to heed the proverb that says, "He that hasteth to be rich hath an evil eye [selfish motives], and considereth not that poverty shall come upon him" (Prov. 28:22 KJV). Christians must be willing to let the Holy Spirit examine their hearts for impure motives and attitudes that would prevent Jesus from being Lord of their finances (see Ps. 139:23–24).

MOVING TOWARD GOD'S PLAN

Let's concentrate now on how to move toward God's plan for managing finances. Simply stated, God's way is not to chance, but to plan. It has been said that if we aim at nothing, we will hit it every time. God expects us to be intelligent producers and consumers. If our money management is sloppy or—even worse—non-existent, we can expect no less than financial problems. We realize that many of us are victims of low incomes, poor products, discriminatory practices, high interest rates, and so on. But these external factors do not excuse us from following God's prescription for dealing with what appears to be overwhelming odds.

There are several steps to successful financial planning. First, one needs to give a tithe (tenth) of one's income to the Lord (see Prov. 3:9–10). Planning actually begins by willingly returning to God a portion of what he has given us. This action is essential if one desires God's guidance in managing money, and is outward proof of an internal commitment to follow his ways. Deuteronomy 14:23 states, "And thou shalt eat before the LORD thy God, in the place which he shall choose to place his name there, the tithe of thy corn, of thy wine, and of thine oil, and the firstlings of thy herds and of thy flocks; that thou mayest learn to fear the LORD thy God always" (KJV). In other words, tithing is more for *our* benefit than for the Lord's! Remember, one does not get closer to God by giving to him. Rather, one returns to the Lord a portion of what one has because one is already committed to his ways (see Prov. 3:5–6). If one wants God's wisdom in finances, practice giving to him.

FINANCIAL BONDAGE

What is financial bondage? In short, it is exactly what the phrase says—bondage related to finances. The average American family (Christians included) is in financial bondage to credit card companies, banks, department stores, and just about any other type of lending institution one could name. America's families have credit outstanding to the tune of some 728.9 billion dollars (U.S. Bureau of Census, 1990). This amounts to anywhere from 20–50 percent of disposable personal income. Such people are shackled by excessive debts, harassed by creditors, and burdened by tension within their families. This is all a result of being in financial bondage.

Why do Black Christians (or any Christian) fall prey to a system that views debt as a way of life? The everybody's-got-to-have-a-little-debt-don't-they? syndrome seems to have become as entrenched in the Christian community as it has in the secular world. We believe that Christians have largely followed the world's lead in this area because they don't know what God's Word says about debt. As a result, they are paying the same consequences ("My people are destroyed for lack of knowledge," Hosea 4:6 KJV).

THE BIBLE AND DEBT

What does the Bible say about debt? Proverbs 22:7 states, "The rich ruleth over the poor, and the borrower is servant to the lender" (NIV).

This means that when someone borrows, that person becomes the *servant* of the lender. Clearly, this suggests that the lender is established as an authority over the borrower. Further (within legal limits), the lender has the power to require full payment of what is owed at any time.

Before the subject of debt is continued, it is important to distinguish between *borrowing* and *debt*. Borrowing is the act of acquiring money and/or goods and services with the promise to pay for them at a later time. One literally makes a vow to pay back the money or provide payment for the previously acquired goods and services. It is *not* wrong for a Christian to borrow! The Bible tells us, however, that we should use caution when borrowing, and that such should not be the norm. As long as the person *repays* what they've borrowed ("The wicked borrow and do not repay, but the righteous give generously," Ps. 37:21 NIV), they are not in violation of God's standards. The minimum expectation is that Christians will repay what they owe.

Debt, on the other hand, is what occurs when a person fails to meet the agreed-upon credit terms of the lender. If the terms of this contract are violated, then what Scripture describes as debt occurs. Debt occurs largely because of a family's lack of understanding *or* lack of adherence to God's principles even when known (cf. Ps. 37:21). Some, if not all, of the attitudes mentioned earlier (greed, covetousness, get rich quick) are usually present in the life of a Christian in debt. When the main goal of Christians is to have the "biggest and the best" and they are not content with what they already have, chances are they will fall prey to the always-borrow-but-hope-that-someone-else-will-pay-it-back philosophy that dominates our society. People who have not learned to spend only what they earn and have a continuous "past-due" lifestyle need far more than "grace periods" and "increased credit limits." They need a complete attitude adjustment! This is needed especially if the aim is to please God in the handling of finances.

Credit Counseling, Inc. has gone on record to say that people who receive budget counseling will experience debt problems again within three years if they don't change their attitude toward credit buying and debt. God expects no less than an attitude change. The Bible states, "Lay not up for yourselves treasures upon earth, where moth and rust doth corrupt, and where thieves break through and steal: but lay up for yourselves treasures in heaven, where neither moth nor rust doth corrupt, and where thieves do not break through nor steal: for where your treasure is, there will your heart be also" (Matt. 6:19–21 KJV).

BUDGETING

Managing your money God's way is next to impossible without a budget. What is a budget? Burkett (1987) indicates,

A budget is nothing more than a short-range plan for how you will spend your money during the coming year. A budget should not restrict your freedom to enjoy life; it should expand it. "How," you say, "can living on a budget expand my freedom?" By helping you live within your means and not go into debt. (p. 30)

A budget then should *not* be viewed as something to restrict spending. Rather, it is a tool that helps you decide how much money you can or would like to spend. To develop a budget, one should take the following steps:

1. List *all* available gross income (income before tax deductions) per month from all sources. This will include wages and salaries, commissions, bonuses, tips, Social Security benefits, interest and dividends, welfare checks, food stamps, rental-property income, etc. Do not include a Christmas bonus that is not certain or money you anticipate receiving. If you regularly live on a non-fixed income such as sales or commissions, divide the previous year's salary by twelve to get a monthly income figure.
2. Determine how much you actually spend each month. If you don't know how much you are presently spending, record your expenses in a notebook for at least thirty to sixty days. List everything! Expenses that don't come due each month, such as car insurance, clothing, and property taxes, can be calculated by taking the previous year's total for each expense and dividing by twelve. For example: if you pay $480 a year for car insurance, your monthly cost would be $40 a month ($480 ÷ 12). Do this for every category not paid out on a monthly basis (See Figure 15.3).
3. Compare your income with your expenses.
   a. If your expenses are greater than your income, you must decide how much your spending can be reduced.
   b. It is especially important at this point to evaluate credit buying. How much of your income is committed to consumer debt? In many families, over 20 percent of net spendable income (income after tithe and taxes) goes toward debt payments, far exceeding what the "average" family can afford.

c. Explore alternate ways to satisfy family needs. Remember that you have committed to live within your means and to *not* spend more than you make. It may require that you purchase less expensive clothing, use public transportation rather than drive your car, or purchase fewer convenience food items when grocery shopping. There are many ways in which a family can save money within their present budget.

d. After adjusting one's spending so that net spendable income is greater than expenses, you are ready to set up a record-keeping system (budget) that will help you decide how much you would like to or can spend for various needs. Suggested budget categories and percentage guidelines *after* tithe, offerings, and taxes are as follows:

— 5% Savings (with a goal to increase as you can)
—30% Housing (includes upkeep and utilities)
—20% Food
—13% Car (gas, upkeep)
— 5% Clothing (new purchases & upkeep of old)
— 5% Doctor, dentist, prescription drugs
— 7% Entertainment, recreation, vacations
        (includes eating out)
— 5% Insurances
— 5% Debts
— 5% Miscellaneous, personal
        Total 100%

e. Next to giving to the Lord, a regular savings plan is of greatest importance in a budget. A savings plan does not represent a lack of faith in God. Rather, it is the practice of a wise person. The Bible states, "In the house of the wise are stores of choice food and oil, but a foolish man devours all he has" (Prov. 21:20 NIV). Which represents better stewardship: to borrow at 18–20 percent interest in order to buy things that wear out, or to save and pay cash for them? Remember: the budget categories are only *suggested* ones. Each family's needs are different. Categories can be added or dropped as necessary. Developing a system of disciplined spending is the goal for which each family should be striving.

f. Developing a budget is not a "one shot deal," but will take several months of work before you feel totally in control of your financial situation. It is not necessary that your new budget fit the guidelines perfectly. It *is* necessary that your new budget *not* exceed your net spendable income. The minimum objective of any budget should be to meet the family's needs without creating further debt.

4. Establish personal and family financial goals which should be reevaluated at least once per year. Having clearly defined goals helps one to clarify needs, wants, and desires. It also gives the individual or the family time to pray about that purchase. This brings God directly into the purchasing picture. It will strengthen the faith of the family so as to trust him in greater matters. Many testimonies have been given as to how God provided the very item needed at a lower cost or no cost at all. Goal setting also provides time to plan for the future.

Financial goals should be divided into three categories:

a. Short-range goals (one to two years). Develop a budget that covers the regular monthly and unexpected expenses. An emergency savings fund should be included in this category.

b. Intermediate goals. What do you want to do in the near future? Purchase a car, plan a major vacation? These could be financial goals within three to five years. Set a specific date for the goal to be reached. Determine the amount of funds you will need; calculate the amount you need to save per month.

c. Long-range goals are projected needs for the next ten, twenty, or thirty years.

All goals should be realistic and subject to reevaluation. Expand the following chart for personal use (see Figure 15.2).

It should be obvious from this discussion of budgeting that one must *act* to implement this plan. No plan is ever going to implement itself. Effort on your part and good communication within your family is necessary. No one person can make the budget work—it is a team effort. Above all, a family needs to pray and allow God to provide wisdom regarding budgeting efforts. God *wants* to guide and give financial wisdom. "In his heart a man plans his course, but the LORD determines his steps" (Prov. 16:9 NIV).

ADDITIONAL SUGGESTIONS FOR A FRUGAL LIFESTYLE

Becoming consumer-wise is important when considering how to live on less. We are not suggesting that believers must live poorly. On

Goals for Year____	Total Cost	Projected Date Needed	Amount saved per month	Amount saved each year
Short-Range				
Intermediate				
Long-Range				

Figure 15.2.

the contrary. Every day we are inundated with advertisers suggesting that their product is a must for our physical, mental, or social well-being. One must keep materialism in perspective. We are living in times when many people are experiencing unexpected changes in their lives. Unemployment, underemployment, less overtime pay, shorter work hours, and reduced commissions, along with increased prices, have caused many families to look for ways to stretch money and other resources.

Develop a positive attitude with the thrifty lifestyle. Make a game of finding ways to cut costs. For example:

— Comparison shop whenever possible. Use the advertisement inserts from your local newspaper that display promotional items.

— Consider both the quality and the cost of a certain product. Where will this product be used, and how frequently?

— Purchase necessary items in quantity when on sale. This is especially wise when considering toiletries, small car products such as oil and air filters, underwear, school supplies, and frozen foods.

— Purchase only necessities. Avoid impulse spending.

— When possible, shop for clothing at outlet stores.

— Coordinate your wardrobe to avoid having clothes that match nothing.

— Resell your slightly used clothing at a consignment shop. If you do not have a consignment shop in your area, begin an annual clothing exchange at your church.

— Keep a calendar of the annual sales activities in your community. Most major businesses will sponsor seasonal sales promotions during holidays such as Memorial Day, the Fourth of July, Labor Day, and President's Day.

— Use an egg timer to limit the length of long distance calls. Take advantage of telephone calling discounts.

— Entertain with "potlucks" or inexpensive meals.

— Join or start a baby-sitting co-op. Exchange child care with another family.

— Carpool to work.

Think of other creative ways to cut costs and live a lifestyle where you can share your surplus with the needy.

CONCLUSION

Historically and currently, the majority of Black families have been and are under financial stress. Most of us fail to protect what we manage to accumulate. We often don't look to the future. As a result, we lose out on inflation-beating opportunities—which mainstream consumers often enjoy—because we are not aware that they exist.

The result is a monthly—sometimes day-to-day—struggle to stay ahead of bills. As consumers, we are often forced to borrow at high interest rates to pay for emergencies; to put off, sometimes permanently, the dreams we have; and even worse, to end up at retirement with little or no money to live securely and comfortably. This is all too often because we fail to heed the wisdom that God has given to us in his Word regarding financial matters. This is why we challenge you to take what has been presented and put it into practice. So elicit the aid of your pastor. If your church does not have a financial counseling program, encourage it to start one. In addition, banks and credit unions usually offer financial and budget counseling. Debt management companies also offer family financial counseling services. If at all possible, seek advice and counsel from Christian financial counselors. "Blessed is the man that walketh not in the counsel of the ungodly . . . " (Ps. 1:1 KJV).

God promises to provide our every need. Nowhere is this more clearly expressed than in Psalm 50:14, 15: "Offer to God the sacrifice of thanksgiving; and pay your vows to the Most High, and call on Me in the day of trouble; I will deliver you, and you shall honor and glorify Me" (AMPLIFIED). These and other promises are available to those who have received Jesus Christ as Savior and Lord. If anyone reading this chapter has not made a confession of faith in Jesus Christ, you are encouraged to do so immediately.

Romans 10:9, 10 (NIV) gives God's promise, "That if you confess with your mouth, 'Jesus is Lord,' and believe in your heart that God raised him from the dead, you will be saved. For it is with your heart that you believe and are justified, and it is with your mouth that you confess [Jesus as Lord] and are saved." All of what has been said earlier will not only mean more to you, but you will have made the most important decision in your life. You will then be in a better position to follow God's financial plan for your life.

Our prayer is that all who read this chapter will seek to glorify God in the overall handling of their financial affairs, and that God's blessing will be on those who are obedient to his financial ways. "The blessing of the LORD, it maketh rich, and he addeth no sorrow with it" (Prov. 10:22 KJV).

Figure 15.3.
Average Monthly Expenses

Church Giving & Tithe   _____
Home Mortgage or Rent   _____
Property Insurance   _____
Property Taxes   _____
Savings & Investment   _____
Life Insurance   _____
Health: Doctor/Dental Fees   _____
Car Insurance   _____
Other Insurance   _____
Union, Club and Other Dues   _____
Home Improvement; Maintenance   _____
Gas   _____
Water   _____
Electricity   _____
Heating   _____
Groceries   _____
Laundry Soap; Toiletries; Cosmetics   _____
Pet Food & Veterinary   _____
Hobbies   _____
Vacations   _____
Entertainment   _____
Auto: Gas & Oil   _____
      Repairs; Licenses, Registration   _____
Public Transportation, Parking, Tolls   _____
Clothing   _____
Subscriptions—Books, Tapes, Etc.   _____
Newspapers   _____
Lunches $_____ Coffee Breaks $_____   _____

School Lunches $____ Supplies $____   ____
Babysitters   ____
Home Furnishings   ____
Allowances   ____
Gifts: Christmas   ____
       Birthdays, Anniversaries, etc.   ____
Education: Music Lessons   ____
       Other Lessons   ____
       Ski, Tennis, Golf Lessons, etc.   ____
       Seminars & Workshops   ____
Haircuts, Hair Styling   ____
Other   ____

Total   ____

Monthly Loan Payments (Credit Obligations)   ____

Total Monthly Expenditures   ____

Net Monthly Spendable Income   ____

Balance   ____

REFERENCES

The Amplified Bible. (1965). Grand Rapids: Zondervan.

Burkett, Larry. (1987). *Answers to Your Family's Financial Questions*, 13. Pomona, Calif.: Focus on the Family.

_____. (1978). *What Husbands Wish Their Wives Knew About Money*. Wheaton: Scripture Press.

_____. (1975). *Your Finances in Changing Times*. Gainesville, Ga.: Christian Financial Concepts. (rev. ed., Chicago: Moody Press, 1982).

The King James Bible. 1909. New York: Oxford University Press.

The New American Standard Bible. (1960). The Lockman Foundation.

The Holy Bible: New International Bible. (1978). Grand Rapids: Zondervan.

U.S. Bureau of the Census. (1990). *Statistical Abstracts of the United States: 1990. (110th Ed.).* Washington, D.C.: U.S. Government Printing Office.